Search for the Truth

Changing the World with the Evidence for Creation

Bruce Malone

3275 E. Monroe Road Midland, MI 48642
989.837.5546
truth@searchforthetruth.net
www.searchforthetruth.net

Dedication

This book is first dedicated to my Lord and Savior, Jesus Christ, in appreciation of the greatest gifts anyone could receive - forgiveness for my sins and the accompanied promise of eternal life in fellowship with Him. It is also dedicated to my wife Robin, without whom my life would not be complete and this book would never have been published.

If this book has changed your outlook on life, strengthened your faith, or deepened your relationship with your Creator, please let us know. If you desire to reproduce copies of this book for others, a CD with the individual articles and illustrations can be obtained upon request. Low cost multiple copies to share with others are available using the order form at the back of the book. May God bless you as you share the truth with others.

E-mail - truth@searchforthetruth.net
Web - www.searchforthetruth.net
Mail - 3275 Monroe Rd.; Midland, MI 48642

Bruce Malone gave his life to Christ over 20 years ago, as the Lord miraculously preserved him through a close call with death. Since that time Bruce has looked for a deeper purpose in life and realized that rejection of Biblical truth, justified by belief in evolution, is the acid which is eating away at the moral foundation of our culture.

Bruce has a degree in chemical engineering and has spent 28 years working as a research leader for the Dow Chemical corporation. He is responsible for key innovations which have resulted in eighteen patents. However, his passion is sharing the relevance and evidence for creation and he left Dow in 2009 to devote full time to creation Ministry.

An adjunct speaker for the Institute for Creation Research, Bruce brings science alive through stories and demonstrations showing that Biblical creation is the most rational explanation for the world around us. The purpose of both his books and lectures is to help the non-scientific layman understand the importance of creation while motivating and equipping them to share these truths.

Bruce resides in Midland, MI with his wife Robin. They have four children who are all actively serving the Lord.

Table of Contents

Acknowledgments

This book has been over ten years in the making and is the fruit of the encouragement, financial support, and prayer support of so many Christian friends that it would be impossible to list everyone involved. I owe a special debt of gratitude to those who patiently reworded so many of these articles. These dear and special friends include my wife Robin, Rob & Beth Kelch, Deanna Windon, Wayne Nichols, Carol & Robin Balderston and Stephen B. Austin. My heartfelt thanks goes to Dr. Tas Walker for his timely technical review of the original manuscript.

Much of this book summarizes the work of brave, true scientists who dare to research outside the evolutionary paradigm which rules modern science. I am indebted and humbled to summarize the work of great men of science such as Dr. Russell Humphreys, Dr. Steven Austin, Dr. John Sanford, and Dr. Baumgardner all of whom work at the Institute for Creation Research.

My deepest appreciation also goes to two of the best editorial cartoonists in the world Chuck Asay and Wayne Stayskal. They not only allowed the use of their work for the newspaper columns (and this book), but greatly encouraged my effort to bring a Christian worldview to public newspapers. Thanks also to Johnny Hart for allowing the use of his insightful cartoons. All of these cartoonists clearly understand the importance of this issue. Thanks also to Master Books, The Institute for Creation Research, Answers in Genesis, Creation Magazine, Alpha Omega Institute, and the Ark Foundation for technical advice and the use of their materials in this book. Further thanks goes to John Adam, Ron Cooper, Lanny & Marilyn Johnson, Pam & Mark Johnson, Dave & Mary Jo Nutting, Tom Wagner and John Whitmore for allowing the use of their excellent articles in this book.

A very special thanks to Patricia Edmund for the final proofreading and Shelley Mordue for the fantastic cover design.

Foreword

There are sermons, tapes, seminars, radio programs, and books galore on every possible subject dealing with Christianity and spirituality. It is neither a lack of knowledge nor understanding that prevents the Christian faith from having a greater impact on the world around us. What limits the power of Christianity is apathy, misplaced priorities, and direct disobedience. In essence, we fail to see the opportunities God gives us. Our national motto is In God we Trust, but we seldom demonstrate any genuine trust with our actions. It is almost as if we as a nation, although, we still acknowledge that God exists, have separated our spiritual beliefs from the physical reality of the world around us. What our actions really demonstrate is a trust in ourselves, not a living relevant God. Does this mean that continuing to talk about who God is and what He has done is a wasted effort? Not at all! One person impacted by truth can change the future of a nation. The primary purpose of this book is to provide a proven method for bringing the truth about what God has done in the past (and therefore is capable of doing in the future) into the public market place of ideas where right now it seldom sees the light of day.

Few people understand how dinosaurs, ice ages, carbon dating, and the big bang fit into their view of the Bible and reality. Therefore, they rather blindly accept whatever they are taught in magazines, museums, and science textbooks without checking out the underlying beliefs upon which the conclusions are built. Even fewer have the time, desire, or patience to read a technical presentation of the Biblical viewpoint in these areas. Yet, the correct understanding of these issues would strengthen their faith, whereas an incorrect interpretation undermines their faith.

There are dozens of excellent books on the scientific evidence for creation. This being true, what is the point of writing another one? Simply that knowledge, properly applied, can change lives. This book not only contains such knowledge, but explains how to present this information in a way in which people will respond. Christianity and truth are not commodities that must be sold like tubes of toothpaste. Our job is not to market or sell our beliefs, but to clearly and humbly explain them. The apostle Peter challenges us to
...be ready always to give an answer to every man that asketh you a reason of the hope that is in you, [do this] with meekness and fear...

(I Peter 3:15). It is not our responsibility to convince people of the truth. We can only make the truth known and leave the convincing to the Holy Spirit. He will then open the eyes and hearts of those who really desire to know the truth. This book is an attempt to share such truth in the areas concerning science.

The heart of the debate over origins is not a discussion of science versus religion, but a clash of how to view reality. We all have the same 'data'. The interpretation of this data is diametrically different because of opposite starting assumptions. The primary assumption of modern science is that God has not interacted with creation from the beginning of time. In other words, everything must be explained without God. Obviously, with this starting assumption, the world is going to arrive at a vastly different conclusion concerning our origin than that of the Bible.

All valid world views must address the questions of where we came from; why there is so much pain and suffering in the world; and how to improve our lives. Darwinism offers a world view that concludes that people exist as the result of purposeless processes. Therefore, ultimately right or wrong do not exist. Evil becomes just a matter of poor training so we can ultimately perfect ourselves. This is in direct opposition to the Biblical world view that starts with an intelligent Creator, explains that death and suffering are a direct result of man's actions, and provides a solution to this problem which are not based on our efforts to make retribution or 'improve ourselves'. Both world views use science to support their conclusions. This book addresses which world view is best supported by the actual scientific evidence.

School age children are receiving a barrage of information from our educational system and media telling them that they are here as the result of a gigantic, purposeless explosion. They are being told that life formed over billions of years as rocks dissolved to form a chemical soup which somehow came alive (by some purposeless force). Since they are old enough to watch cartoons on television they have been indoctrinated with the idea that they are here as the result of random-chance processes (evolution). The most basic brainwashing technique is to repeat something over and over again as if it were a fact. With enough repetition even the most outlandish lie can be molded as fact in people's minds. Once this has happened, it becomes very difficult to overcome because the lie becomes the filter through which the individual views reality.

If parents do nothing to explain the scientific problems with the evolutionary world view; don't be surprised when your children reach their teenage years without any real faith in a relevant God. Don't be surprised if, by the time they enter college, they totally turn their backs on God. And don't be surprised if, by the time they leave college, they have totally rejected your standards of right and wrong while setting their own arbitrary, relative values.

The purpose of this book is to reverse 100 years of indoctrination in evolutionary dogma by taking the offensive in an area where Christianity has been on the defensive for far too long. In a larger sense, this is a book about reality the reality of our past, the existence of absolute values, and the nature of God. It is my hope that this book will serve as a reference and encourage people to publish evidence for creation in their own communities. As you will read in the introduction and from testimonies from unsolicited letters (a few of which are shared throughout this book), presenting the evidence for creation changes people's lives!

Introduction

"... upon this rock I will build my church: and the gates of hell shall not prevail against it."

- Matthew 16:18

Only a spiritually blind person can miss the fact that there is something terribly wrong with this world. Even though beauty abounds in both nature and people, it is not difficult to see that things are not as they ought to be. On a personal level, why can't you always do what you know is right? If you are honest with yourself, you will realize that you can't and you don't. We are all selfish and cruel (often with the people we love most). The Bible call this evil 'sin', explains where it comes from, and prescribes a cure for this problem.

It has been said that Christians are not really part of this world, but just passing through on their way to their permanent home (Philippians 3:20). With this perspective in mind, look again at the promise which Jesus made to His followers in Matthew 16:18 – *"The gates of hell will not prevail against [my church.]"* This is not a comfort, but a command. Christians are not called to cower in their churches hoping that they can somehow hang onto their faith in the midst of the onslaught from this world. God blesses us to be a blessing. We are to be about His business so that someday we may hear those words, *"Well done, my good and faithful servant."*

The Bible contains no example of God praising people for hiding themselves from the world. On the contrary, we are told to be a light on the hill and the seasoning to food. It was not by accident that the Promised Land (Israel) was located at the very crossroads of the two major world civilizations of that day. Everyone from east and west had to pass right though the midst of God's chosen people in order to conduct trade and commerce. Jewish people were forced to interact with the world so that the World could see what was different about their faith. God expects no less from us, but how do we do this today?

Search for the Truth ("*Search*" for short) shares one method of tearing down the gates of deceit that grip our world. One of the wonderful things about Christianity is the realization that a creative God did not make us from a cookie cutter. He has an individual plan for each of our lives. Not everyone is called to put the material in this book to use. However, if you feel an excitement and stirring in your spirit as you read this book…if you start to think, "I could do this in my church or community."…or… "This really could make a difference." … Act on the thought. If just one person in every community would do so; it would lead many people toward a saving knowledge of God. By understanding what God has done in the past we can better understand what He is doing in the present and what He will do in the future.

This book is divided into six sections corresponding to the different scientific disciplines dealing with the evidence for, or relevance of, creation. Each section contains individual articles about evidence for creation from these varied scientific disciplines. Anything in this book can be copied and shared with others or put to use as suggested in the last section by printing it in local newspapers. The short chapters between the *Search* articles provide a running narrative of how this book came to be, how God has used my life and this material in miraculous ways, and how you can put the same information to use.

Can sharing the actual physical evidence for creation make a difference in people's lives? Let's contrast two examples of what happened with school boards which attempted to present a balanced view of origins. Currently incredible pressure and resources are in place within our public education system to prevent students from viewing any of the evidence for creation. Any attempt to present the evidence for creation is immediately labeled as religion or "creationism" (note that the opposing belief system is never labeled "evolutionism") and the national media and atheist organizations, unknowingly aided and abetted by teachers and others who know essentially nothing about evidence for creation, pull out all stops to prevent any crack developing in the edifice of evolutionary dogma.

In 1999, the state school board in the state of Kansas changed the requirements for the science curriculum to allow for the evidence for intelligent design to be studied alongside the evidence for evolution. The national media went nuts and totally distorted the ruling of the board stating that evolution would no longer be taught in

Kansas and that students were being dragged back into the dark ages. The end result, after this extensive misinformation campaign ran its course, was that every member of the state school board lost their job. As a result, the decision was reversed, returning the curriculum to an "evolution only" approach. In 2004, the State of Georgia wanted to place a simple sticker on biology textbooks stating that evolution was an unproven theory and not a fact. Again the national media moved in with a publicity blitz distorting the facts without presenting any of the evidence for creation. The result -- a federal judge ordered that the stickers be removed. In Pennsylvania in 2006, a local school board required that the science curriculum include some of the evidence for intelligent design along with the usual one sided presentation of evolution. Atheist organizations immediately sued and due to the much publicized media barrage, the school board decision was again reversed by a Federal judge and school board members again lost their jobs.

Contrast this with what happened in the small community of Grantsburg, WI. In 2004, the school board of this small town of 1,364 voted to change the science curriculum to allow evolution to be critically examined in the light of true science. The national media and state atheist organizations once again descended upon the town like buzzards on road kill. They promoted the usual 'creation is religion and evolution is science' propaganda and warned how the children of the school system would be warped and ruined. However, this time instead of remaining silent, one family organized a group of friends and over the next six months started purchasing space in their town's weekly newspaper and publishing a column containing articles from this book. Week after week, citizens of Grantsburg were exposed to concise, interesting articles that laid out the evidence for a Biblical worldview from every area of science. The school board election for those brave souls who dared to allow the evidence for creation to be viewed by students was held in April of 2005. To the astonishment of many, every board member who had voted to allow students the freedom to think was re-elected (albeit by a razor thin margin). [For the whole story of this victory for truth, see page 114.] We may not always see immediate results, but presenting the truth does make a difference in people's lives.

This book is the fourth edition of Search for the Truth. If you wish to print these articles in your community a CD with the text and illustrations can be requested at no cost. Contact me at www.searchforthetruth.net to request this resource. Low cost multiple copies of this book also make an excellent teaching tool and are available via the order form in the back of the book.

Section I:
Evidence for Creation from Biology and BioChemistry

Dear Bruce & Family,
Hey, just wanted you to know what God did with _Search for the Truth_ in Amsterdam. Check this story:

Our first day there in Amsterdam, we went to Vrije Universiteit (Free University) to pray and pass out invitations to an international praise and worship meeting. While in the dorms we met a young man named R.C. We shared with him for awhile about the meeting and Christ. Before coming, I believe God wanted me to bring your _Search for the Truth_ manuscript on the mission trip and now I know why. While talking, R.C. mentioned a few things about evolution and how he believed that although it was not a perfect science, it answered more questions than creation. After our discussion, he mentioned he would like to know about "our truth"...that is when I felt the leading to give him your book. He was thankful. The best part came, by God's design, when we ran into him two days later and gave him a Dutch Bible. He said, "I read the Truth book and now I have to question what I believe." PRAISE GOD!!! Seeds planted and I believe a harvest to come. But you know what this means – I am left without a copy of your book. My roommates and I enjoy reading it, (we keep it in the bathroom!)
Your missionary in training,

– James Damude

Chapter 1

"My people are destroyed for lack of knowledge: because thou hast rejected knowledge, I will also reject thee...

- Hosea 4:6

If this book was just another fact filled volume expounding on the scientific evidences for creation it would have little impact on the world around us. Many books have been published that explain the impossibility of evolution in great technical detail. Yet with each passing year, the belief in evolution strengthens. Very few people read books on creation and even fewer attend seminars on the subject. The voice of truth in this area is actually a whisper in the midst of a tempest from our education system and the media shouting
evolution is a fact.

This book presents the scientific evidences for creation in ways not typically used.

I was first exposed to the evidence for creation in the summer of 1988. At the time, I was attending a Presbyterian Church led by Reverend Leonard Phelps, a man with a deep faith in the Lord and a respect for the Bible. That summer, he invited a guest lecturer to speak on the topic of creation. Even though, I was at that time a Christian in a real sense (rather than by birth or tradition), I was still a complete product of our public school system.

In 1981, I had graduated cum laude from the University of Cincinnati with a BA in chemical engineering and was working as a new product development researcher for the Dow Chemical Co. I had loved science for as long as I could remember and had naively accepted evolution as fact. Therefore, when a speaker came to our church to present the idea that man had not come from apes and that the Bible could be understood literally, I was idly curious, but not particularly interested. Had the speaker based his fruitfulness on my reaction, he would have considered his time wasted because I only attended two of the four Sunday night lectures. I can also remember some older ladies in the church commenting how incredible it was that anyone could believe that an ape could turn into a man. I distinctly remember commenting (under my breath) that they themselves must be the missing links in order to believe otherwise. My overall arrogant attitude was,
how dare a bunch of religious fanatics question the findings of science

.

However, the second of the two lectures totally changed my perspective on life. The speaker talked about the evidence of a worldwide flood and showed how this event explained fossil records better than billions of years of gradual accumulation. In 23 years of education and church attendance, not one person had ever presented the flood of Noah as a factual historical happening. The ramifications of this on everything I had been taught in biology, geology, physics, anthropology, and the origin of the earth and universe became immediately apparent. The implication on the age of the earth was mind boggling. It was as if a light had suddenly been uncovered so that for the first time I could see things around me clearly. The evidence for the rapid accumulation of the fossil record simply made more sense than what I had been taught for years. I spent the next 8 months reading everything I could find on the scientific evidence for creation and evolution (including the Bible from cover to cover). This culminated with spending a week with scientists from the Institute for Creation Research in Cedarville, Ohio in July of 1989. During a field trip to study the geology of the surrounding area, I made a comment to Dr. John Morris that launched me on the adventure that culminated in publishing this book. I stated that,
If just one person in every community would dedicate themselves to making the evidence for creation known; God could return our country to its Christian foundation.

This book, and the CD containing these articles, provide one method for doing just that.

Search for the Truth

By Bruce Malone

Western civilization was founded on the realization that an infinite creator God exists. It was upon this basis (that the universe was the orderly product of an intelligent being) that the founders of modern science had the confidence to develop the scientific method and modern science. However, in recent years, this open acknowledgment of a personal creator has been replaced by science as the source of ultimate reality. This viewpoint shift is primarily justified by the acceptance of evolution (both biological and cosmic) as fact. The late Christian philosopher, Francis Schaeffer, put it best, "Modern man has two feet firmly planted in midair."

In essence, modern man has put science in place of God as the foundation for understanding reality. Instead of the starting point, "In the beginning God created…" we now have "In the beginning hydrogen gas…" However, science can never define reality because it is merely a tool which organizes observations in such a way as to attempt to explain the physical world. Current observations are extrapolated to explain the past (which can no longer be observed) or to predict the future (which also cannot be observed). As more observations are gathered, predictions of science (known as hypotheses, theories, and laws)

constantly change. For example, the universal laws of motion developed by Newton in the 1600's have been expanded by Einstein's theory of relativity in the 1900's.

Used by permission of Chuck Asay

This in turn has been expanded to include other discoveries of modern physics.

The realization that scientific discoveries are ever changing has been incorrectly extended to all areas of life and has led to the conclusion that there is no absolute truth. However, just because scientific interpretations are ever changing does not prove that truth does not exist. Science can neither prove nor disprove the existence of God. Furthermore, what we believe about the existence of God has absolutely no bearing on the reality of His existence. If we only know a fraction of all reality; who are we to assume that the knowledge of God does not exist in the areas we have not mastered?

If God does exist, and has interacted with mankind in the past;

there should be some physical evidence for both His existence and this interaction. The quantity and quality of this evidence is the subject of these articles.

Is it possible to discover objective truth? Is there sufficient evidence to support belief in the existence of a creator God? Is this God an impersonal force or a personal God who has interacted and communicated with humans? These are the questions which will be addressed. The foundational assumption of every article is that truth does exist. Jesus Christ repeatedly claimed to be God.[1] Either He is the creator of the universe or He is not. The Bible claims to be inspired by God.[2] Either this is true or the Bible is just a compilation of men's ideas. The Bible describes as factual events an instantaneous creation of separate plant and animal types and a worldwide water catastrophe. Either these events happened or they did not. If they did; there should be evidence supporting these events. These articles will thus examine all areas of science to determine just what is the truth of our past.

1. *The Bible - John 8:19, John 8:58 John 1:1-17, John 5:34 - 39,*
2. *The Bible - Isaiah 40:8, Matthew 5:18, 2 Timothy 3:16*

No Chance of Life By Chance

By Bruce Malone

In the 1700's, many scientists believed that life spontaneously generated from non-living matter (such as raw meat or sewage). In the 1800's, using careful experimentation, Louis Pasteur proved this concept wrong and verified that life only comes from previously existing life. Ironically, many scientists have once again returned to the belief that life came from nonlife…in spite of the fact that there is no experimental evidence to show how that could have happened. The reason for the return of this unsupported belief is that science has been defined to eliminate the consideration of the only other alternative—the creation of life by an intelligent designer.

Even the simplest living cell is an incredibly complex machine. It must be capable of detecting malfunctions, repairing itself, and reproducing itself. Man has never succeeded in building a machine capable of these same functions. Yet, most scientists accept the belief that life arose from non-life despite the ever increasing amount of evidence clearly indicating that it did not and could never happen. It would be easier to believe that a chemical manufacturing facility found on Mars had built itself.

A classic experiment used to support the belief that life "built itself" was first proposed in 1953 by Stanley Miller. In this experiment, sparks were discharged into an apparatus through which common gases were circulated. These gases reacted to form various organic products which were then collected and analyzed. The experiment succeeded in producing *a few* of the 20 amino acids required by living cells. These results have been heralded as proof that life could have arisen by itself. However, dozens of *major*

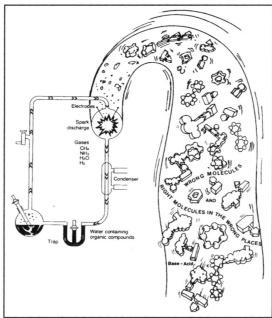

problems with this experiment, (clearly understood for more than 30 years), still go unanswered and are not even mentioned to students.[1]

For instance, our early atmosphere is assumed to have had no oxygen because this would stop amino acid formation. However, with no oxygen, there would be no ozone shield. With no ozone shield, life would be impossible. The fact that oxidized rocks throughout the geological record indicate that oxygen has always been present is ignored.

In addition, the same gases which can react to form amino acids in the presence of sunlight undergo known reactions which remove them from the atmosphere. The required gases simply could not have been around long enough for life to have developed. Furthermore, a cold trap was used to keep the reaction products from being destroyed as fast as they formed. Where is this "cold trap" in nature?

The biggest problem is that the amino acids formed in this experiment are always a 50/50 mixture of stereotypes (L and D forms). Stereotypes are like a drawer full of right-hand and left-hand gloves, identical in every way except a mirror image of each other. Life uses only L stereotypes of these random amino acids. Yet, equal proportions of both types are always produced. How could the first cell have selected only L stereotypes from the random, equally reactive mixture produced in this experiment? And what about the other required types of amino acids which have *never* been formed in this experiment?

These are just some of the myriad problems regarding the fanciful idea that life generated itself. What this experiment really proves is that life could not possibly have developed in this manner. Yet, students are told just the opposite.

No experiment has ever shown that matter has the ability to come alive. The best explanation for life is still that life only comes from pre-existing life. As you search for the truth, perhaps you should consider the possibility that the source of all life... is God.

1. Thaxton, C.B., Bradley, W.L., Olsen, R.L., *__The Mystery of Life's Origin,__* Chapter 4, Philosophical Library, 1984.

The Invevitable Extinction of Humanity

By Bruce Malone

For the last 200 years, science has increasingly become ruled by a single "prime directive." Those who remember the original Star Trek series will recall that every starship in the Federation fleet was bound by one unbreakable rule—they were never to interfere with the development of another culture. In a similar way, one unbreakable rule guides all modern scientific endeavors. Richard Dickerson, a prominent biochemist and member of the elite National Academy of Sciences, states it this way, *"Science, fundamentally is a game. It is a game with one overriding and defining rule: Let us see how far and to what extent we can explain the behavior of the physical and material universe in terms of purely physical and material causes, without ever invoking the supernatural... A chess player is perfectly capable of moving his opponent's king physically from the board and smashing it in the midst of a tournament. This would not make him the champion because the rules have not been followed."* [1]

It is because of the "prime directive" of science (i.e. we must explain everything via evolution) that no matter how conclusive the evidence for our recent creation, it will not be acknowledged. Further-more, the evidence pointing to this reality will be buried, ignored, and at times not even seen by those whose paradigm of reality is that the prime directive must be upheld even at the cost of intellectual honesty.

For the last 50 years, it has been acknowledged that if there is more than one minor mistake on the genetic code of a species per generation, that species is ultimately doomed to extinction. For instance, if cockroaches have been around for 300 million years and they have

one minor random change to their DNA every generation, over a billion meaningless mistakes would have built up - dooming them to extinction. No mechanism exists

> **"if there is more than one minor mistake on the genetic code of a species per generation, that species is ultimately doomed to extinction."**

which can eliminate these minor mistakes. Natural selection can act as a quality control mechanism which can eliminate individuals with major genetic problems because such offspring are less fit for survival. However, natural selection cannot remove mistakes in the genetic code that build up having minimal survival effect.

For instance, suppose our genetic code was similar to a textbook full of information and each subsequent copy of the textbook had a few letters randomly changed. Natural selection would be like the test taken by everyone who had read each unique textbook with its individual set of errors. Very few, if any of the textbooks, could be eliminated based on the results of end of the year student testing. The next generation of books would have a few more errors, and the third generation a few more..etc...until the textbook ultimately became meaningless nonsense. Yet, for any given textbook generation, natural selection (the testing of students using all of the textbooks from that generation of books) would have no ability to eliminate any but the most blatantly erroneous textbooks. This is why it has been acknowledged that more than one minor error per generation will ultimately doom a

species to extinction due to the "genetic load" of errors building up on its DNA code. [2]

It is not widely reported that every generation of humans has not one random error in their DNA code but thousands of random and permanent changes. These random changes are actually a loss of functioning information—the same way that random changes in the letters of a textbook result in the loss of information content.

The obvious question of 'where did all of the original information come from?' is also being ignored, as is the rate of detrimental changes -- orders of magnitude greater than any yet to be identified source of adding information. Furthermore, the rate at which mistakes are increasing on the human genome provides compelling evidence that the human genome cannot possibly have been around more than a few hundred generations nor can it survive indefinitely.

Never has there been so much scientific evidence supporting the reality that humans were recently created by an unimaginably intelligent designer. It is this evidence which makes it obvious that our hope lies not in this life nor in this physical universe—which is winding down, not up. Our hope lies in reconciling ourselves with the designer of this universe and in what He has done to provide for us in the eternity which will follow our physical extinction.

1. Dr. Michael Behe, *__Darwin's Black Box: The Biochemical Challenge to Evolution__*, Simon & Schuster, p. 240.
2. Dr. J.C. Sanford, *__Genetic Entropy: The Mystery of the Genome__*, Ivan Press, 2005.

Proteins: Life's Molecular Machines

By Bruce Malone

Proteins are huge molecules made by linking together hundreds, or even thousands, of different amino acids like beads on a long necklace. These proteins are not found in random arrangements, but are specifically designed to carry out unique biological functions. In order to function properly, they must have exactly the right amino acids, in exactly the right positions, and be of exactly the right length. It is the specific sequence of the 'beads' on a protein chain that allows each one to form the perfect 3-dimensional configuration needed to perform the required functions within our bodies.

It is estimated that the human body contains over 200,000 different proteins.[1] The following description of proteins is given by molecular biologist Michael Denton: *"If a cell were magnified a thousand million times...in every direction we looked, we would see all sorts of robot-like machines. We would notice that these simplest of the functional components of the cell -- the protein molecules -- were astonishingly, complex pieces of molecular machinery, each one consisting of about three thousand individual atoms arranged in highly organized 3-D spatial configurations...the task of designing even one such molecular machine - that is, a single functioning protein molecule - would be completely beyond our capacity..."[2]*

One example of a very common protein is the hemoglobin molecule. Hemoglobin is a protein in our red blood cells that transports oxygen throughout our bodies. The molecule is perfectly designed to transport the optimal amount of oxygen in exactly the right way. If just one of the 287 amino acids which make up the hemoglobin molecule is out of place, an often fatal disease called sickle-cell

> **The task of designing even one such molecular machine - that is, a single functioning protein molecule - would be completely beyond our capacity..."**

anemia results. Because of this misplacement of just 1 out of 287 specific amino acids, the defective hemoglobin molecules bind together when the amount of oxygen in the bloodstream becomes low. This in turn stretches the red blood cells into a sickle shape which cannot easily flow through small blood vessels.

If this is the consequence of the misplacement of just one amino acid out of 287; how could all of the very specific proteins needed by the first form of life have developed by random chance processes? The simplest known form of life has over 100 different (and specific) proteins. These are all formed from only L-type amino acids and are arranged in a very specific order by the DNA molecule. Yet in the words of John Horgan, *"The DNA cannot do its work, including forming more DNA, without the help of proteins. In short, proteins cannot form without DNA, but neither can DNA form without proteins."[3]* This is the classic chicken or egg mystery. You need both to be present simultaneously because one cannot form without the other.

Further complicating the process is the fact that all laboratory experiments simulating the conditions necessary for the formation of life produce a random mixture of 50:50 R and L stereotypes. The odds of just one protein forming (such as the 287 amino acid hemoglobin molecule) with all L stereotypes, could be compared to flipping a coin and getting "heads" 287 times in a row. This could statistically only happen only once in every 10^{124} tries. Most scientists agree that any specific event with odds greater than 10^{50} will never happen. It gets even more impossible, though, because proteins are not just random molecules, but need all the amino acids to be in a specific order to function correctly. The odds of getting the specific 100 proteins required for the simplest form of life, with all L stereotypes, and all in the specific order needed, is greater than $1/10^{10,000}$. Yet, a single human body uses not a mere 100, but 100,000 such specifically designed proteins!

These outlandish odds demonstrate the scientific impossibility of the formation of life by chance reactions. However, these problems are almost never presented in textbooks. Our children deserve better than an indoctrination which ignores these overwhelming problems.

1. James Perloff, **_Tornado in a Junkyard_**, Refuge, 1999, p. 66.
2. Michael Denton, **_Evolution: A theory in Crisis_**, Adler & Adler, p. 328.
3. John Horgan, "In the Beginning", **_Scientific American_**, 2/91, p. 119.

Not Enough Monkeys in the Universe

By Bruce Malone

The DNA molecule stores specific information by lining up four chemical compounds in a very specific order similar to the way Morse Code lines up three symbols (a dot, a dash, and a space) to convey a unique message. The order in which these four chemicals are arranged not only determines the distinguishing characteristics of an animal, but also if the organism will grow into a man or a marigold. Biochemists around the world are involved in a major undertaking to decode the language written on the human DNA molecule. But where did this fantastic molecule come from?

Scientists have had great success splicing new sections of DNA onto the DNA molecule, duplicating sections of DNA, producing the building blocks of DNA from basic chemicals, and unraveling the DNA molecular code. All too often, it is inferred that because we can do these things, we know how the molecule originated. However, this is a total distortion of reality.

Science has not even come close to explaining how the DNA molecule could have originated without intelligent guidance (i.e. creation). Here are just a few of the problems naturalistic scientists need to solve before making any sweeping statements concerning life's origin:

1. When the building blocks of DNA are mixed together, they do react and link up...but not in the spiral shape of the DNA molecule. How did the shape originally occur when it doesn't happen now?

2. Great amounts of energy would be required to produce a molecule as complicated and as large as even the simplest segment of DNA. Yet the molecule is so energy sensitive that it easily comes apart. Many mechanisms are in place within a cell to protect the

DNA molecule from degeneration. How could DNA have survived before all the protective mechanisms existed?

3. DNA is not a random, meaningless molecule. It carries specific and useful information needed for the formation and development of an organism. Where did this coded information come from?

4. Specific proteins function to construct copies of the DNA, but DNA is required to create the needed proteins. How could one exist without the other being there first?

There are many other major problems which have no answer aside from the acknowledgment of an intelligent designer. Yet, chance processes continue to be the only possibilities taught. It has been said that given enough time, anything can happen (such as a monkey typing the entire contents of the Encyclopedia Britannica). Rather than just accept such statements, let's use the science of probability to ask, "How many monkeys (or how much time) would it take to randomly type just the title 'Encyclopedia Britannica'?"

The odds of a monkey typing the 'e' of the title in the first place is 1 in 39 (the number of keys on a typical keyboard). The odds of getting an 'e' followed by an 'n' is (1/39 x 1/39). The odds of a monkey getting just the title 'Encyclopedia Britannica' correct (one time) is $1/10^{36}$. If these monkeys are extremely proficient and persistent typists and make one attempt every second for the entire assumed age of the universe (15 billion years) it would still require 100,000,000,000,000,000,000 monkeys. In other words, enough monkeys to cover every square foot of the Earth's surface, stacked over one mile deep, making one attempt every second for 15 billion years <u>MIGHT</u> type the title right...once. But even if one monkey did type the title right once, how would we ever recognize it among billions of trillions of wrong ones?

The useful information coded into the simplest DNA molecule is unimaginably more complicated that the simple title 'Encyclopedia Britannica'. The odds of the useful code found on the DNA molecule forming by chance processes is astronomically smaller. In actuality, it is an absolute impossibility. Science clearly reveals that life can not form by evolutionary processes. Why aren't we teaching our children these facts of science?

Is it a Bird..a Fish...or a Mammal?

By Bruce Malone

Loons have been documented diving 200 feet under the water and swimming with the agility of a fish. Indoctrination from our school, museum, and media system presents such abilities as having evolved over time by some natural mechanism. Believers in evolution provide only a superficial explanation for such specialized abilities, while totally ignoring the problems posed by such speculation. To see this dichotomy more clearly, let's examine in detail just one remarkable characteristic of the common loon.

The loon is the only bird that has solid bones similar to a mammal. Bones form the framework of bodies upon which the muscles, ligaments, and other tissue have a place to anchor and function. In animals, other than birds, bones are the densest and the mechanically strongest parts of the body. However, in birds, the bones have been designed hollow in order to reduce the overall weight of the bird, allowing it to fly while expending the least possible energy. The bones of birds, while remarkably strong for their weight, are less dense than surrounding tissue and can actually float on water -- except for the bones of a loon. It turns out that the loon has solid bones like mammals, rather than hollow bones like all other birds. Why is this and how could it have happened?

Every part of the loon is designed for it to function perfectly as a deep water diver. Its relatively small wings allow quick movement and direction changes under water. Its large webbed feet allow it to not only propel itself underwater, but to run on top of the water for assisted take-offs. And most importantly, its solid bones give it low enough buoyancy so it can rapidly descend to great depths when searching for fish. Other water birds such as

Notice how low the Loon Floats

ducks and swans, ride high in the water due to their hollow bones, but they cannot dive deep in search of fish. If the loon had hollow bones; diving deep would be as difficult as SCUBA diving with an inflated life vest.

Believers in evolution would argue that the loon developed its solid bones over time as small changes in DNA gave some pre-loon type bird increasingly denser bones resulting in the advantage of being able to dive deeper. This sounds logical, ***BUT*** the problems with such a scenario have been ignored. First, the whole idea of a bone slowly changing from hollow to solid is just story telling. There is no fossil or factual evidence to suggest it ever happened. Similar storytelling is repeatedly presented as science by evolutionary believers as they talk about their faith. Second, the structure of the two types of bone is completely different and involves a totally unique DNA sequence. Expecting random changes in the DNA code to change one type of bone to another would be like a cardboard factory suddenly turning out solid lumber due to random changes over time in the fiber processing machinery. It could simply never ever happen. Finally, the bone structure supports the surrounding tissue. Not only would the bones have to change, all the DNA code for each of the surrounding tissues, ligaments, muscle types, and blood generation apparatus within the bones would have to change simultaneously and function perfectly while the bones themselves were transforming from hollow to solid. Upon close examination the whole concept of slow change over time is preposterous.

If students were given all of this information, when presented with the unique features of an individual organism, and were then asked to ponder the relevant question - *how did this organism develop its unique features?* – they would be far more likely to discover the truth.

Only two possibilities exist -- the DNA information was programmed by a designer (creation) or this information developed by random mutational changes (evolution). The reason this choice of possibilities is not presented to students is that they would invariably choose creation - leaving naturalistic scientists with no followers. Furthermore, these same students would be far more likely to place the reality of God's existence at the center of every other choice they face in life.

Try Looking into the Microscope

By Bruce Malone

NASA has spent hundreds of millions of dollars scanning every minute portion of the sky with radio telescopes. Its goal is to locate signals coming to earth from extraterrestrial life forms. Although NASA has backed off on these efforts, private funds are still being solicited in order to continue the search. How would we identify a signal as coming from an intelligent source? It would have to consist of *a complex pattern with occasionally repeated segments* which could not be generated by a formula or a natural cause. An example of a repeated complex pattern is any human language. The carrier of the sequence could be as varied as ink on paper, electro-magnetic signals in space, sound through air, or smoke signals in the sky. **Whenever and wherever such a pattern is found it is proof of an intelligent originator.** This is why a pilot flying over a deserted beach could immediately recognize a message for help spelled out in the alignment of rocks on the beach even if he did not know the language in which the message was formed. The pattern itself would be immediately recognizable as having an intelligent source.

The series of simple repeated patterns emitted by rapidly rotating stars (quasars) is not evidence of intelligence because the sequence is too regular and contains no information. Random non-repeating patterns are merely noise and are

also not evidence of intelligent origin. It is only when there is *a complex pattern with occasionally repeated segments* that an intelligent originator must have been involved. If such a pattern coming from outer space

were to be discovered; it would be proof that we are not alone in our universe.

The primary motivation for the effort to find this pattern coming from a source outside of our solar system is philosophic and not scientific. If evidence of other life forms was found; it would be heralded as proof that life had developed elsewhere. In other words, given the right conditions... life could pop up anywhere. Yet, there is not a single shred of evidence that life exists anywhere else in the physical universe. Since the effort is philosophically rather than scientifically motivated, negative results seldom change the motivation or beliefs of the experimenters.

The same individuals who are

willing to spend millions of taxpayer dollars in an effort to find such a pattern in electromagnetic signals from space are unwilling to acknowledge that the same type of complex pattern, found in all living cells, came from an intelligent source. In our search for intelligent extra-terrestrial life, why don't we take our eyes off the telescope and put them on the microscope? Inside every living organism is a marvelous blueprint for life known as the DNA molecule. Guess what this organic molecule contains? *A complex pattern with occasionally repeated segments* which could not be generated by a formula or a natural cause! This is the same type of evidence which scientists would immediately accept as proof of intelligent origin - if it was found coming from outer space.

Why isn't the coded sequence of the DNA molecule heralded as evidence of intelligent origin? Can it be that many scientists are blind to the evidence for supernatural design because they have been trained to believe that an intelligent, creator God cannot be considered? Does peer pressure from the scientific community stop the open acknowledgment of this obvious evidence for the divine origin of biological life? Furthermore, as knowledge of our universe increases, do we have more or less reason to believe in its supernatural origin?

The Builder will Eventually Return

By Bruce Malone

Parables are stories about familiar things which illustrate a deeper meaning. The following parable has its roots in modern man's search for the origin of life.

In an isolated jungle lived a tribe of primitive people with no knowledge of the world outside their village. They had never been in contact with any modern technology and lived in constant struggle with other tribal groups. One day as members of the tribe were hunting in unknown territory, they stumbled upon the wreckage of a crashed airplane. Approaching the plane with caution they touched the metal surface and ran their hands over the smooth glass of the cockpit window. As they ran back to the village to report the find to the village elders many questions ran through their minds. Where could this huge structure have come from? A debate over the origin of this strange object soon raged - had the gods sent it to them as a sign? The village polarized into opposing viewpoints.

One opinion was that the object was built by humans. After all, the skeletal remains of several humans were found within the decaying structure. Others believed the object must have had a natural origin. To believe it was created by other humans would acknowledge an intelligence surpassing their own.

Those believing that the airplane was designed and built by other intelligent humans argued that this was obvious, but could not prove how, why, or when. All attempts to explain how, why, or when, which were not based on a belief in random natural processes, were severely ridiculed. The tribal elders believed that all of the knowledge needed to explain the

Used by permission of Pamela Van Noose

world around them was in the possession of their tribal counsel and any attempt to persuade them otherwise was met with severe punishment. The first group soon became silent.

Those believing in the natural origin of the object strengthened their argument by showing that the same rubber-like substance found in the tires could be found oozing from trees. Likewise, a substance similar to the glass could be found on beaches where lightning had struck the sand. The paint and fluids in the structure could also be shown to occur naturally. By throwing one of the screws into the air with just the right spinning motion and catching it in just the right hole, the screw would even partially spin into place.

Amongst themselves they agreed that, given enough time, the structure could have built itself (although the exact mechanism was not yet known).

Even more convincing evidence was forthcoming as the deteriorating airplane was repaired and the parts rearranged. Since the natives eventually understood so much about the structure, this was accepted as proof that the plane had built itself. A project was even started to map, catalogue, and understand every piece of the structure. All of these observations confirmed to the primitive natives that they had been correct in their understanding of the natural origin of the object.

Those stubborn few who continued to believe the object was created by other intelligent people were considered backward and ignorant. They were ignored, and village schools were organized so that all of the children would be taught only the naturalistic "scientific" explanation.

Within several generations, there was no longer any dissension because everyone now knew that random processes had produced the wrecked airplane. So the mystery was solved ... until the builder of the airplane returned.

Life is Irreducibly Complex

By Bruce Malone

As we learn more about biological life, it becomes increasingly apparent that its similarity to complex machines is startlingly strong. Yet, because science has been redefined to exclude the possibility of a designer, we are left without any plausible explanation of how life developed.

Michael Behe is a biochemistry professor at Lehigh University who wonderfully illustrates the similarity between mechanical machines and biological life in his book, **_Darwin's Black Box: The Biochemical Challenge to Evolution_**. According to Dr. Behe, even at the smallest biochemical level, life is made up of irreducibly complex machines. Although these machines are made of proteins instead of metal, their complexity is proof that they could only have been produced by an incomprehensibly intelligent designer.

The perfect example of an irreducibly complex machine is the simple mouse trap. This machine consists of at least five parts: the platform, the spring, the hammer, the catch, and the hold-down latch bar. The absence of any one of these components will turn the machine into a piece of useless junk. Furthermore, each of the components has to be designed to a specific size and positioned in a specific place in order for the mouse trap to function. Thus, the simple mousetrap is irreducibly complex … it will not function unless all five pieces are in place. It is this interdependence of the individual parts which makes it so obvious that the simple mousetrap has a designer.

Biological life is also made from irreducibly complex structures, even at the smallest molecular level. For instance, there are millions of organisms, including human bodies, which use a structure called a cilium to either swim or move things around within a creature. Cilia are hair-like structures attached to cells which beat like a whip in order to move foreign particles out of our lungs. Sperm also use cilia to swim.

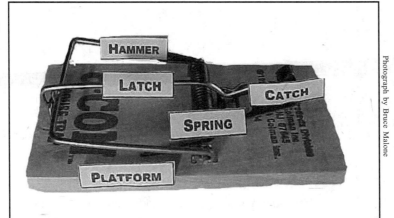

HAMMER
LATCH
CATCH
SPRING
PLATFORM

Photograph by Bruce Malone

Because these structures are so biologically important and so widespread throughout the animal kingdom, Dr. Behe estimates that TEN THOUSAND technical papers have been published on various aspects of cilia.

Like the mouse trap, cilia require several components in order to operate. In the case of a mousetrap, the components are specifically sized pieces of metal and wood. In the case of cilia, they are specifically shaped proteins. The absolute minimum number of components needed for a cilium to operate are three: proteins forming the hair-like fibers (the rotor), proteins linking the adjacent fibers so that they do not fly apart (links), and proteins which contract to cause its whipping motion (the motor). Without all three of these components - the structure would not function. Thus, cilia are irreducibly complex machines. In reality, cilia contain hundreds of different proteins and all are required for its operation. But even these three specific proteins could never have formed by chance mutations. All three are specifically designed to function together and if any one as missing, the cilia could not operate. Thus, the cilia would become a useless drag line hindering the motion of the organism rather than aiding its survival.

In Dr. Behe's words, "The amount of scientific research which has been done... leads many people to assume that even if they don't know how cilia evolved, somebody must know. But the search of professional literature proves them wrong. Nobody knows."

Nobody knows where cilia came from because cilia are irreducibly complex and can never be explained without a supernatural designer. Yet most biochemists are trained to ignore this possibility when examining biological features. If the correct answer has been eliminated; is it any wonder that ten thousand papers can be written on cilia and not one can explain their origin?

A Squashed Mosquito is Dead Forever

By Tom Wagner

Have you ever squashed a mosquito? Interestingly, the squashing of a mosquito may help us understand what makes life possible and what makes the spontaneous generation of life impossible.

When a mosquito is slapped, what happens? Obviously it's shape changes and it dies. But what makes it die? All of the thousands of sophisticated chemicals which make up its body are still there, relatively unaltered. At the moment of impact its cellular components are still intact including the all-important DNA. So why is it now dead?

Prior to being smashed, the mosquito was a highly organized system with much organized information. But when hit, it became disordered, causing critical information in the design of its body to become jumbled. There arose confusion in the finely tuned coordination of chemistry (including the chemicals involved in its overall structure) which culminated in an overall breakdown, resulting in death. And you thought you just slapped it!

For another example, let's say you were to take 100 million bacteria and concentrate them in the bottom of a test tube. Now if you were to physically lyse (break open) the membrane of each of the cells, the insides would spill out, forming a concentrated mixture of incredibly complex "life-giving" chemicals. Yet, even though all of the right 'stuff' for life is there, not even one of the 100 million critters will come back to life, nor would any new creature arise.

For a third example lets consider the food industry. Each year over a billion containers of previously living

chemical ingredients are placed into containers where light and/or heat can pass through (an open thermo-dynamic system.) Everything needed for life to form is present in each jar or can. Yet not once, in any can or jar, does new life form.

If the already complex chemistry of minuscule bacteria or canned food cannot reorganize itself back into a living cell, even when concentrated in the test tube environment under carefully controlled conditions, then how could life have evolved in the first place, from basically uncomplicated chemicals in conditions FAR less appropriate? It simply never could have happened!

As with the mosquito, in order for life to exist the chemistry must be specifically organized and controlled in time as well as space.

For a cell to live, it must be surrounded by a sophisticated membrane that allows only certain chemicals in and out, according to when they are needed, not just at any time. Inside the cell, the amount of any chemical must be exactly correct, otherwise the whole system would be thrown off balance and the organism would die. Furthermore, the entire living organism must be controlled by the fantastically complex three dimensional genetic coded structure of DNA.

All this means that in order for the chemistry to have come together in the first place, the individual atoms must have been purposefully and simultaneously organized by a creator having the knowledge and power to do such a thing. It could not possibly have happened by the right chemicals just "coming together".

It is Jesus, the Son of the Living God, who deserves our praise for the awesome things He has accomplished in this creation of His. There is no other plausible explanation for the complex life we find all around us. Yet, this plausible explanation is the only one not allowed to be discussed in our public schools!

Tom Wagner is a nature photographer and science teacher living in Iowa who writes on the evidence for creation. This article was first published in Creation magazine, www.answersingenesis.org

What Good is Part of an Animal?

By Bruce Malone

The late Dr. Werher von Braun, a renowned space scientist and former director of NASA, made the following statement concerning our origin, *"One cannot be exposed to the law and order of the universe without concluding that there must be design and purpose behind it all...To be forced to believe only*

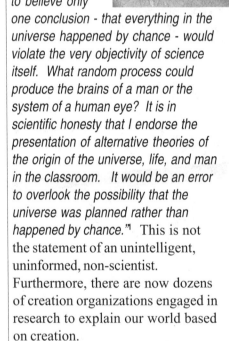

one conclusion - that everything in the universe happened by chance - would violate the very objectivity of science itself. What random process could produce the brains of a man or the system of a human eye? It is in scientific honesty that I endorse the presentation of alternative theories of the origin of the universe, life, and man in the classroom. It would be an error to overlook the possibility that the universe was planned rather than happened by chance." This is not the statement of an unintelligent, uninformed, non-scientist. Furthermore, there are now dozens of creation organizations engaged in research to explain our world based on creation.

A powerful example of the evidence for creation is the interdependence of the parts within an organism. Could completely different yet fully functioning parts of an organism have all arisen in a step-by-step fashion? If not, their origin must have been simultaneous creation. The butterfly is a perfect example. How could some worm-like creature have mutated with both the ability *and* desire to seal itself inside a cocoon? For either to happen would require thousands of simultaneous and useful changes to the chemical structure of this mysterious "pre-butterfly" type creature. What would have

happened to some worm-like creature that sealed itself

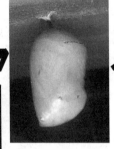

inside of a cocoon but did not yet have the ability to rearrange its biomatter into an adult butterfly? There has never been a logical explanation of how an insect other than a caterpillar (which already possesses the necessary information to become a butterfly) could transform itself into a butterfly by a series of small genetic changes.

Another example is the woodpecker. Evolution teaches that some kind of bird turned into a woodpecker at some time in the distant past. But what would happen to the first bird born with its feet modified with a backwards claw... yet without the instinct to search for insects while holding onto a vertical tree trunk? Or to the first bird born with backwards talons and the desire to beat its head against a tree... but the incorrect bill? Or the correct feet, desire, and bill...but no instinct to blink its eyes at the moment of impact to keep its eyeballs from popping out? Or the correct feet, desire, bill, and blinking ability... but with a tongue too short to reach the insects inside the hole which it had just beaten into the tree? Or the correct feet, desire, bill, blinking ability, shock-

absorbing membranes in the back of the skull, and tongue...but now the tongue too long to fit into its mouth because its skull was not yet redesigned to hold the tongue? In each case, the bird would be at an incredible disadvantage and natural selection would have brought its evolutionary development to an end.

There are thousands of other examples in nature. It is easy to look at a perfectly designed organism and say, *"Look at how well this creature is adapted to its environment!"* The critical question

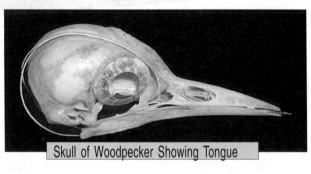
Skull of Woodpecker Showing Tongue

is ignored by evolutionists and not presented to students - *"Is it logical that this animal could have developed by one small change at a time?"*

1. Excerpts from an original interview in "Applied Christianity", from the **Bible-Science Newsletter**, May 1974, p.8.

NOTE:
Throughout this book 'evolution' will refer to its original meaning: the transformation of one type of animal into a completely different type. No one disputes that there can be minor variations within a given class of organism (micro-evolution). However, this has never been shown to lead to completely new features or types of creatures.

Mutations Always Result in a Loss

By Bruce Malone

Darwin's original theory of evolution included the idea that environmental changes could cause structural changes to occur in plants and animals. He also postulated that these acquired characteristics could be transmitted to offspring. In other words, a horse-like animal, by stretching its neck to reach the leaves in a tree, would be at an advantage if it had a longer neck. So after a life time of using its body in this way, it might develop a longer neck and would pass on this characteristic (which was acquired during its lifetime) to its offspring. This original belief, known as Lamarckism, has been shown false and has been replaced by the belief that mutations are the driving force behind evolution.

Mutations are mistakes made during the transfer of information from the genes of one generation to the next (birth defects are examples of these.) Believers in evolution postulate that if these mistakes are beneficial to the animal it will give the mutated animal an advantage, and natural selection will then preferentially select these animals for survival. Although this belief seems logical, it does not fit reality.

Mutations are mistakes which have never produced a long term benefit. Even examples of "beneficial" mutations, such as sickle cell anemia (a fatal disease which imparts a resistance to malaria) do not create new features or improve overall survivability. One hundred years of experimentation has shown that mutations can not develop new organisms or even cause useful

changes to existing organisms. This is because mutations never add useful information. They are exactly analogous to random misspellings in a book. Therefore this mechanism for evolution, even in combination with natural selection, fails to explain how new functional structures could arise.

During the last century millions of fruit flies have been irradiated in

laboratory experiments to observe the effect of mutations. The mutation rate has been increased by as much as 15,000 times[1]. The results of this experiment simulate millions of years of evolutionary progress. What has resulted are big-winged, small-winged, wrinkled-winged, and no-winged fruit flies; large-bodied, small bodied, and no-bodied fruit flies; red-eyed, speckled-eyed, leg-in-place of eye fruit flies; many bristled or no bristled fruit flies; but mainly dead or sterile fruit flies. In conclusion, researchers began with fruit flies and end up with...well...fruit flies - defective ones.

Furthermore, after several generations, even changes in the number of bristles on the irradiated fruit flies reverted back to the original number.[2] No new organ or useful functioning feature has ever

developed.

The belief that mutations could slowly change an animal into some other animal is analogous to believing that an old vacuum tube black and white television could be changed into an color liquid crystal monitor by throwing random parts at it. The impacts will definitely produce changes (given the quality of current TV shows it could even

be argued that these changes would be beneficial), but they certainly will not change the unit into a color TV.

In the same way, mutations may produce changes, and it is remotely possible that some may be beneficial, but they will not change an organism into some other type of organism. For that to happen, useful information would have to be added to the DNA of the creature. This simply is not going to happen as a result of random mutations.

It would seem that this commonly accepted evolutionary mechanism (mutations) has serious flaws which are seldom reported to students or to the general public.

1. E.J. Gardner, ***Principles of Genetics***, (N.Y.: Wily, 1964) p. 180.
2. N. MacBeth, ***"The Question: Darwinism Revisited"***, <u>Yale Review</u>, June, 1967, p. 622.

Darwin's Magic Potion

By Bruce Malone

When Charles Darwin published *The Origin of Species* in 1859, he brought scientific credibility to the concept that man developed slowly from previous life forms. Most people do not realize that the concept of evolution did not actually originate with Darwin, but predates him by thousands of years. As far back in history as the ancient Greeks there were ideas about life coming from previous forms of life. Even the mechanisms proposed by Darwin can be attributed, in a large part, to others.[1] What sets Darwin apart is the timing of his work. The intellectual community of Northern Europe was ripe for a naturalistic explanation of life. The distortion of Biblical Christianity was bringing faith in the supernatural under increasing ridicule, and humanism (man making himself the center of all things) was rapidly replacing the Christian belief in absolute truth.

Thus, when an alternative to creation seemed to have been found, it was rapidly accepted as fact. The easiest way to reject the authority of a creator is to remove the existence of that creator. In actuality, Darwin proved neither where life came from nor how it developed. He merely proposed a method whereby this transformation from beast to man *seemed* possible. With the exception of mutations as the source of new genetic information, the belief in evolution as the explanation for our origin has progressed little in the last 150 years. The concepts popularized by Darwin continue to be taught with the fervor of religious dogma.

Darwin proposed several things concerning the origin of the enormous variety of life on our planet. The first was that *"the species are not immutable"* (i.e. we came from a previous simpler form of life). Darwin's second

Pepper Moth Color Variation

proposal was that this transformation of one life form into another was driven by a process called natural selection (popularized as "survival of the fittest"). His third assumption was the rejection of a Biblical time frame and a world wide flood as an explanation for the geology of the planet. This allowed him to accept the increasingly popular huge time periods needed for this transformation to take place. Believers in evolution still assume that given enough time, there is essentially no limit to biological variation. But can this seemingly magical force transform amoebas into man?

Almost every biology textbook has the following example of natural selection in action. In England, before the industrial revolution, it was common to find the peppered moth in proportions of 95 percent light-colored to 5 percent dark-colored. This was believed to be caused by the majority of the trees in a certain area being light so the light-colored moths were better camouflaged. Thus fewer light-colored moths were eaten by predators. After the industrial revolution, the trees became primarily dark-colored (due to pollution) and the light-colored moths were now at a disadvantage to the predators. Thus, the peppered moth population shifted from light colored to 95 percent dark. This is a classic example of the powerful ability of natural selection to adapt an organism to its environment. But how far does this go to explain the development of completely different types of animals? We started with light and dark moths and we ended up with...light and dark moths. Nothing new developed. The population merely shifted.

There does not exist even one example of natural selection producing a new type of animal, a new organ, or even a major permanent change in an existing organism. This is because "natural selection" is just that - selection. It can create nothing new. It can only select the most advantageous information which is already present in the molecular blueprint of the organism. Natural selection cannot cause new useful information to be added to the DNA of an animal. Darwin was simply wrong when presenting this mechanism as the explanation for life's development.

1. Ian Taylor, ***In the Minds of Men***, TFE Publishing, 1987.

Natural Selection to the Rescue?

By Bruce Malone

It is assumed by believers in evolution that some mutations find a useful purpose. It is proposed that even a slight advantage will be passed onto the next generation, which, exceedingly slowly, transforms one type of creature to another. This process is known as natural selection, but how does natural selection hold up under the light of scientific scrutiny as the directing force behind life's origin and diversity? Dr. John Sanford, retired Cornell University geneticist, inventor of the "gene gun" and 25 other patented discoveries, uses the following illustration to expose the fallacy of this evolutionary belief.[1]

According to Dr. Sanford, the amount of information required to transform a single-celled organism into a human being would be greater than the information required to transform the manufacturing plant for a Little Red Wagon™ into the Star Ship Enterprise -- complete with warp drive engines and holodeck! Can natural selection, acting on accidental changes to the assembly directions of the little red wagon, accomplish this transformation?

Natural selection is similar to the quality control department at the wagon assembly plant and our genetic code is similar to a document containing the entire manufacturing process for the red wagon. Everything needed to manufacture the wagon, including the specifications for all of the materials of construction...all of the individual components...the

processes needed to manufacture them...all of the metal press specifications...all of the robotics and programming language...the assembly instructions...the paint specifications...the employee benefits manual... EVERYTHING needed for the wagon's construction needs to be attached as a manual to the bottom of the wagon. The next wagon to be produced must use only the information in the existing wagon to make the next copy. The quality department (natural selection) can only see the finished enormous

wagon, not the amount of information in the manufacturing manual (the genetic code of the wagon). The question is: can random changes in the assembly manual (the genetic code) allow the quality control department (natural selection) to transform the little red wagon into a better wagon and ultimately into the USS Enterprise?

The amount of information contained within the simplest single cell organism (similar to the information required to build a wagon assembly plant) would fill a small library. Suppose you started with a perfect set of instructions in this library and randomly changed hundreds of individual letters throughout the instructions. Very few of these changes would be critical for assembly or cause a faulty wagon which the quality control department (natural selection) would reject. It is far

more likely that almost all of the random changes (these are called mutations in living organisms) would result in no noticeable change and the wagons would roll off the assembly line with mistakes in their manuals intact -- to be used in the creation of the next generation of wagons. This next generation would then have another set of barely noticeable mistakes added, one random letter mistake at a time. Given enough generations of the wagons, and with every increasing letter-by-letter mistake in their assembly manuals; eventually the point would be reached when wagons could no longer be produced from the instructions because there are so many tiny mistakes present. Large mistakes can be eliminated by natural selection, but not the small mistakes because, one wrong "letter" at a time, they are essentially undetectable in the final product. Yet, in the end they will drive the manufacturing process to extinction the same way one rust molecule at a time will destroy a car. This is exactly what is happening to the human genome at an alarming rate. Thousands of tiny mistakes are building up with each generation.

It would seem that neither mutations, nor natural selection, can remotely justify the dogmatic belief in evolution as the explanation for either life's development or its origin.

1. Dr. J.C. Sanford, *Genetic Entropy: The Mystery of the Genome,* Ivan Press, 2005.

Concepts have Consequences

By Bruce Malone

Concepts have consequences. **People act on what they believe to be true.** If children are indoctrinated through a public education system which allows only evidence which fits neatly into a naturalistic explanation of life; we will increasingly become a society which looks only to ourselves for answers to life's questions.

If we have evolved from apes; if we are just another animal ...then who sets the rules? Whose standard should define right from wrong, good from bad, helpful from harmful, lawful from unlawful? Without an absolute basis for morals, the distinction between these opposites disappear. The result is a spiraling descent toward meaninglessness and a degeneration in the value of human life. Acknowledgment of creation provides answers to foundational questions about life that are based on factual scientific and historical evidence. If we evolved from pond slime; on what factual basis could anyone say their belief is right, while someone else's belief is wrong?

A common consequence of the belief in evolution can be found in most high school biology books that contain a section on comparative embryology. This is the concept that humans and animals have a common ancestor because their embryos have a similar physical appearance. This concept was popularized in 1866 by Ernst Haeckel as he traveled throughout Europe showing the similarity of different animal embryos. Yet, as early as 1874 he was reprimanded by his own university for using fraudulent drawings. Amazingly, his teachings remain in textbooks to this day. Since the 1950's, it has

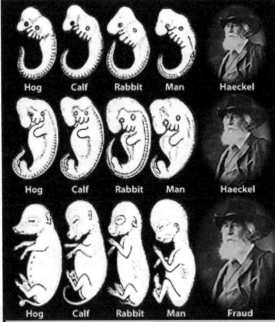

Haeckel's fraudulent drawings - he changed the head and eye size, moved eyes to different positions, and modified body lengths.

been proven that a woman's fertilized egg is a complete human being. Only time and nutrition are required for it to grow larger. From the moment of conception, a pregnant woman's body is two bodies, not one. The second body from the moment of conception, can never be anything but a human.

Examples of developing baby parts which have been said to be evidence of evolution are the "gill slits" and the "yolk sac". In a growing baby, the "gill slits" and "yolk sac" serve completely different functions from those of animals from which they are supposed to be descended. Gill slits form gills in fish. In humans, they are merely folds forming various glands and facial features. The yolk sac contains food for a reptile or a bird; while for a human, it has a radically different function. In a growing baby, the heart and circulatory system develop before the bones (which will ultimately be the baby's blood source). A baby's heart actually starts to beat 18 days from conception. Yet, the developing baby may have a different blood type than its mother, so it cannot use her blood. With no bone marrow to make its own blood, how can the baby continue to develop? The simplest engineering answer would be to provide a temporary alternative supply. The yolk sac does exactly that, then it disappears!

Comparative embryology does nothing to support the concept of evolution. The primary reason that it still remains in textbooks is that it is used to justify abortion. A woman does not have an abortion because she believes in evolution: although, it makes it much easier to justify killing a baby if you believe it is just a blob going through some stage of comparative embryology. How easy to justify moral disobedience; if we are just animals accountable to no one but ourselves.

It is a historical fact that mankind is sinful and rebellious. The taking of human life by abortion is just one more example of this sinful nature. Fortunately, God has provided a bridge to span the moral abyss between sinful mankind and Himself. This bridge is called Jesus and it is open to anyone willing to repent (change direction) and believe that Jesus is their Maker and Lord who paid the price for their sins.

Our Design is no Accident

By Bruce Malone

Vestigial features are those parts of an organism thought to be useless leftovers from its ancestor, as the creature has evolved to a new way of life. Our tailbone is commonly taught to be such a feature. The idea of vestigial features has been used as evidence for evolution since 1859 when Darwin first proposed that such features were evidence for the descent of one organism from a completely different one. The logical consequence of this alleged transformation is that the "new" creature would be left with some features which are no longer needed in its new environmental niche.

Belief in evolution demands that we believe that each type of animal on earth is a result of its descent from some previous life form. If this were the case; almost every creature should have many leftover features which are no longer needed. Yet, the more we learn about biology, the more we discover that every part of an organism serves some useful function. For example, the appendix is often said to be a useless leftover from our ape ancestry. We now know that the appendix serves as a type of lymphatic tissue in the first few months of life to fight disease. It is no more a useless feature than one of your lungs is useless just because you can survive with only one lung.

The acceptance of the idea that some parts of the human body are useless leftovers has led to many tragic consequences. Based on the misguided concept that the human colon was a vestige of the past, Sir William Land and dozens of other surgeons stripped the colons from

thousands of patients in order to "cure" a variety of symptoms[2]. Many died. As late as the 1960's many people routinely had their tonsils removed. This practice was again fueled by the mistaken belief that the tonsils were a useless leftover feature from our past. It is now known that they serve an

important disease fighting function and should not normally be removed.

Some possible vestigial features exist such as the blind eyes of cave salamanders. Blind salamanders have non-functional eyes because they live their entire lives in total darkness. At some time in the past, salamanders may have found a niche in dark caves and apparently only those which mutated to blindness had a need to stay in the total darkness where they could compete for existence without blindness being a disadvantage. However, these salamanders are still salamanders, a mutation to blindness is hardly an upward improvement in complexity, and no new information has been added to the DNA of the salamander.

The human tailbone is frequently

listed as a vestigial feature but anatomists tell us that the tailbone serves a very important function in human physiology. The coccyx (tailbone) is the point of insertion of several muscles and ligaments including the one which allows man to walk completely upright. Without a tailbone, people could not walk in a completely upright manner, dance a ballet, perform gymnastics, or stroll down the street with their arm around their spouse. Hardly a useless, leftover -- vestigial feature! The human body is designed for maximum versatility -- it is far more versatile than the body of any other creature. What other animal can perform the range of movement required for activities as diverse as ice skating, pearl diving, pole vaulting, snow boarding and gymnastics? This range of movement would be impossible without the tailbone!

In summary, evolution predicts that there should be leftover features as one organism slowly turned into another. Based on this theory, over 150 human features were at one time listed as useless. Creation predicts that although some life forms have degenerated and lost use of an original function; every part of an organism was designed to serve some useful purpose. As we learn more about the biology of living organisms, including ourselves, it is readily apparent which theory best fits the facts.

1. Robert Wiedersheim, ***The Structure of Man***, p. 200, 1895.

The Eyes Have it - Creation is Reality

By Bruce Malone

Charles Darwin expressed confidence that natural selection could explain the development of the eye[1], but how does this confidence stand up to the light of reason? Today, we are in the curious intellectual situation of allowing only naturalistic explanations in public schools. This is done in spite of the fact that the alternative (creation or intelligent design) more adequately explains the observations. It would take a miraculous number of design changes to transform a light sensitive patch into an eyeball. Furthermore, each change would have to be coded onto the DNA of the "new" creature in order for the change to pass to the next generation. It has never been explained how this could have happened. Each new feature would need to be independently useful or natural selection would not have allowed the new creature to live.

- An eyeball with no retina would be a tumor, not an improvement to be passed on to the next generation.
- An eyeball without a focusing lens would be worthless except as a light detector.
- An eyeball without a functioning optic nerve to carry the signal to the brain would be worthless.
- An eyeball without the perfect balance of fluid pressure would explode or implode.

- An eyeball without a brain designed to interpret the signals would be sightless.
- There are over 100,000 different proteins in our body. The only one with a molecular structure to make it perfectly transparent to light is used to construct the lens of our eye.

Labels: Lateral Rectus M., Sclera, Retina, Choroid, Ciliary Muscle, Foyea Centralis, Vitreous Body, Upper lid, Central Artery And Vein, Lens, Cornea, Hyaloid Canal, Suspensory Lig., Optic Nerve

The Incredibly Complex Eye

It is beyond credibility that chance mutations could have produced any of these changes, let alone all of them at once. Any one of these changes would result in a worthless tumor. All are needed simultaneously for sight to result.

Yet, the chance development of this "hardware" for the eye pales in comparison to the impossibility of the "software" development. The brain must be wired to both accept and understand the signal coming to it from the eyeball. An analogy would be the multi-pixel image from a digital camera. Each part of the image is wired to a specific spot in the receptor screen of the camera to reproduce an image of what the camera is viewing. As the "first eye" was developing, how could the

brain have known what the randomly wired image received from the pixels of the optic nerve represented? Before there was sight, the image would be wired like the white snowy image of an out of tune television screen. It can be statistically proven that randomly changing the location of a few of the millions of available pixels would never produce a clear image and sight could never develop in this way.[2]

In Darwin's time, the complex design of the eyeball was forceful evidence in favor of creation. Our more advanced knowledge of the intricate design of the eye provides even stronger evidence for its creation.

The complexity of the eye still argues for the reality of its instantaneous formation by an incredibly intelligent designer. There is neither a fossil record showing that the eye evolved nor any testable observations to explain how it could possibly have happened. The fanciful story that a light receptive patch turned into the complex eyeball is nothing but the dogmatic faith of a religious belief system. Why do we allow textbook selection which leaves out both the problems with evolution and the evidence for intelligent design? This is indoctrination, not education.

1. Charles Darwin, ***The Origin of the Species,*** republished by J.M. Dent & Sons Ltd., London, 1971, p. 167.
2. Stoltzmann, David, ***The Specified Complexity of Retinal Imagery,*** Creation Research Society Quarterly, June 2006.

Common Creation Question Answered

By Bruce Malone

Many questions are raised by believers in evolution when presented with the evidence for creation. This article addresses some of these common questions.

How did marsupials get to Australia?

Noah was charged with building the vessel to safeguard certain animals during the first flood (a massive and complex worldwide disaster) not with distributing them afterwards. Once Noah released the animals on Mount Ararat, natural instincts and climatic conditions determined how the redistribution of the animal population took place. As subsequent generations of animals spread across the globe, territorial prowess or chance movements would send certain groups in certain directions. Those animals least suited for or least able to defend a territory would either be forced further from the landing site or exterminated. A consequence of the worldwide flood was a brief but severe ice age which locked ocean water into vast ice fields. This lowered ocean levels and created a land bridge to Australia. A similar land bridge connected Asia to Alaska during this period of Earth history allowing for the free movement of man and animals between these continents. Land movements during the ice age or the subsequent melting of the ice cut off the connection between Australia and Asia effectively isolating the unique animal life to Australia.

How could worldwide coal deposits form rapidly?

The first effect of the worldwide flood would have been the ripping up of vegetation and erosion on an unimaginable scale. As the water receded from one area, vegetation would have been deposited only to be subsequently buried as the area sank and water brought in more sediment. Thus, layer upon layer of coal would have been formed. Furthermore, it has been shown in the laboratory that vegetation can

> "Denying that survival of the fittest is part of the evolutionary process is akin to denying that one type of animal will drive another to extinction."

be turned in to coal in as little as one hour with sufficient heat and pressure. A recent model of coal formation is provided by a study of the catastrophic explosion of Mount St. Helens in 1980. This explosion knocked down millions of trees which ended up floating on Spirit Lake. Underneath this floating vegetation mat is a thick layer of peat consisting of tree bark and organic matter. If that organic matter were buried by a subsequent eruption, the result would be a coal seam covered by sedimentary rock. Repeated cycles would rapidly produce a series of coal seams with sediment on top of each seam. It is perfectly reasonable to believe that an enormous global flood would have rapidly created the extensive coal seams we find today.

Is "Survival of the Fittest" part of evolution?

Modern evolutionists have tried to distance themselves from this concept due to the obvious negative consequences of applying the principle to the social realm. Denying that survival of the fittest is part of the evolutionary process is akin to denying that one type of animal will drive another to extinction given the right conditions. Contrary to the rosy picture of animal cooperation which evolutionists like to portray, one type of animal has no qualms wiping out another in its quest to propagate itself. Wild dogs introduced to Australia are endangering native species because they are more aggressive and have no natural enemies. Sounds like "survival of the fittest" doesn't it? Survival of the fittest has always been an integral part of the evolutionary theory.

If we are also animals that have evolved according to this basic principle of evolution; why shouldn't we extend this principle to the social realm? Why shouldn't we eliminate weaker classes of humans that compete for what we feel we need? Evolution taken to its logical conclusion leads to a savage world akin to Hitler's Nazi Germany when the strong determine what is right. It was no coincidence that Hitler was strongly influenced by the writings of Darwin.

It is a slap in God's face and a distortion of Scripture to believe that evolution, with its driving mechanism of survival of the fittest, would be a loving God's method for creating and preserving us.

Stasis - Yesterday Once More

By Bruce Malone

Illustrated throughout this article are a few of the thousands of organisms which have remained literally unchanged while millions of years supposedly passed. Meanwhile, other forms of life were supposedly changing - all the way from fish to people - without leaving a transitional record.[1] This is one of many problems with the belief in evolutionism. The pictures in this article show the fossilized or amber encapsulated organisms (often assumed to be over 100 million years old) compared with identical modern living specimens (in the smaller inset picture).

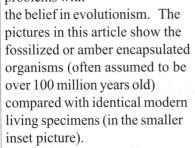

It is a fact of biology that organisms have an incredible ability to accurately reproduce copies of themselves. So where do new types of animals come from? Believers in evolution theorize that new animals arise when a reproductive mistake happens. They believe the "old" creature slowly turns into a completely different type of creature (apparently without leaving any fossil remains of the transitional forms). Meanwhile, other animals of the same type remained identical for millions of years!

There is an acknowledged lack of evidence for the transitional forms between vastly different types of animals. The current explanation concerning the lack of fossil evidence for evolution is called "punctuated equilibrium". This is really just a smoke screen for a lack of evidence. According to punctuated equilibrium, animals stay the same for long periods of time but when they change, they change rapidly. Thus, they leave no fossil record of their transformation because it happens so fast in relatively small or isolated locations. Thus for believers in evolution, the lack of evidence becomes evidence!

LOGIC CHECK TIME:

What does the biological record show? - stasis (lack of change).

Evolution explanation:
Macro-evolution is happening *so slowly* that we do not even see it today.

What does the fossil record show? - no intermediate forms between different animal groups.

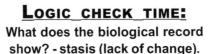

Evolution explanation:
Macro-evolution happened *so fast* that the fossil record did not record it.

Apparently, I am not the only person unconvinced by the evolution believer's religious adherence to such inconsistent reasoning because a 2004 Barna poll showed that 45% of the people in the United States still believe that God created human beings within the last 10,000 years.

1. Dr. Colin Patterson, senior paleontologist at the prestigious British Museum of Natural History, and the author of the book, ***Evolution***, made the following written comment when questioned why he did not include any illustrations of transitional forms in his book, "...if I knew of any, I certainly would have included them..." . The full text of his statement is documented in ***Darwin's Enigma*** by Luther Sunderland, pp. 88 - 90. There are no transitional forms in the fossil record simply because creatures have never turned into completely new

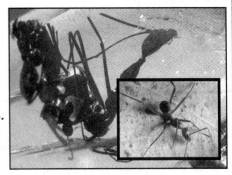

different types of creatures.
The illustrations used in this article were kindly provided by Dr. Joachim Scheven, LEBENDIGE VORWELT Museum.

Only God Can Make an Instinct

By Lanny and Marilyn Johnson

The Mallee Fowl is a mound building bird that lives in Australia. It is about the size of a chicken and is an incredibly busy worker. In the fall of each year, the male begins to dig a hole about three feet deep. After the hole is dug, he piles leaves and twigs into the pit. After each rain he covers a layer of vegetation with sand sealing in the moisture. The mound he builds can be up to 35 feet across and 15 feet high. He will move as much as 6000 pounds of material to build his mound. As the wet vegetation decays, it produces heat. So as the leaves and twigs rot, the pile warms up.

The Mallee Fowl keeps checking the temperature of the mound by pushing his heat sensitive beak and tongue into the mound. It may take four months for the mound to reach the perfect temperature (92 °F). When it is warm enough, the male digs an egg chamber and the female starts to lay eggs over a period of many days. After each egg is laid, the male covers it with sand. He continually tests the temperature of the mound with his bill and adjusts the insulating layer of sand to raise or lower the interior temperature of the mound.

If the nest is too hot because of the rotting plants under the eggs; he removes sand from the egg chamber to let it cool down. If the nest is too hot from the sun heating the nest from above; he adds sand to the nest to insulate it better. If the nest is too cold and the sun is out he will remove insulation so that the sun's heat can warm the mound. The Mallee Fowl keeps the nest within 1°F at all times.

The female will visit the nest

A Mallee Fowl Nest in Australia

every few days until she has laid from 6 to 30 eggs. The eggs hatch after 9 weeks buried in the mound. Each chick, once it has hatched, will struggle from 2 to 15 hours to dig its way to the surface of the mound. They then totter to the shade to rest. Within 24 hours of hatching, they can fly! The baby birds then have no contact with their parents. They are on their own as soon as they hatch. The parents rest for a month and then start the whole process over again. The male Mallee Fowl spends up to 11 months a year taking care of the nest. That's dedication!

When Mallee Fowl mature at 2 years of age, they find mates and start their own nests. How do they know how to do that? They were never taught by their parents. No one taught them that as soon as they hatch they need to dig their way out of the mound of rotting vegetation. No one taught them which way is up. How do they know to find shelter in shade? How do they know to eat seeds? How do they know that their tongue can be used to sense exactly 92 °F? How do they know to add sand or remove it to keep a steady temperature? How do they know to bury plants because rotting vegetation gives off heat?

Even if one bird somehow discovered some of these things; countless scientific experiments have shown that learned knowledge is not biologically passed from one generation to the next.

The way animals know how to survive is called instinct. Instinct is knowledge which is programmed into a creature before birth. Man has never been able to explain how it could have developed by any evolutionary process. Such programmed wisdom demands an intelligent programmer. Such intelligence testifies to a creator. Psalm 104:24 says it best, *"O Lord, how manifold are thy works! In wisdom Thou hast made them all. The earth is full of Thy riches."* God is the one Who made instincts.

Lanny and Marilyn Johnson run the children's ministry at Alpha-Omega Institute. Alpha-Omega reaches thousands of people worldwide with the evidence of creation. They can be reached at their website: **discovercreation.org**

How did Cain Find a Wife?

By Bruce Malone

The following is the paraphrased essence of one of the most critical junctures in the most famous trial of the twentieth century. The scene is the 1925 Scopes Monkey Trial, and defense attorney Clarence Darrow had goaded prosecuting attorney Williams Jennings Bryan to take the stand in defense of the Bible.

Mr. Bryan,"Where did Cain find a wife?"

"I don't know."

"Could you repeat your answer Mr. Bryan? The entire nation is listening via radio broadcast and this is a pretty basic and simple question. Let me rephrase it. If, as the Bible claims, Adam and Eve were the first man and women, and no other people existed, who did their son Cain find to marry?"

"I don't know."

Darrow made Bryan appear foolish because he did not know scripture well enough to defend the most basic of questions. This trial marked a turning point in American education because, for the first time, the Bible was openly ridiculed. Bryan's inability to answer simple and logical questions was one factor that allowed the American educational establishment to accept evolution hook, line, and sinker, while rejecting the historical creation account of the Bible.

Even today, most Christians do not know the answer to questions as basic as "Where did Cain find a wife?" The problem with not having reasonable answers to logical questions is that it brings all Christianity into question. Why should people believe in a God that they cannot see; if believers in God cannot answer life's questions about our origin?

The reason that the answer to

this question is not immediately apparent is that we have been trained to think like evolutionists. Evolution was founded on a principle of modern geology called 'uniformitarianism.' This is the belief that small changes over vast periods of time caused the massive geological changes (Darwin added biological changes.) In essence, we

> **"Why should people believe in a God whom they cannot see if believers in that God cannot answers life's simplest inquires about the past and our origin?"**

are trained to believe that every thing has always operated as we see it today. This is not what the Bible teaches. It teaches that mankind was created perfect, without flaws. It was only after man's disobedience that imperfection entered God's creation. Thus mankind, as originally created, would not have had the myriad of genetic mistakes now present in our DNA. Mutations do not lead to better and

improved humans. These mistakes cause hundreds of debilitating illnesses and birth defects. The reason all of us are not born with enormous numbers of medical problems is because our genes are a combination of the characteristics of both our parents. Only when both parents have the same DNA mistake, do their children manifest the resulting genetic problem.

Furthermore, these genetic mistakes accumulate and increase with time. In other words, the information in our DNA gets more garbled, it never increases in clarity. Since mistakes are accumulating in our DNA, it is logical to assume that as we go back in time, there would be fewer mistakes. The reason brothers and sisters cannot marry today is because they are likely to have similar DNA errors which only lead to children with birth defects. However, there were no moral laws against children intermarrying until after the time of Moses. This was approximately 4000 years ago and at least 2000 years after the creation of mankind. Before that time, sibling marriage was quite common. The Bible states that Adam and Eve had *many* sons *and* daughters. Cain merely married his sister.

The reason we don't realize this obvious answer is because we have been trained to believe things have always been the way they are today. The past and the present become far more understandable when we view it from a Biblical perspective. This viewpoint acknowledges that the past was very different from the present.

Section II:
Evidence for Creation from Geology, Anthropology, and Paleontology

Dear Mr. Malone,

Thank you for the books you sent. When the mail man delivered the box to our door, he noticed the cross we have hanging inside our door and said, "Wow, I like delivering packages to people with crosses in their houses." I told him about the books he was delivering and asked if he would like a copy and his eyes got big. So I opened the box and gave him one.

We are using your materials to dialogue with the Lutheran school that our children attend. I think we are the last church in our area to still have a "remnant" of Bible believing Christians in it. However, many of our leaders still fall into the "just-trust-Jesus-and-nothing-else-matters" camp. So we have a lot of work to do because we are losing our Christian culture. Our lives have changed since understanding the importance of creation. We are engaged in the battle, and we, like you, are trying to win hearts over to the Lord, the Creator, and the Redeemer.

If death came into the world before the disobedience of man, there is no need for a savior because death is not caused by our sins. May God continue to bless you, your family, and your work.

In God we trust!

— Steven L. Busch

Chapter 2

"If my people, which are called by my name, shall humble themselves, and pray, and seek my face, and turn from their wicked ways; then I will hear from heaven, and forgive their sin, and heal their land."

- 2 Chronicles 7:14

The "scientific establishment" has redefined science to accept only naturalistic explanations for the physical world. Furthermore, the modern media has provided an overwhelming publicity barrage implying that anything to do with creation is religious belief, while anything to do with evolution is empirical proven scientific fact. Even the language used to discuss the subject is tilted toward this viewpoint with the discussion couched in terms of creationism vs. evolution. Thus, even before the discussion starts creation is a religious "ism" while evolution is "reality". As the articles throughout this book show, the exact opposite is true. The typical Christian knows little or nothing of the evidence for creation, instead just being satisfied in their belief that "God is creator" and seldom caring to learn more about the issue. Yet, the Biblical model of a real and recent supernatural creation, a real curse of the entire universe due to the rebellion of mankind, and a real global worldwide flood in judgement for mankind's sin is so foundational to Christianity that everyone who considers themselves a Christian should be aware of how well modern science supports this reality of the past.

Prior to graduation from college, I had not once been shown any of the scientific evidence for creation either in school or church. Little wonder, that by the time I started my career, God had little relevance in my life. It wasn't as though I had any animosity toward God or religion. It simply held no relevance to the world around me. This should be no surprise when the subject never came up in school and everything seemed to be explained without reference to a creator. The decline of Christianity as a moral force in Europe correlates almost perfectly with European's widespread acceptance of evolution as a fact. This is no coincidence. The increasing rejection of absolute truth in America is also intimately connected to the rising belief that we are all just the result of purposeless natural forces. The faulty logic and poor assumptions of evolutionism are at the heart of our culture's moral slide. Once I had made this connection and realized the foundational connection between evolutionary teaching and the moral decline of our nation, I decided to fight the root cause of the moral decline and culture war which is raging in America.

With this in mind, I set about developing a series of lectures on the scientific evidence for creation. I decided that the class should be held in a church and received approval to do so. However, I was also hoping to reach non-Christians so I advertised with flyers posted at two local colleges and purchased a full-page newspaper ad. Rather than just list what the class was about, the top half told about the class and the bottom half listed people in the community who believed in the Biblical creation model . In order to add credibility, the educational background of these Christians was also listed (see ad in appendix I on page 133.)

As a new Christian, I made the naive assumption that older Christians had taken the time to study and verify God's Word. I had only recently discovered the fact that if God exists, He should have the ability to communicate to humans what He means and unless this God is a liar, He must mean what He says. The Bible repeatedly claims to be the inspired Word of God (2 Timothy 3:16). Furthermore, the prophecies of the Bible are statistical proof that the book has been inspired by God because specific details of future happenings were written down in advance (see page 95.) This could only have been done by someone outside of time and space, i.e. the creator of time and space. I assumed that other Christians acknowledged the same basic facts about God's Word and trusted it to mean what it said. However, as I approached Christians with a scientific background, I was surprised how many refused to be part of a public proclamation that God was a literal creator and were not even interested in hearing about the scientific evidence for the Biblical model of creation. Many of those with scientific backgrounds didn't have a clue how well the scientific evidence confirmed the Biblical teaching of a worldwide flood and an intelligent designer of biological life. My biggest surprise was when I approached a highly awarded high school science teacher who frequently taught adult education classes in our church. Not only did she refuse to be associated with the ad, but also refused to attend any of the classes stating that, "She was satisfied with her present beliefs". I was shocked that a highly honored teacher would not even view the evidence for creation or consider the possibility that the Biblical model of creation could be true. The problem seems to be that most people, including Christians, have been conditioned to believe that anything to do with biblical creation is equivalent to studying the evidence for a flat earth. They have been so convinced by the propaganda for evolution and an old earth that they are totally uninterested in even viewing the evidence for a recent creation.

However, the trail of those who believed in the recent Biblical creation model, understood the scientific evidence supporting this belief, and were willing to publicly proclaim the truth led throughout the city to a wide diversity of denominations, scientific disciplines, and personalities. It was like the larger picture of Christianity - scattered throughout every part of society. There were also an unexpectedly large percentage of engineers among those who accepted creation. This may be because engineers tend to be practical rather than theoretical in their approach to life and the Biblical model of creation is extremely practical and well supported by evidence.

I need to digress at this point to clearly state that being a Christian does not depend upon belief in creation. Your eternal destiny depends on only one thing - what you personally have done with your knowledge of the finished and final work of Jesus Christ. Jesus Christ is not the 'New Age' inner consciousness but the Creator God who became a man and died for our sins. We may not understand much about the details of creation or how it was done, but we must have a desire to know Jesus personally (John 1, Colossians 1, Hebrews 1, Romans 10:9). If you choose to spit in God's face and reject His sacrifice by not acknowledging your own sinfulness, not accepting the death of Jesus as payment for your sins, and not making him Lord of your life...there is nothing else God can possibly do to save you. You can attempt to be a perfect person, believe God is creator, and go to church every time the doors are open, but you have just insulted God if you think these things will earn you an eternal place in the presence of a totally holy Creator. If we could earn our way to heaven by working to be a "good" enough person; then Jesus died for nothing. Why should He have died in our place if we could earn our way to heaven by being a "good" person? This is the message of the bible from cover to cover and unless we accept that Jesus did it all; Christianity becomes just another man-made religion and the Bible is simply a book of myths and lies.

***However**, rejection of what the Bible has to say about creation does have consequences. In order to accept evolution, much of the Bible must be ignored or "spiritualized" rather than understood to mean what it clearly says. The atheists know exactly what the Bible says and laugh every time Christians, who claim to believe in God's Word, spin tangled webs of confusion trying to explain away clear statements of Scripture. Where does this practice stop? A Christian who rejects God's Word when it clearly describes a recent creation (Exodus 20:11, Genesis chapters 1-5) and a worldwide flood (Genesis chapter 6-11, Job 22:15-17, Matthew 24:39, 2Peter 3:6), especially, when there is so much evidence supporting the factual nature of these events, will find their Christian walk hindered, their witness weakened, and will have to answer for undermining God's Word when they do face their Creator.*

*The biggest problem with blending evolution and billions of years with Christianity is the question of death. The Bible states that death is the penalty for man's sin and that the entire universe is fallen as a consequence of the sin of one man (Romans 8:22). If man caused death to occur by his actions, how could death have been around for billions of years before man appeared? How could creation **be restored** to its original splendor where the wolf shall dwell [in peace] with the lamb if it wasn't doing so in the original creation (Isaiah 11:6-9)? How can Christ's death be the payment for our sins if there is nothing special about death and death has always been around. As a matter of fact, if evolution is true, then death, struggle, and disease is actually God's method of creating us in the first place. So how can death be the consequence of our sins? Acceptance of evolution, and its required billions of years, undermines the very message of Christianity and allows people to separate "religion" from the physical world around us. Is it any wonder that the more strongly a society becomes influenced by evolution and billions of years, the more rapidly Christianity becomes irrelevant in such a culture?*

The newspaper ad, shown in appendix I, immediately created a controversy which ultimately generated a series of 40 letters to the editor by 20 different authors spanning several months. Over the ensuing years, hundreds of other letters have been written as I have laid out the evidence for creation in various newspapers. A few of these letters are included in Appendix II on pages 135-137.

The original Sunday morning class lasted 10 weeks and covered a wide variety of scientific disciplines. The weekly attendance was a modest 60-80 with an average of 20 visitors (including several professors from a local university). Yet people traveled from other towns to hear this information that they were not getting elsewhere and many who attended told me they truly understood Christianity for the first time or that I had answered questions they had their whole lives. At the end of 10 weeks, I had enough feedback to know that this was indeed useful and proceeded to contact other churches with a condensed 4 to 6 week class. It was at this point that my second layer of naiveté was removed.

I approached about a dozen churches over the next year. I tried to teach the creation class at many of the churches in my hometown of Granville, Ohio, but not one of the churches would allow the class to be taught. In one case, the pastor approved the class, but was overruled by an ex-professor on his church board. In another case, I was approved to teach by both the pastor and the church board and was scheduled to advertise the class in the newspaper when I got a call to attend a special church meeting. I was informed that the church could not allow the class because the property committee had vetoed it! Over the next few years, I taught at half a dozen churches, but was turned down by far more. So, just as Paul started with God's people then moved on to unbelievers, it was time to try a different approach.

Our Mysterious Past

By Bruce Malone

Just beneath the lush vegetation and majestic scenery of our planet is a massive worldwide graveyard. Plants and animals are buried by the billions under countless tons of mud and sediment which have subsequently turned to rock. How did all those organisms get there? The answer to that question is **THE KEY** to understanding our origin.

Starting in the early 1800's geologists have chosen to interpret fossils and sediments based on a presupposition of slow accumulation, or more recently, multiple local catastrophes over billions of years (uniformitarianism). Thousands of geologists have been indoctrinated in this belief and have spent the last 150 years working to fit the evidence into this interpretation of earth history. Yet, many facts remain unexplained by this interpretation. Most of these "mysteries" disappear, if the reality of a recent worldwide flood is acknowledged. A jury looking for the truth starts with eye witness accounts. In addition to the Bible, which clearly presents the global flood as a factual event, every major culture in the world has a flood story. From the Aztecs to the Chinese...Aborigines to the ancient Greeks...all cultures have an ancient account of a universal flood. Many of these stories include details of a righteous man being saved on a floating vessel and attribute the event to judgment from

God. If this really happened; people would have spread across the globe after the catastrophe. As centuries passed, the account of the flood would have become distorted. This is exactly what we find.

More evidence comes from fossils. The very existence of fossils is evidence of rapid burial. Fossils do not form today unless animals are rapidly buried. Yet many fossil deposits contain billions of tightly packed and intricately preserved creatures indicating that they had been washed together and rapidly buried. The extent, frequency, and lack of decay found in most fossil beds testify to the worldwide extent of the catastrophe.

The nature of the rock record is also a testimony to a worldwide flood. At many locations around the world, often resting just above those rock layers containing very few indications of life, there is a conglomeration of rocks and boulders. The Great Unconformity in the Grand Canyon is an example of this. The Great Unconformity represents a supposed 500 million years of missing earth history. But is there really any "missing" time? Along this interface great boulders

of Shinumo Quartite are buried exactly as if they were transported into place by energetic flood waters.[1] The expected consequence of an extensive and energetic flood would be the rapid erosion of massive amounts of sediment and the redeposit of these sediments at other locations. Rocks and boulders would drop to the bottom of these flood waters and come to rest at the top of newly scoured surfaces. This is what we find between the Tapeats sandstone/ Dox sandstone border in the Grand Canyon. Evolutionists assume there is a "missing" 500 million years at this border. Creationists see the evidence as a conformation of a worldwide flood with no "missing" time.

Creation geologists have only been working to explain the massive sedimentary rock layers of our planet by a worldwide flood for a few decades and there is still much to be explained. However, the creation model explains many problems which the uniformitarian model does not - despite 150 years of study from an evolutionary perspective.

The truth can only be found if all of the evidence is examined. Does our current scientific and education establishment allow for this freedom of investigation?

1. Austin, Steve, *Grand Canyon Monument to Catastrophe - Field Study Guide Tour book,* pp.44, ICR, 1993.

Fossils Do Not Prove Evolution

By Bruce Malone

Fossils. The very name brings to mind images of untold ages past...dinosaurs roaming ancient swamps...slow but steady progression as simple sea life was transformed into today's complex variety. Is this an accurate reconstruction of the past or is a worldwide flood the correct explanation of the fossil record?

Fossils are the preserved evidence of past life. They are found in every part of the world, including the tops of the highest mountains. They may be as simple as a seashell which has left a permanent impression in sandstone or as grandiose as a giant plesiosaur whose bones have turned to rock after rapid burial. The fossils themselves tell us neither their age nor how they became encased in the rock layers. Rather, they must be interpreted within some view of earth history. Many people have been led to believe that the existence of fossils proves that millions of years have passed. In reality, fossils can form quite rapidly. Heat and pressure from rapid burial can accelerate the fossilization process. Geological conditions following a worldwide flood would have exceeded anything imaginable today and thus led to the rapid fossilization of the plants and animals on a massive scale.

Fossilization can happen rapidly under the right conditions, although it is a rare event today. Yet, there are mass burial sites throughout the

Used by permission of Creation Ex Nihilo Magazine

world that are tightly packed with millions of fossils. Apparently, billions of organisms were washed together by the mass destruction of the worldwide flood, buried by massive amounts of sediment, and rapidly fossilized. These extensive fossil graveyards would be the predictable result of a worldwide flood, but would hardly fit the slow accumulation model which continues to be taught as the primary explanation of the fossil record. Something dramatically different must have happened in the past to have caused the wide spread fossilization which we find all over our planet. Noah's flood would have been this event.

Geologists and paleontologists operating from a Christian world view acknowledge the possibility that a worldwide catastrophe buried unimaginable amounts of plants and animals. This was the disaster documented in the first book of the Bible. It lasted over a year and had reverberations lasting for centuries.

Although any order of burial in a flood would be possible, the general tendency would be for sea life to be buried in the lower rock layers and land animals to be buried in higher rock layers corresponding to their ecological niche. This tendency is generally found. Sea creatures would have been buried first because the salinity and temperature of the oceans would have changed during the catastrophe, wiping out massive numbers of these sea creatures. Ninety-five percent of all fossils found are sea creatures. Even after the flood, plant and animal extinction would have been common as many types of creatures failed to adapt to the dramatically changing conditions.

Creation geologists (and there are many of them) believe that the majority of the geological record is a result of geological activity during and subsequent to the year-long, worldwide flood. This flood would have been an incredibly complex event. It must have involved rapidly moving continental plates, changing climatic conditions, and massive volcanism for decades.

Geologists and paleontologists operating from an evolutionary world view acknowledge local catastrophes, but do not allow consideration of a worldwide flood. This would wipe out the "slow change over eons of time" interpretation of the fossils which is needed to continue believing in evolution.

Only one interpretation of the evidence can be correct and only one interpretation of the evidence agrees with what the Bible claims is the history of our planet.

Explosive Evidence for Creation

By Bruce Malone

In order to determine what happened in the past, geologists study current processes and use these observations to determine how rock layers came to cover our planet. Before the 1800's, geology was dominated by the acknowledgment that a worldwide flood was the cause of most rock layers. This changed when the founders of modern geology, James Hutton and Charles Lyell, succeeded in replacing this interpretation with the belief in uniformitarianism.

Uniformitarianism is the belief that slow-and-gradual processes, like we see today, account for the geological features of our planet. It also assumes that there never was a massive and rapid accumulation of sediment caused by a worldwide catastrophe. Charles Darwin was heavily influenced by this type of thought when he extended the concept of slow and gradual geological change to include slow and gradual biological change. In the last 30 years, many geologists have come to accept as fact that the past saw rapid geological changes far surpassing anything we see happening today. However, the majority of geologists still cling to the belief that there has never been a worldwide flood.

The foundational assumption of the creation model is that there was a worldwide flood in the recent past. If this assumption is correct; there should be evidence for this event. A worldwide flood would have caused massive destruction of plant and animal life followed by a redeposition of this biomatter and sediment. This would result in enormous fossil beds at locations throughout the planet. This is exactly what the fossil record reveals.

One criticism of the Biblical explanation for our past is the lack

of a natural model which duplicates the processes that were happening during Noah's flood. However, in 1980, the explosion of Mt. St.

Rapidly Formed New Toutle River Canyon

Helens in Washington provided just such a model. When it erupted, an estimated 18 billion cubic feet of rock, ash, dirt, steam and melted snow flowed down the side of the mountain at speeds estimated at 90 MPH. This, and subsequent ash flows, laid down as much as 600 feet of sediment on the north face of the mountain slope. In essence, a massive flood event was modeled for the scientific community.

The sediments laid down during this violent mud and ash flow were not a homogenized mixture but rather a series of finely layered horizontal strata. They look quite similar to the horizontal layers of rocks which can be observed in road cuts as we travel our interstate highways. This type of horizontal rock strata is often assumed to indicate millions of years of earth history, but Mt. St. Helens has provided geologists with a scale model of how such strata could be laid down rapidly by flowing water.

Subsequent to the Mt. St. Helens explosion, a new river canyon was formed in one day (March 19, 1982) as backed up water broke through the newly deposited sediment. This canyon is over 100 feet deep and looks amazingly like a 1/40th scale model of the Grand Canyon. Had no one been present to see this area form, we might assume that the small stream at present located at the bottom of the canyon had cut the canyon over millions of years. This is the story most of us have been taught about the Colorado River and the Grand Canyon. Many geologists are now coming to acknowledge that just as the Toutle River canyon at Mt. St. Helens formed rapidly, the Grand Canyon was also formed over a short period of time by a massive flow of water. Yet the majority of the geological community continues to believe that low energy processes and long time periods account for the geological record. Creationists believe that high energy processes and short periods of time account for the geological record. Only one viewpoint is correct and only one viewpoint agrees with the biblical record. Guess which one?

Water CAN Move Mountains - Rapidly

By Bruce Malone

Four million people per year visit the Grand Canyon and ponder the incredible forces which cut this chasm out of the earth. Did the small river at the bottom carve through the many layers of sediment over eons of time or did a catastrophic event carve the canyon more rapidly? These are the competing explanations for the origin of the Grand Canyon. How could a flood, though, have accomplished so much? As the following examples show, moving water has enormous erosion capabilities.

In the spring of 1983 the spillway tunnel of the Glen Canyon Dam had to be opened to allow drainage of water from Lake Powell. When one of the spillways was fully opened the flow pattern changed and blocks of rock were seen hurtling out of the spillway exit. The water became red with dissolved sandstone and there were noticeable earth tremors. The spillway was immediately closed for inspection. The survey team discovered incredible erosion damage to the spillway tunnel caused by cavitation of the flowing water. In a matter of minutes, flowing water had penetrated the three foot thick, steel reinforced, walls and ripped a 150 foot diameter hole into the surrounding rock requiring 63,000 cubic feet of concrete to repair.

In the scab lands of eastern Washington is an even more dramatic example of the incredible erosion force of rapidly flowing water. An ancient lake was blocked at the end of the ice age by an ice dam in northern Idaho. When the water breached the dam it ripped through Montana, Idaho, and Washington leaving 16,000

<- Flood Flow

water surface

Cavitation bubbles

hydraulic plucking

hydraulic vortex "kolk"

suction

suction

square miles of scarred terrain and deeply cut valleys. At one location, the flood cut a 50-mile long trench 6 miles wide and 900 feet deep through solid rock! An estimated 10 cubic miles of Columbia Plateau basalt was eroded in a matter of hours by this single event. The process by which moving water can cause such extensive damage is illustrated above.

Could the Grand Canyon have been carved out by similar catastrophic events and processes? Many qualified geologists are coming to believe this is exactly what has happened. These geologists have proposed that a large area of the southwestern United States was covered by water which apparently broke through a natural dam and very rapidly eroded much of the Grand Canyon to its current depth. The water for this rapid erosion came from water left on the plateau when the global flood receded.

There are many other examples of moving water accomplishing

massive geological changes. Yet all of these local examples pale in comparison with the effect a worldwide flood would have on regional geological features. If there were a worldwide flood; the illustrated destructive forces would be in operation during and subsequent to the event. The result would be the rapid accumulation of very thick sedimentary deposits over massive regions. During such an event, valleys would be filled with sediment thousands of feet thick.

A single worldwide flood is still the best explanation for the sedimentary rock layers that cover our planet. Geologists who believe in an old Earth do not reject the evidence for this flood based on scientific observations. They simply choose to interpret the evidence based on the assumption that there never was such a flood. Could it be a philosophical aversion to accepting that which is supernatural in its origin? Would a geologist who accepted a worldwide flood as the formation of our planet's geological features be welcome in the present science community? Or would this "politically incorrect" interpretation cause him to be ostracized? To accept a worldwide flood as a factual event would profoundly affect other areas of science, as well: including biology, paleontology, and anthropology. Would such an interpretation be allowed by the scientific community?

Science is Only a Tool

By Bruce Malone

SCIENCE IS A TOOL. Sweeping statements by scientists concerning what happened in the past should never be confused with facts because the former are always based on limited knowledge.

Conclusions often change as more knowledge, data, and mechanisms are discovered. Science is just the tool used to uncover the truth. It is not, nor should it be confused with, absolute truth. One area of science where this misunderstanding is especially prevalent is with scientific statements regarding the age of the earth. Over the last 200 years, the "accepted" age of the earth has risen from 6000 to 5 billion years.

One classic argument for the great age of a geologic feature comes from Specimen Ridge in Yellowstone National Park. At this

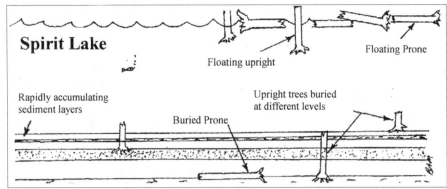

Spirit Lake

Floating upright

Floating Prone

Rapidly accumulating sediment layers

Buried Prone

Upright trees buried at different levels

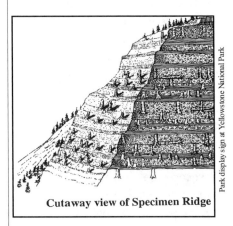

Cutaway view of Specimen Ridge

location there is an eroded hillside with petrified trees standing upright through exposed sediment. The classic interpretation is that these layers of trees represent 32 subsequent forests. As the lowest forest was destroyed and buried under the sediment, another forest grew on top. It is taught that this area represents earth history in excess of 100,000 years old. For many years, this interpretation was

written in geology textbooks and placed on interpretive park signs. Bible believing Christians had no better explanation. However, in 1980 Mt. St. Helens erupted, knocking down thousands of acres of trees. Over one million of these trees ended up floating on Spirit Lake. Dr. Steve Austin, a Ph.D. geologist for the Institute of Creation Research, realized that as these trees became water logged, many sank to the lake bottom in an upright position. As tree bark and sediment dropped to the bottom of the lake these upright trees became buried at different levels. Sonar tracking of the lake bottom has revealed as many as 10,000 dead trees standing in upright positions on the lake bottom. If the trees were buried under a subsequent volcanic event; the area would have the appearance of many forests which have grown one on top of the other over thousands of years. Yet, this sedimentary deposit was formed rapidly by a single flood-like event.

Returning our focus to the evidence from Specimen Ridge, it is interesting to note that the buried trees do not have the extensive roots which would be expected from trees which had grown in place. Rather, they have abruptly ending root bundles. This provides additional support that this extensive area was formed during a flood of

mind boggling proportions, not by multiple forests over thousands of years. Could the primary reason that this explanation for Specimen Ridge is not widely accepted is that the idea of a global flood would destroy the current scientific paradigm?

This is just one example of the evidence, which at first glance, seems to be ironclad in its implication that the earth is much older than the Bible indicates. However, additional knowledge always vindicates the clear statements of this remarkable book.

Evolutionary geologists prefer to choose interpretations which indicate that long time periods have been involved in geologic processes. To do otherwise would leave no explanation other than supernatural creation for the formation of our planet. Christians who take the Bible seriously acknowledge that a catastrophic event, such as the worldwide flood, account for areas such as Specimen Ridge.

It is only by examining all the evidence in light of both interpretations that the truth can be found. Unfortunately, modern geological interpretation starts by excluding the consideration of a worldwide flood. With this possibility eliminated at the start, how can the truth be found?

Still Missing After All These Years

By Bruce Malone

If the creation model of life's origin is correct; the fossil record should show a pattern of distinct breaks between very different "kinds" of creatures. If the classic evolutionary model is correct; the fossil record should be a blurred continuum of creatures.

The most fundamental grouping of animals is the phylum. There are dozens of phyla in the animal kingdom and each phylum represents a vastly different body structure. For instance, all animals with a backbone are in one phylum; most insects are in another; external-shelled creatures, such as clams, are grouped together, while jellyfish are in yet another. The phyla comprises the broadest distinction among life forms. If any group of animals should have transitional forms; it should be the phylum.

Creationists predict that as we examine the fossil record, we should not find organisms which bridge the gap between the very different created body types. Believers in evolution, on the other hand, reject divine creation, believing instead that all life slowly changed from a simple single cell into the complex forms we see all around us. If they are correct; there should be thousands of "in-between" forms as one basic body type changed into another. This necessitates millions of changes to an organism, (such as an amoeba) before it could have turned into a clam. If these transitions between phyla cannot be found, something must be very wrong with the theory of evolution.

What does the fossil record thus show concerning the appearance of these most basic animal groups? The following quotes are representative of what has been

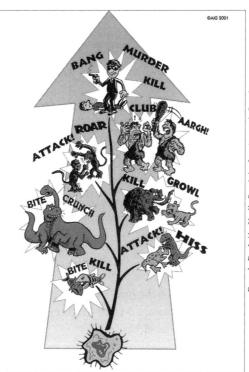

found after extensive search by an army of evolutionary paleontologists over the last 150 years. These statements are both contextual and relevant to what the fossil record actually reveals:

⇒ *"All paleontologists know that the fossil record contains precious little in the way of intermediate forms; transitions between major groups are characteristically abrupt."* [1]

⇒ *"Despite the bright promise that paleontology provides of 'seeing' evolution, it has presented some nasty difficulties for evolutionists, the most notorious of which is the presence of 'gaps' in the fossil record."* [2]

⇒ *"...no real evolutionist, whether gradualist or punctuationist, uses the fossil record as evidence in favor of the theory of evolution as opposed to special creation..."* [3]

⇒ *"The known fossil record fails to document a single example of phyletic evolution accomplishing a major morphologic transition"* [4]

Evolutionists have lined up some fossils which seem to fill small gaps between closely related creatures. However, accepting small transitions as evidence in support of the grand evolution scenario is like believing a single stepping stone can bridge the Atlantic Ocean.

Evolution requires transitional forms between the most basic animal groups... yet none exist. Whereas, creation asserts that there have never been transitions between very different kinds of life. This is exactly what the fossil record shows. What better evidence for creation could there be?

Evolutionary scientists continue to search for an acceptable explanation for how one type of animal could have turned into a completely different type of animal. Yet, precious little fossil evidence shows that this has happened, there is no undisputed evidence showing that it is currently happening, and there is no adequate theoretical explanation for how it could have happened. One must wonder if the belief in evolution is based on wishful thinking and faith, NOT objectivity and science.

1. Gould, Stephen, "The Return of the Hopeful Monster", *Natural History*, Vol. LXXXVI(6), 1977, p.24.
2. Kitts, David, "Paleontology and the Evolutionary Theory", *Evolution*, vol. 28, 1974, p.467.
3. Ridley, Mark, "Who Doubts Evolution?", *New Scientist*, Vol. 90, No. 1259, (June 25, 1981),

Contrasting Views of Reality

By Bruce Malone

The Macro-Evolution Framework of History:

In the beginning, something exploded (we really don't know what, how, or where it came from) and then our current universe slowly formed and cooled. The rock surface of earth dissolved to form a chemical soup which somehow became the first self-replicating cell. This cell somehow adapted itself to its environment, becoming increasingly complex with time. Billions of years passed as useful information was added to the chemical blueprint of simple organisms and caused the variety of life forms to increase. The end result is the current diversity of life we see all around us. Thus, what we are really being taught is that rocks (or basic elements) turned into people.

As shown in previous articles, the commonly proposed evolution mechanisms simply do not justify the belief in this miraculous story of life's development. Mutations are random mistakes which demonstrably do not add useful information to the DNA molecule. Natural selection cannot begin to eliminate the vast majority of harmful mutations and does not explain how useful complex interrelated new functioning features could have developed. And despite enormous efforts in laboratories all over the world, it has never been shown how chemicals could be mixed together and "come alive". Thus, evolution is firmly based on faith, not scientific observation.

The Biblical Framework of History:

This framework acknowledges four major interventions by God in history. The first is the instantaneous creation of the

> **"Thus, what we are really being taught is that rocks turned into people."**

universe and diverse forms of life. The second is the curse of this creation in response to the disobedience of the only organisms created with free will (mankind). The third is a worldwide flood as judgment for the almost total rebellion of humanity. The last was God's appearance on earth as Jesus Christ in order to deal with the human sin problem. This framework is also based on faith.

The evidence supporting the first three interventions of God is either ignored or undermined by our public education system. Is it any surprise that the reality of the fourth major intervention by God often seems to have even less relevance in our children's lives?

True Science Points to the Correct View

The rocks don't talk. No fossil has ever been uncovered with a label attached. All must be interpreted within a framework. An evolution geologist and a creation geologist shown the same rock or fossil will arrive at a

different conclusion concerning its origin and age. They will interpret the data based on the framework which they believe to be true. The best way to determine who is correct is to see how many contradictions arise from interpreting the data within each framework. An example of this is the black shales of the Hartford rock formation in Connecticut. Evolution geologists commonly interpret these rocks as having formed from plant and animal sediments slowly collecting at the bottom of a deep lake.[1] Creation geologists interpret this deposit as the result of a rapid deposit of sediment during the worldwide flood which has subsequently turned to stone.

Interestingly, portions of this formation contain hundreds of well preserved and tightly packed fish fossils per cubic meter of shale. This is what would be expected from a catastrophic burial, but does not match the observations of slow settling at the bottom of a deep lake or shallow sea. Dead fish can occasionally settle and be well preserved but not in the tightly packed manner observed in this formation. To reinterpret this large rock formation as a catastrophic deposit would upset the entire uniformitarian foundation of geology. Therefore, the sediments continue to be interpreted in a way which doesn't match observations.[2]

1. McDonald, N.G., "Paleontology of the Mesozoic Rocks of the Conn. Valley", **State Geo. and Natural History Survey of Conn. , 1982.**
2. Whitmore, John, "The Hartford Basin of Central Conn.: Multiple evidences of Catastrophism", **Proceedings of the 2nd International Conference On Creationism,** 1990.

What Happened to the Dinosaurs?

By John Whitmore

Although the monstrous creature was obviously a vegetarian, its size was overwhelming. Its hips could withstand the enormous force of each pounding step and its midsection was a mass of muscle. Its gigantic tail extended far behind him, not unlike a giant cedar tree swaying behind his body. Its bones were like steel girders with ribs like iron bars to support his enormous weight. This is the greatest creature to roam the swamps and rivers of the earth.

Is this a scene from the blockbuster movie, **Jurassic Park**? It could be, but it isn't. This description, which perfectly fits an Apatosaurus, is a paraphrased description taken from one of the oldest books of the Bible, Job 40: 15-24. If dinosaurs have been extinct for 65 million years, how could a writer of the Bible have accurately described the appearance, food, and habitat of this creature?

The vast majority of books on dinosaurs are written from an evolutionary perspective which assumes that the dinosaurs died out 65 million years ago. The leading model for the demise of the dinosaur involves a large asteroid hitting the earth. Yet, the most obvious alternative explanation is almost always ignored. Almost all fossils are the remains of creatures buried by waterborne sediment which has subsequently turned to rock. During the flood, as the water flowed over all the land surfaces, animals would have been drowned and rapidly buried by massive amounts of accumulating sediment. It is not at all surprising

Ancient petrograph of an dinosaur-like creature by the Kuku Yanlanji People

to generally find animals from similar ecological zones buried together. Thus "simple" sea creatures like coral and shellfish would be buried first (and lowest) with more mobile creatures higher in the rock layers.

Genesis 7:2 states that Noah saved two of every representative "kind" of land animal on the ark. Noah would have taken young specimens, not huge, older creatures. Dinosaurs would have emerged from the ark to inhabit an entirely different world. Instead of a warm, mild climate worldwide, they would have found a harsh climate which soon settled into an ice age. If climatic hardships did not cause the dinosaur's extinction, man's tendency to destroy large animals probably did.

In the early 1900's on the Doheny expedition into the Grand Canyon, Indian cave drawings were found which closely resembled a duck-billed dinosaur. Legends from ancient China to ancient England have recorded descriptions of dinosaur-like creatures. The Kuku Yalanji aboriginal people have paintings which look exactly like plesiosaurs. These and other intriguing evidences seem to indicate that the age of the dinosaurs ended more recently than is commonly taught. Christians do not need to feel foolish about standing on Scripture in their understanding of the world around us. There is ample evidence to support the Biblical record.

Evolution is the foundational basis for the religions of humanism and atheism. These world views are popular because man, instead of God, decides on rules and moral standards. Creation serves as the foundational basis for Christianity which acknowledges that all things were created by God, we live in a fallen universe that will be restored to perfection in the future.

There is a danger of becoming so indoctrinated by evolutionary thinking that we become closed to Christianity. We need to be diligent to understand what our children are taught and make sure they are hearing all the facts. By teaching them the evidence for creation and the fallacies of evolutionary explanations, they will be directed toward God, instead of away from Him.

John Whitmore is a MS geologist and professor of geology at Cedarville College in Cedarville, Ohio.

The Missing Link was Never There

By Bruce Malone

The following statement was made by Ph.D. anthropologist John Cole[1] and is typical of what is commonly taught throughout the world concerning human origins. *"There are extreme numbers, hundreds and hundreds, of known fossilized individual humans at various stages of evolution from the most primitive semi-humans to the present. ... You can see a very nice progression."*

Variations on this theme are repeated everywhere. From the cartoons to EPCOT center, from advertisements to zoos, from museums of science to your child's textbook ... the assumption that humans came from ape-like creatures is presented as fact. However, a closer examination of these fossils justifies some valid skepticism of these "hundreds and hundreds" of intermediate links.

Creationists are often accused of presupposing the Bible to be true and interpreting data in light of that presupposition. Believers in evolution, especially in the field of human anthropology, also start with a presupposition - that man has evolved from some apelike creature. Evolutionary anthropologists will **ALWAYS** interpret fragments of animal bones from the presupposition that evolution is a fact. This can blind even the most honest researcher from the truth and cause a faulty interpretation of the physical evidence.

A classic example is the now defunct ape-to-man link known as "Piltdown Man". In 1912, a human skull fragment was found along with an ape's jaw fragment. The teeth of the creature were intermediate between the two. For the next 41 years this was proclaimed as definitive proof of the transformation from ape-to-man.

> **"Descriptions of fossils from people who yearn to cradle their ancestors in their hands ought to be scrutinized as carefully as a letter of recommendation from a job applicant's mother."**

Most top paleontologists of the day were in agreement and hundreds of papers were written on the find. Two generations of students were shown this "proof" of evolution and many were ridiculed if they dared to voice doubts on its validity. It was only after someone **OUTSIDE** the field of paleontology was given permission to date the fragments that it was discovered that they were of vastly varying ages. **The whole thing had been a hoax!**

Upon closer examination it was even noticed that file marks were clearly visible on the teeth. How could honest, qualified experts have been duped for so long? Because "Piltdown Man" was exactly what believers in evolution had expected to find. Their presuppositions had overshadowed careful scientific analysis. Although science can be a self correcting endeavor, there is strong pressure to conform to the majority opinion. It is often someone outside a particular scientific discipline who must expose faulty assumptions and make new discoveries. This is especially true if these assumptions form the very basis of the thinking in that scientific discipline.

In 1984, there was a major show of man's supposed ancestors at the American Museum of Natural History. The following excerpt is from Phillip Johnson's book, ___Darwin on Trial___. It is very revealing concerning the anthropologist's bias toward interpreting fossil fragments within the presupposition of evolution: *"This is how Roger Lewin described the scene at the 1984 Ancestors exhibition. The 'priceless and fragile relics' were carried by anxious curators ... to be admired by a select preview audience of anthropologists who spoke in hushed voices because 'It was like discussing theology in a cathedral'. Lewin considers it understandable that anthropologists observing the bones of their ancestors should be more emotionally involved with their subject than other kinds of scientists. 'There is a difference. There is something inexpressibly moving about cradling in one's hands a cranium drawn from one's own ancestry'... Descriptions of fossils from people who yearn to cradle their ancestors in their hands ought to be scrutinized as carefully as a letter of recommendation from a job applicant's mother."*

Creation anthropologists are also highly biased. They are far more likely to interpret an apelike skull as an extinct ape. The problem arises because **only** the evolution interpretation is allowed in schools and museums.

1. *WOSU radio debate; John Cole vs. Bruce Malone; Columbus, Oh. 3/27/91*

Continental Drift or Continental Race?

By Bruce Malone

The continents of the world are large rock masses which "float" on a vast layer of hot material located miles below the surface of the earth. For many years, it has been taught that the continents are slowly drifting apart as the plates on which they ride are slowly spreading apart in some places; while in others, they are being subducted (plunged into the hot layer below.) Current measurements place the speed of this process at an excruciatingly slow 3 cm per year. If the European, African, and American continents were once one large land mass, it would have taken 100 million years for them to drift to their current position at 3 cm per year. This is part of the evidence that evolutionary geologists use to support their belief in an extremely old earth.

However, work by geophysicist, Dr. John Baumgardner, has shown that this continental movement to their present positions could have happened extremely rapidly.[1] Until recently, Dr. Baumgardner worked at the Los Alamos National Laboratory as an expert in modeling geophysical movements of the Earth's crust. He was instrumental in developing

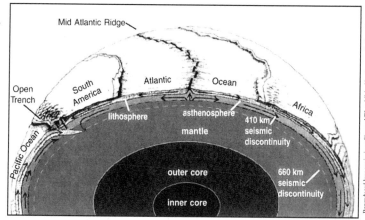

Reproduced by permission of journal TJ, published by Answers in Genesis

one of the world's most complex and comprehensive computer models on continental movement. In the process of developing this model, Dr. Baumgardner discovered the importance of including in his model the shear thinning of the underlying rock. This happens when thick fluids "thin out" under a shearing force (movement). This thinning tendency has been confirmed by

Himalaya Mountains - Note Folded but Unbroken Sediment Layers

Pictured used by permission of Don Slinger

laboratory experiments on rock at high temperature and pressure. It is this mechanism (fluid thinning of the earth's underlying rock layers) which explains the rapid movement of the earth's continental plates.

Once this shear thinning had started, it would trigger a rapid subduction of the continental plates

so that the continents would move into their current positions in a matter of months rather than over millions of years. Dr. Baumgardner's model shows that the sinking plates would have moved at billions of centimeters per year rather than at the current rate of only a few centimeters per year.

The ability of modern science to model the past is only as good as the starting assumptions. A large meteor impact or massive earthquake could have triggered a runaway subduction process that moved the continents to their current positions quite rapidly. Dr. Baumgardner thus believes that the worldwide Biblical catastrophe in Genesis chapters 7 and 8 (commonly known as Noah's flood) could have easily triggered this runaway subduction of the earth's continents. If Dr. Baumgardner is correct; massive land movements would have accompanied the flood.

This rapid movement of the various continental plates also would have caused rapid mountain formation around the world as the moving plates collided near the end of Noah's flood. The folded and vertical sedimentary layers of the Himalaya Mountains formed rapidly while the sediment was still relatively soft after Noah's flood as the Indian continent slammed into the European continent.

There is more than sufficient scientific data to support the contention that our continents moved to their current positions quite recently and rapidly.

1. John Baumgardner, Ph.D, *__Computer Modeling of Large-scale Tectonics Associated with the Genesis Flood__*, The Proceeding of the 3rd Internat. Conference on Creationism, 1994.

Grand Canyon Mystery Solved

By Bruce Malone

One of the most distinctive rock layers in the Grand Canyon is a formation known as the red wall limestone which extends from Las Vegas in Nevada through Arizona, Colorado, and into New Mexico. It is widely reported that this rock layer represents millions of years of earth history as carbonate containing sea creatures slowly settled to the bottom of a sea that for eons of time covered a huge area of western United States. This 400-foot thick rock layer is assumed to have formed 335 million years ago.

No rock layer comes with a label attached. All scientific data must be interpreted so the interpretation depends upon the presuppositions (assumptions) of the researcher. For the last 200 years, the majority of geologists have approached the interpretation of the rock layers on our planet with the assumption that there was never a single worldwide, globe covering flood. They have assumed that gradual or local events produced the geological features of our planet. Recent discoveries in the redwall limestone layer of the Grand Canyon revealed that this assumption of slow accumulation over huge periods of time is totally wrong. This should come to no surprise to Christians who take God's Word seriously because it was predicted almost 2000 years ago that *"In the last days scoffers would come... [denying both a literal creation and a worldwide flood]"*[1]

Steven Austin (Ph.D. in geology from the University of Pennsylvania) has led dozens of tours through the Grand Canyon and spent many years studying its unique geological features. One of the fossil finds that Steve noticed was ancient extinct nautiloid shells fossilized in this redwall limestone layer. For many years, these fossils were labeled as extremely rare

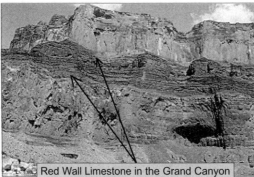
Red Wall Limestone in the Grand Canyon

within the canyon. Yet, Dr. Austin managed to find dozens of them. This anomaly prompted him to examine this geologic feature more closely.

What he discovered was a layer of nautiloid shells at the very center of the limestone which contains not just a few rare nautiloid shells, but an estimated ***20 billion shells*** all located near the exact center of this layer.

These nautiloids are apparently now extinct, but they were squid-like creatures with long, hard cone shaped shells up to two feet in length. Even more intriguing than the huge number of shells, is their location and position within the limestone layer. It turns out that all of the billions of shells are located essentially at the very center of this 400 feet thick rock layer and they are statistically oriented in the same general direction. Had this layer been laid down over eons of time as dead creatures slowly settled to the bottom of a seabed, why would all of these creatures be found in a narrow layer at the center of the formation and why would they statistically be lined up in a single flow direction?

Dr. Austin discovered a research paper explaining how highly sediment laden water, flowing at high rates causes large objects in the flow stream to become oriented at the exact center of the fluid flow.[2] This is exactly what we find in the red wall limestone layer. This layer is not a geological feature demonstrating millions of years of earth history, but a testimony to the mass extinction of billions of nautiloids during a flood flow event of unimaginable proportions! The nautiloid shells are found at the center of this huge and extensive rock layer because this was just one of many sedimentary layers laid down on our planet during the worldwide flood of Noah only a few thousands years ago.

Scientists operating from a billion year old earth perspective missed this discovery because they were blinded by preconceived notions of an ancient earth. For this reason they were not looking for this type of evidence. Studying the earth from a Biblical perspective provides enormous opportunities for fruitful research discoveries about the world God has made. It also yields abundant evidence for both a young creation and worldwide flood.

1. II Peter 3:13-16
2. Dr. Steve Austin, 'Nautiloid Mass Kill and Burial Event, Redwall Lime stone', ***Proceedings of the Fifth International Conference on Creationism***, 2003, pp.55-100.

Man's Slippery Family Tree

By Bruce Malone

The popularized notion of half-humans scraping together a bare existence of berries and prehistoric animal meat is so common that most people believe that there is total agreement in the scientific community over this concept of our past. However, this idea is based far more on conjecture than on fact. Thus considerable disagreement exists as to its validity. Listed below is a very brief summary of just a few of the key ape-to-man links which have been used to "prove" human evolution.

Neanderthal (homo neanderthalis)

After Darwin's theory on evolution was published in 1859, the search for man's ape-like ancestor began in earnest. Throughout Europe, many apparently human skeletons were found which had thicker than normal bones and eyebrow ridges. These skeletons were reconstructed with a hunched over, ape-like appearance. They were rapidly presented to the public as "ape-man" links in spite of the fact that many experts of the day disagreed with this conclusion. If fully clothed and placed in a modern city, it is unlikely these people would even be noticed. The differences in bone structure are easily attributed to pathological diseases or minor genetic variations. A probable explanation for their existence in caves was because of their attempt to repopulate the world north of the warmer equatorial regions during the ice age (which immediately followed Noah's flood). Neanderthal Man is classified by most scientists as fully human and is merely a minor variation of the human family.

Java Man (homo erectus)

In 1892, Eugene Dubois found a thick boned skull cap in the same general vicinity as a human thigh

Early Anthropologists Examining "ape-man" Skulls

Classic Painting of anthropologists examining Piltdown man

bone. This is still presented as evidence of an early transformation from ape to man. However, many years after this supposed creature was widely accepted as an "ape-man" link, Dubois admitted that the skull cap and leg bone were separated by 46 feet in a gravel deposit. These details are omitted when Java man is discussed.

Peking Man (homo erectus)

In the 1920's, a group of researchers found a large number of ape-like skull fragments in a cave near Peking China in the direct vicinity of fire pits and tools. Although all of the original skulls disappeared during WWII, it is still assumed that since the skulls and tools were found together this was an ape-man link. However, students are seldom presented with a more plausible explanation. Monkey meat is very tough, but monkey brains are still considered a delicacy in that part of the world. Since only the skull fragments were found, it is quite likely that Peking man was man's meal ... not man's ancestor.

Lucy (australopithecus)

This very ape-like creature supposedly preceded *homo erectus* in the evolutionary progression from ape to man. The most famous example was found in the early 1970's by Donald Johanson and brought him instant fame. The 40% complete set of bones was missing most of the skull. It is thus still debated whether this creature walked upright in a human manner. Many respected evolutionists still reject the claim that "Lucy" was an ape-to-man link. For instance, British anatomist Lord Solly Zuckerman conducted an extensive examination of a wide variety of *australopithecus* fossils concluding that they were not upright walkers.[1] He and a team of scientists spent 15 years studying the anatomical features of humans, monkeys, apes, and *australopithecus* fossils before coming to this conclusion. If "Lucy" did not walk upright; the obvious conclusion is that Lucy was an ape. Further studies by Dr. Charles Oxnard also came to the conclusion that *australopithecus* were not intermediates between man and ape.[2]

There are similar problems with every fossil link between humans and apes. Not only is there considerable disagreement between evolutionary researchers but the evidence is sparse, fragmentary, and open to other interpretations.

1. S. Zuckerman, ***Beyond the Ivory Tower***, Taplinger Pub. Co., New York, 1970, pp. 75-94.
2. C. Oxnard, ***Fossils, Teeth, and Sex - A new Perspective on Human Evolution***, Univ. of Wash. Press, 1987, p.277.

Are Birds Really Dinosaurs?

By Bruce Malone

From magazines to newspapers... from museums to textbooks... the concept that dinosaurs turned into birds is presented as fact. Yet, this concept, like all the other supposed "facts" of evolution, is wrought with problems which are seldom exposed. Whenever dinosaurs with a bone structure remotely similar to birds are found, the link between dinosaurs and birds is assumed to exist. Bird fossils such as Archaeopteryx (right) are presented as proof of evolution because the bones have some characteristics reminiscent of reptiles. Yet this whole idea of dinosaurs turning into birds is based more on faith than scientific fact. Here are a few observations which are seldom reported:

1. Birds have a totally different respiratory system to that of reptiles. For a reptilian respiratory system to change into an avian respiratory system would be analogous to a steam engine changing into an electric motor by randomly removing or modifying one component at a time, without disrupting the motor operation. It is simply an impossibility.

2. The hollow bones, muscle design, keen eyesight, neurological signals, instincts, feathers, and a hundred other unique bird features are completely different from that of reptiles. In particular, a bird's lungs and feathers indicate brilliant design. Either would be totally useless to perform their designed function unless complete. A step by step transformation from scale to feather makes a nice story but "the devil is in the details". And the details simply do not add up to a workable intermediate creature. The building blocks of scales and feathers aren't even the same - they are made from radically different types of protein.

The Most Complete of Only Four Known Archaeopteryx Fossils

3. Many recent dinosaur to bird "links" are "dated" between 120 - 140 million years. Yet, archaeopteryx (which exhibits all the characteristics of a fully formed bird) is "dated" at 150 million years. How could a fully formed bird be older than the transitional links between birds and dinosaurs? Alan Feduccia, a world authority on birds (and an evolutionist) states, *"Paleontologists have tried to turn Archaeopteryx into an earthbound, feathered dinosaur. But it is not. It is a bird -- a perching bird. And no amount of 'paleobabble' is going to change that."*[1]

University of Kansas paleontologist, Larry Martin, gives an excellent summation of this presentation of this dinosaur to bird fossils: *"You have to put this into perspective. To the people who wrote this paper (linking dinosaurs to birds), the chicken would be a feathered dinosaur."*[2]

Those who reject the possibility of the sudden appearance of birds have no alternative but to accept the remarkably inadequate evidence proposed for evolution. However, the actual evidence for evolution (merely variation within a particular kind of animal group) does not support the fact that one type of animal could ever turn into a completely different creature. Evolution is the only alternative shown to students because the other alternative (creation by God) has been arbitrarily eliminated.

Rather than blindly accepting the latest evolutionary find, dig into the details and determine if real science can prove that reptiles could have turned into birds or lifeless chemicals could have ever "come alive". An honest scientist will follow the data wherever it leads -- even if it leads to an encounter with their personal creator.

1. *Science*, 259(5096): pg. 764
2. CNN website, June 24, 1998.

Ape or Man, but no Apeman

By Bruce Malone

Charts showing a progression from ape-like creature to man are extremely common and leave readers with the impression that the search for man's ancestors is essentially finished. These types of charts seldom acknowledge the massive body of evidence that reveals discrepancies and outright fraud which has accompanied the search for man's ancestry. It is beyond the scope of this article to refute each of the supposed fossil fragments in the ancestral line leading to man, but a few will be highlighted. For a balanced view of the evidence concerning our origin read ***Bones of Contention, A Creationist Assessment of Human Fossils*** by Martin Lubenow. It is a well documented assessment of all the fossils which have been placed in the line of human lineage and clearly shows the bias that enters into both the arrangement and acceptance of fossil evidence. Lubenow shows that those fossils which do not fit into the accepted evolutionary time frame are either ignored or reclassified. The only alternative is to discard the entire evolutionary scenario. For instance, in 1978, associates of Mary Leakey found human footprints in Tanzania at a rock level which should not have contained fully human prints. Russell Tuttle of the University of Chicago was asked to study the footprints and came to the conclusion that they "...are indistinguishable from those of habitually barefoot *Homo sapiens* (modern humans)."[1] Yet, because

they were found in deeply buried rock, they were arbitrarily assumed to be from an ape-like creature in the process of becoming a modern human.

Another example is the skull

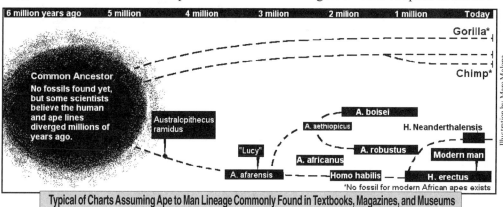

Typical of Charts Assuming Ape to Man Lineage Commonly Found in Textbooks, Magazines, and Museums

labeled KNM-ER 1470 which was found by Richard Leakey in 1972 in Kenya. This skull had an 800 cc brain capacity. **It is not widely known that the cranial capacity for modern humans ranges from 700 to 2200 cc and that cranial capacity has absolutely nothing to do with intelligence.** The skull had a modern appearance including a high dome, thin cranial walls, and evidence of a Broca's area (speech center). Yet, because the skull was found in a stratum which should have contained no modern humans, the fragments were pieced together to give the skull a very ape-like appearance. It could just as easily have been pieced together to look completely human. Roger Lewin describes the following comment by Michael Day as he and Richard Leakey were studying the skull fragments, *"You can hold the [upper jaw] forward, and give it a long face, or you can tuck it in, making a short face,"* he recalls. *"How you held it really depended on your preconceptions."* Without a preconceived bias that evolution is a fact, the entire group

of humanoids known as *Homo habilis* could just as easily be classified as a variation of modern humans.

Martin Lubenow spends the largest amount of space in his 295 page book discussing the group known as *Homo erectus*. There are over 200 known fossil fragments which fit into this category. However, almost all of them are well within the range of human variation currently present on our planet. In reality, no compelling reason exists for them to not be considered mere variations of modern humans.

Only the australopithecine is left as a potential human ancestor once the other possibilities have been fairly evaluated. These creatures are so ape-like that they bear little or no resemblance to humans. They are simply the bones of some extinct ape-like creature. The bones truly are in contention with the evolutionary theory of human origins.

1. R.H. Tuttle and D.M. Webb, "The Pattern of Little Feet", ***American Journal of Physical Anthropology*** 78:2, (2/89):316.
2. Roger Lewin, ***Bones of Contention: Controversies in the Search for Human Origin***, New York: Simon & Schuster, 1987, pg. 160.

Noah's Ark Was No Little Boat

By Bruce Malone

If "Noah's Ark" is found, it will be the greatest archeological discovery of all time. Finding an ancient wooden sea vessel, buried high on Mt. Ararat, large enough to hold two of every basic type of land dwelling animal, would have the following implications:

⇒ *It would supplement and reinforce confidence in the geological evidence that the entire surface of our planet had been covered by water within the last 6000 years.*

⇒ *It would provide an additional factual basis for the flood legends which are present within the oral history of almost every human culture.*

⇒ *It would again confirm the reliability of the early Biblical record of the human race.*

⇒ *It would support the Biblical model that every land animal (including humans) has descended from those animals taken on the ark.*

The discovery of Noah's ark is yet to be confirmed by a qualified team of scientists, but many seemingly reliable sources have claimed to have seen it.[1]

According to the Biblical text, Noah had over 50 years to build the ark which would have been an unmistakable witness to the impending judgment of God. Jesus not only referred to this event as a fact of history, but tied his imminent return to a time when the state of affairs on earth would be similar to those at the time of Noah, i.e. widespread evil but going about life as normal as if nothing would ever change (Matthew 24:37-39).

Assuming the ark is found (there have been many sightings but no definitively proof), there will once again be an enormous monument pointing toward impending judgment. When this event occurs, I pray that many who have not placed their faith in Christ will wake up and do so because their opportunity will soon be gone. God never brings judgement without adequate warning - His desire is that none would choose to perish (2 Peter 3:9).

The most common question asked about the validity of Noah's ark is, "How could millions of different animals fit on one small boat?"

♦ First, there were not millions of animals. Not every "kind" of animal needed to be on board. Only land-dwelling, air-breathing animals were present. Fish and insects could have survived well outside of the Ark and would not need to have been taken aboard. Furthermore, every minor variation of animal (species) was not present. Wolves, foxes, coyotes, and dogs could have come from an original dog kind.

♦ If the average animal size was as large as a sheep, and between 2 to 7 of each kind of animal was taken, 16,000 sheep-size animals, at the most, would have been on board. This number could have been as low as 2000 if the Biblical "kind" is equivalent to the family level of modern animal classification. These numbers include every known living and extinct type of mammal, bird, amphibian, and reptile.

♦ This was no small boat. Noah built a vessel longer than a football field and three stories high. The total space available was equivalent to 522 railroad stock cars. A stock car holds 240 sheep so the ark could have held 125,000 animals.

♦ At most, only 40% of the total space was needed for all of the animals![2] The remainder would have been used for food storage or could have been used to rescue thousands of people from impending judgement - had there been any who accepted God's grace.

The account of Noah's flood is similar to many other Biblical stories. It makes perfect sense–if you assume it means exactly what it says and take time to study it carefully.

1. B.J. Corbin, **The Explorers of Ararat**, Great Commision Illistrated Books, 1999.
2. Woodmorappe, John, **Noah's Ark: A Feasibility Study**, Institute for Creation Research Publications, 1996.

Dinosaur Discoveries Rock Evolution

By Bruce Malone

Only seven *Tyrannosaurus Rex* specimens have been found which are more than 50% complete. Because these fossils are assumed to be over 60 million years old, evolution believers have historically failed to look for unfossilized material within the bones. Dinosaur bones are generally found in a fossilized condition with silica and other minerals having completely replaced the carbon structure of the original bones—although bones with the appearance of recent burial have been documented.[1] Fossilization is a well understood process that can take place very rapidly under proper conditions. There are many documented cases of the rapid fossilization of organic matter in silica rich water exposure.[2]

Yet, a recent *T. Rex* discovery sent shockwaves through the scientific community. Evolution believer, Mary H. Schweitzer, of North Carolina State University has discovered flexible blood vessels inside the fossilized bones of a "68-70 million year old" *T. Rex* from the Hell Creek formation in eastern Montana.[3] In fresh bones, any weak acid can be used to remove the calcium, leaving only organic material such as fibrous connective tissue, blood vessels and various cells. By comparison, if one were to use acid to demineralize a typical mineralized fossil, nothing would be left because everything has been turned to stone. Yet, this acid-treated *T. Rex* bone fragment left flexible and elastic structures very similar to what one would get from a fresh bone which appeared, *"so flexible and resilient that when stretched would return to its original shape"*[4]

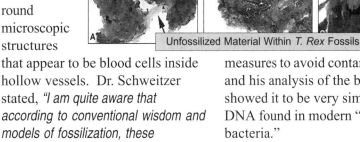

Unfossilized Material Within *T. Rex* Fossils

Close examination of the broken thigh bone also revealed round microscopic structures that appear to be blood cells inside hollow vessels. Dr. Schweitzer stated, *"I am quite aware that according to conventional wisdom and models of fossilization, these structures aren't supposed to be there, but there they are. I was pretty shocked."*[5]

Unfossilized Blood Vessels and Red Blood Cells

The entire evolutionary community should be far more than shocked. They should be rethinking their dogmatic faith system requiring millions of years of earth history. How could a fossilized bone, buried under enormous heat and pressure, and after millions of years exposure to the environment have intact organic structures? The soft tissue would have completely degraded, no matter how fortuitous the preservation process.

This is not the first soft tissue to be unearthed. Nucleic acid (DNA) with up to 800 base pairs has been taken from "fossil" magnolia leaves allegedly "17-20 million years old."[6] Yet, DNA exposed to water and oxygen rapidly degrades. A "25-40 million year old" bee was also found encased in amber containing living bacteria spores.[7] Dr. Cano, the discoverer, took careful measures to avoid contamination and his analysis of the bacteria showed it to be very similar to the DNA found in modern "bee bacteria."

These finds -- soft tissue, bacteria spores, and DNA in fossils and amber -- are not isolated examples, but part of a growing number of scientific discoveries which are rocking the evolutionary time frame to its core! However, don't expect to hear about them in your child's textbook, popular science magazines, or museums any time soon. Why? Because it is easier to deny, ignore, or explain away the implications of these finds rather than to admit that the presuppositional assumptions of the evolutionary belief system -- huge periods of time, no recent worldwide flood, and no interaction of God with creation -- could be wrong.

1. Buddy Davis, Mike Liston, John Whitmore, **The Great Alaskian Dinosaur Adventure**, Master Books, 1998.
2. Carl Wieland, 'The Earth: How Old Does it Look?', *Creation ex nihilo* **23**(1):8–13, December 2000.
3. Schweitzer, M. H., et al.,*Science*, 307, no. 5717, pp. 1952-1955, 25 March 2005.
4. www.msnbc.msn.com/id/7285683/, March 2005.
5. Boswell, E., *Montana State University News Service*, 24 March 2005.
6. Golenberg, E., et al., *Nature* **344**:656-8.
7. Cano, S., *Science*, vol. 268, no. 5213, p. 977, *Research News*, 19 May 1995.

Transitional Forms of Life

By Bruce Malone

Believers in evolution claim that the fossil record is filled with transitional forms of life that prove one form of life turned into another over vast periods of time. Those who acknowledge the evidence that we have an intelligent designer claim that there are no transitional fossils showing how one animal turned into another. Both groups have the same rocks, fossils, and data, so why do they come to such different conclusions? And how can the non-scientist know who is correct?

Any set of objects can be lined up to claim a transition from one form to another. A tricycle, a bicycle, a motorcycle, and a car can be aligned to show massive changes in the "evolution" of transportation. Yet, one did not "evolve" into the other by random mutational changes and natural selection. All exist because of intelligence and controlled energy input by a common designer to create each mode of transportation. Small changes from a Volkswagen to a Volvo might represent microevolution–but again even this change is by intelligent design, not chance.

The same is true when we view the fossil record. Billions of creatures died and were buried during the global catastrophe commonly known as Noah's flood that covered the world. Thousands of creatures alive before this flood bcame extinct as the ocean salinity and temperature changed. They could not adapt well to life on a completely altered planet after this catastrophic event. Is it any wonder that, across the world and throughout the sedimentary rock layers (those layers laid down by water), we find trillions of bones and fossils of creatures deposited by this enormous event? Is it any wonder that these fossilized bones range from creatures completely different from creatures alive today to slight variations of creatures alive today? Why the assumption that

"Fishapod" Fossil - Where are the Legs?

any variation from a modern creature is a transition between very different forms of life?

Even in Darwin's day the enormous variability of creatures coming from a common ancestry was known. Darwin acknowledged the wide variety of pigeons with different sized beaks and skulls could be bred from a common pigeon. Yet, this variability was built into the original pigeon's DNA. What is not addressed by lining up supposedly transitional forms is the question of where did all this information originate? Neither mutational changes nor natural selection can explain it.

A revealing look at just how desperate evolution believers are to suggest transitional forms is revealed by the fossils proposed as transitions from fish to land animals. In the early 1900's, the fossil of a fish call the coelacanth, found in "70 million year old rock layers", was commonly proposed as a

transition between fish and land animals because it was assumed that the bones in its fins were "in the process of turning into legs". For decades, this was definitive proof that "evolution is a fact". Yet in 1938, a living coelacanth was found. It was discovered that they lived deep in the ocean (not near shore) and that the bones in their fins were used to survive in their environment (not as legs). They were quietly dropped as a supposed evolutionary transition between fish and land animals. It was never explained how they could have remained alive for "70 million years" without leaving a single fossilized remain.

More recently, a four foot fishlike creature called the tiktaalik roseae (nicknamed the fishapod), supposedly alive 375 million years ago, was proposed as the definitive link between fish and land animals.[1] Why? Again because of bones in its fins.

For fins to turn to limbs would require enormous information added to the creature's DNA. Ligaments, muscles, nerves, and instincts would all have to function perfectly in each useful step by step change. This is story telling, not science. The fishapod is no more a transition between fish and land animals than a duck billed platypus is the transition between a duck and a beaver. Should the fishapod be found alive today, it would no doubt be yet another marvel of God's creative genius -- perfectly adapted for its environment, bones in the fins and all.

1. Michael Novacek, '*Darwin Would Have Loved It*', **Time Magazine**, 4/17/06.

Section III:
Creation and Education: Truth vs. Indoctrination

Dear Bruce,
I really cannot express to you what your coming to Lawrence Technical University and speaking to our students has meant to me, or to our students—in the most positive way! Your presentation and books strengthened my understanding and have given our students much to chew on.
Thank you, thank you, thank you!

- Martha Langrill, Campus Crusade for Christ

Dear Bruce,
I really enjoyed your presentation and I know the stuff you talked about will be valuable when I talk to my friends about the Gospel. A lot of my friends put a lot of stock in evolution to explain the world. It'll be cool to share info with them that shows that our faith is logical, based on reality, and not simply blind faith. I hope all is well with you and the work that God has called you to.
Your brother in Christ,
Ben Salazar, Detroit Mercy University

Chapter 3

"...I found an altar with this inscription, 'to the unknown God', whom therefore you ignorantly worship, Him I declare to you."

- Acts 17:23

Acts chapter 17:16-34 is a fascinating study in how best to introduce Jesus to a culture which knows nothing about Him. In every country that the Apostle Paul visited, there were Jews who had a clear understanding of God. They had experienced the supernatural intervention of God in miraculous ways throughout their history. They understood that God was a supernatural Creator who was not part of the physical world around them, but who was capable of interacting with mankind and performing miracles whenever it suited His perfect and holy purposes. Therefore, when Paul spoke to the Jews he did not need to start by explaining the character and reality of God's existence. In synagogues, Paul could start by directly explaining that mankind could not earn its way into favor with a perfectly holy God, but needed an intermediary who could Himself make the payment that we deserve to pay for our sins, (i.e. God Himself in human form) -- Jesus Christ.

However, in Athens, Greece, Paul had no common foundation upon which to build. Therefore, he went to Mars Hill, the spot in the city where philosophic ideas were discussed, and laid out the case for Christianity by starting from a point of common understanding -- the "unknown God" of the Greeks. Paul first explained that this unknown God was the creator of all things, *"God made the world and all things therein, seeing that He is Lord of heaven and earth, dwelling not in temples made with hands...He gives all life, and breath, and all things; and has made of one blood all nations of men..."* (Acts 17:24-26).

Paul next explained that this God personally interacts with us, *"...He is not far from any one of us. For in Him we live, and move, and have our being."* (Acts 17:27-28).

Paul thirdly explained that this God was not invented by man, *"...we ought not think that God is like gold, or silver, or stone, shaped by art and man's device."* (Acts 17:29).

It was only after laying this foundation that Paul went on to talk about Jesus Christ, *"Truly, these times of ignorance God overlooked, but now commands all men everywhere to repent, because He has appointed a day in which he will judge the world in righteousness by a Man whom He has ordained."* (Acts 17:30)

The result of starting with creation rather than starting in the "middle of the story" with Jesus Christ was that *"many rejected what Paul had to say"* (acts 30:32), BUT many others were convicted and a great church movement began. This will always be the case when presenting the truth of who God is, what He has done for us, and what He expects from us. Many will reject Him, but the Holy Spirit will use our efforts to convict and draw others. To tell someone who has no understanding of the Bible that Jesus died to be our Savior is like starting a novel in the middle. It simply makes no sense. Until someone understands that he had a Creator, and that mankind has rebelled against this Creator, (i.e., we are sinners), why would he need a Savior? Thus, Paul started with creation not with Jesus Christ. We are in the same situation today. The majority of people in our culture no longer have an understanding of either Jesus Christ or of a Biblical God. Re-establishing a foundational understanding of God as Creator will lead directly to understanding His personal nature and His interaction with humanity. Establishing this groundwork is critical if people are really going to understand who Jesus Christ is and what He has done. So where is the Mars Hill of today where this message can be proclaimed? Where is the best place for a public give and take of ideas?

Some would suggest that our public school and university system are the best places for examining ideas. Those who have tried to bring a balanced view of origins into the public education system (by teaching evidence for creation) have quickly found just how closed our education system is to evidence for our supernatural origin. Our entire education and media system currently operate with one underlying prime directive. No one talks about the underlying and often unstated rule that strongly guides the actions of educators and media professionals alike but anyone breaking this rule will quickly find themselves censored or fired. The rule is -- under no circumstances will any direct reference or acknowledgment of the Biblical God or Biblical model of reality be acknowledged as true. Because this prime directive is in operation, no matter how strong the evidence is for the Biblical model of a recent creation, the fall of man, and for a worldwide flood; some other explanation for the world around is always shown. Therefore, very little access to the public education or media system is allowed for any true Biblical model of reality. Even baby steps in the direction of acknowledging that the overwhelming scientific evidence supports an "intelligent designer" are venomously opposed by the educational establishment.

So how can Christians best proclaim the truth in our rapidly darkening culture? Most Christian denominations and even para-church organizations such as Campus Crusade for Christ see creation as a side issue which keeps people from focusing on Christ and creates too much controversy. They work hard to present Jesus Christ as the answer people are looking for, but the vast majority of people in our culture are too busy with their lives to bother with Jesus. A few are saved, yet culture as a whole continues to slide downhill so the pool of people who are interested in anything that has to do with Christianity continues to shrink. People are not being shown the connection between the reality of the world around them and what the Bible has to say about why the earth operates the way it does and where everything came from. They act on exactly what they have been taught by the educational system and media, i.e., the world will pretty much go on forever the way it is today (uniformitarianism). The church is, therefore, doing very little to help people see the truth -- we were very recently created; a holy God does and will always judge sinful behavior; the world is rapidly running downhill; and the final judgement of this world is not far off and our individual judgement is only one heartbeat away. Since the church at large is ignoring the message of creation and how this message brings the Bible alive by tying the physical world to the spiritual aspects of God's Word, how can individual Christians get the truth out?

Some would suggest that the internet or public access TV provide for the free flow of ideas at little or no cost. However, because of the overwhelming barrage of propaganda stating that "evolution is a fact", relatively few people bother to attend lectures on creation so getting people to visit a creation web site is similarly difficult. There are enormous amounts of in-depth research information on the Internet, but it is like a drop of water in a swimming pool of information. There is just too much out there. Another option is writing books or religious magazines. However, these seem to reach only those who have already heard the message. With rare exception, Christians find themselves preaching to each other instead of impacting our culture!

I believe the Mars Hill of today is the public newspaper. This is especially true for small community newspapers. This resource influences a large percentage of the population, still has good credibility, and allows for the give and take of ideas via the letters to the editor. A few of the hundreds of letters to the editor which resulted from placing Search for the Truth articles in newspapers are shown in appendix II. With this goal in mind of getting the truth into public view in such a way that it would be seen and understood, I thus set out to produce an appealing newspaper column showing the scientific evidence for creation to people who were not likely to be exposed to it in any other way. This book is the result of this effort. The articles in this book have also been reproduced in over a dozen small papers across the nation, always with controversial results which raise people's awareness that they are not getting the whole truth through our educational system. In at least one case a school system was allowed to continue showing the evidence for creation because these articles were published (see page 114) and many people have written to say Search for the Truth has been instrumental in the salvation of friends and relatives.

Science Defined to Exclude Creation

By Bruce Malone

The following strategy is repeatedly used by those who advocate "evolution only" education. They:

1. Define science to exclude the possibility of a creator.

2. Claim that all the evidence for our designer is "not science" and, therefore cannot be shown.

3. Repeat, like a mantra, statements such as "evolution is the basis of science" and imply that microbes to man evolution is a proven fact.

4. Then give examples of minor changes within organisms as "proof" that one organism can change into a completely different type, while using the same word, 'evolution' for both the small and the enormous changes.

Actual scientific evidence for any major evolutionary transformation is non-existent. No experiment ever performed has come even remotely close to showing how life could form from chemicals. Major problems with origin of life experiments are systematically hidden from students – after all, we can't have students considering the only other alternative (creation), can we?

No experiment has shown how useful functioning information can be added to the DNA molecule by random changes. Yet, it can be experimentally demonstrated that every known mutation results in a net loss of original functioning information. Why aren't we training students to ask the big question - where did all of this original functional information come from? Acknowledgment of a designer gives a mechanism that agrees with known scientific observations; evolution relies on faith that denies experimental reality.

It is commonly parroted by evolution believers that creation is not science because it is not testable or repeatable. In actuality, the creation model is far more testable than the concept that microbes turned into man by random mutational changes. Any sequence pattern even remotely similar in form or function to the DNA code, beamed to earth from outer space, would immediately be acknowledged as evidence of an intelligent originator. Yet, the same evidence for a designer, found in every DNA molecule, cannot be acknowledged as such in classrooms! Mutation rates have been accelerated a million-fold with fruit flies, yet no new creature or even any new functioning feature has ever developed. Fossils are an undeniable record of the sudden appearance of distinctly different animal forms with huge gaps between enormously diverse creatures. The creation model explains the fossil record as a consequence of a real worldwide flood and the reality of this ancient global flood has been repeatedly confirmed by careful scientific observations. Yet, these evidences are systematically suppressed because of a dogmatic faith in evolution, which survives by defining "science" so that it leaves out the better creation alternative.

Those setting the standards for our public school science curriculum have merely replaced the acknowledgement of our Creator's existence with a definition of "science" that excludes the possibility of God's interaction with His creation. In essence modern man has decided to use the public education system to pretend that there is no God (at least not one worth mentioning). In reality what is being taught is that there is no God except naturalism. God, who desires for us to have a personal relationship with Him, has a response to this sad situation. Psalms 14:1 states, *"The fool says in his heart, 'There is no God.' "* We have become a nation of fools in the way we have allowed our children to be educated.

Education - Redefined

By Bruce Malone

The goal of public education should be training children to think, reason, and discover truth. Yet, the methods used by our education system seem more directed toward molding young minds in such a way as to guarantee agreement with the majority opinion. This teaching method is most apparent when it comes to evolution.

Whenever there is even the slightest hint of criticism or opposition to the naturalistic evolution found in our textbooks, schools, or museums, the charge of bringing religion into public schools is leveled against concerned parents. However, *it is a fact* that the very different types of creatures on our planet were either created as distinctly different types *or* they exist because one type of creature gradually turned into another. *It is a fact* that either the sedimentary fossil record exists because there has been a world covering deluge which rapidly formed these rock layers on the earth *or* there have been huge periods of time where slow gradual processes created them. *It is a fact* that the enormous amount of information found in the genome of living creatures has resulted from either intelligent design *or* random chance processes (such as mutations) that created this information. *It is a fact* that the earth was either created quite recently *or* it is billions of years old.

The correct possibility in each of these cases can only be answered by scientific inquiry, not by philosophy or religious study. In any other scientific inquiry the evidence for or against these two opposing possibilities (involving evidences in areas of geology,

biology, biochemistry, physics and cosmology) would be examined in laboratories and classrooms to discover which model best fits the available evidence. Yet, when presenting anything concerning evolution, students are only allowed to view evidence which fits the evolutionary belief. It is as if allowing students to even view the data that would lead them to question the validity of the "billions-of-years evolutionary model" is off limits. Science has been redefined to eliminate consideration of anything except natural causes and students are only shown evidence and theories which support this definition. Let's examine what it would be like for any other area of knowledge to be taught in a similar fashion:

"Today students, we are going to discuss the subject of geography, but first we must define geography. Very smart people have decided that geography is the study of only land surfaces. Therefore children, any surface of the planet covered with large areas of open water is outside the definition of geography. You will not be allowed to view such maps. It does not matter that

The new (less water) World Map

large oceans exist. Since the definition of geography excludes areas covered by water, these areas cannot be shown to you."

"You will notice that this model of our globe is much simpler and far more convenient to understand. Since our global community is connected by the internet and rapid transportation, open water is irrelevant to travel anyway. Therefore, we are going to pretend that our oceans are much smaller. If we say it often enough, and train each other to cover our eyes when crossing over them; I'm sure everyone will eventually believe it."

"Most importantly children, we must never, ever allow maps showing large oceans into our schools. Any evidence supposedly showing the existence of large oceans cannot be allowed. After all, the very definition of geography excludes the possibility that such a thing could exist."

DING... *"Well, that's all for geography today, children. Now, its time for your English class, where you will learn that English has been defined as a language which does not contain verbs..."*

Magic, Science, and Great Mysteries

By Bruce Malone

The best kept secret of a magician is to get the observer to eliminate the obvious while focusing on the illusion. For instance, the magician will display empty hands or an ordinary scarf before putting something back into his hand (which you assume is still empty) or switching to a trick scarf (which you assume is still ordinary). His skill as a magician depends upon getting the observer to disregard the correct answer so that the mystery remains. Believers in evolution use the same method as they present students with only the natural possibilities for the appearance and advancement of life, while hiding the evidence for creation.

Magazines occasionally publish lists of "great mysteries." *U.S. News and World Report* devoted the cover story of the 8/18/97 issue to 18 "Great Science Mysteries." Yet, most of these mysteries simply disappear if we assume the Bible is true. They are only mysteries if the correct answer has been eliminated before starting the investigation.

One of these "great mysteries" was titled, "Is there life on other planets?" Most biochemists know the answer to this question, but they have been trained not to consider the obvious. Life is far too complex to have developed by natural processes. The information inherent within any living cell requires direct intervention from an outside intelligence (God). Furthermore, even with billions of dollars and thousands of scientists attempting to produce life using purified chemicals and sophisticated laboratory equipment, not one scientist has even come remotely close to producing a living organism from a mixture of chemicals.[1] Yet we are being led to believe that it happens by random processes all over the universe.

Another "mystery" was - "How old is the universe?" Subsequent

> **" Like the magician preparing an audience for a magic trick, the correct answer has been removed from consideration before the investigation begins."**

articles will explain why no dating method is 100% reliable because all are based on unprovable assumptions. However, the vast majority of dating methods indicate that the earth is thousands, not billions, of years old. A straight-forward reading of Scripture would also indicate that the earth has only been around for about 6000 years. A thorough understanding of dating methods shows this to be a perfectly reasonable scientific position. Dr. Russell Humphreys, a highly regarded Ph.D. theoretical physicist who recently retired from Sandia National Laboratories, has mathematically demonstrated how Einstein's theory of relativity explains why the universe "looks" billions of years old, yet could have been created quite recently.[2]

Science cannot even explain why both males and females exist. This is because evolutionists assume that all life came from a sexless single-celled organism. Evolution cannot explain why (or how) this cell could have turned into two radically different types of creatures (male and female) and how these creatures miraculously 'found' each other. Again, the Biblical answer is obvious and straight forward. Sex was created by God and no creature other than a woman can provide a suitable mate for a man.

Yet, another of the scientific mysteries was, "what caused the ice ages?" Creationists have demonstrated for years that the worldwide flood was accompanied by massive volcanism and increased ocean water temperature. This would have caused both the massive destruction of life (which we find as fossils all over the world) and greatly increased evaporation rates. The increased evaporation and volcanic cloud cover would have caused a buildup of snow in northern latitudes. The inevitable consequence of this, in any global climate model, would have been an ice age lasting for centuries.[3]

Almost all of the other "mysteries" also disappear when one applies a straightforward Biblical world view. They are only mysteries when, like the magician preparing an audience for a magic trick, the correct answer has been eliminated from consideration before the investigation begins.

1. Michael Behe, *Darwin's Black Box: The Biochemical Challenge to Evolution,* Free Press, 1996.
2. Russell Humphreys, *Starlight and Time*, Master Books, 1994.
3. Michael Oard, *The Evidence for Only One Ice Age - Proceedings of the Third International Conference on Creation,* 1994.

Science Can Never Define Reality

By Bruce Malone

America's founders centered their discussions of almost every topic around what the Bible taught. Although not all were believing Christians, they did recognize the unique authority of the Bible. One study conducted by the University of Houston found that 92% of all important quotes by America's Founding Fathers from 1750 to 1790 were either direct or indirect references to Biblical teachings.[1]

Today, if a person were to state that his viewpoint was based on Biblical teaching; he would be met with either a blank stare or open ridicule. America's culture is post Christian in nature because Christianity is no longer the primary influencing philosophy. The belief that science can define reality has replaced Christianity as the primary source of truth.

Science is a powerful tool that has helped mankind develop the technological marvels of our modern age. Because of this, many people are under the false impression that science can prove what has happened from the beginning of time, predict what will happen eons into the future, and explain everything in between. This false conception of the capability of science is promoted by false philosophic ideas, such as evolution, which have masqueraded as true science for over 150 years. Understanding the limits of science can help put this discipline into a proper perspective.

Science Can't Define Reality

Science cannot explain what life is or define the difference between human and animal life. Science can describe how things work but not what makes life "alive" or even what makes life exist.

Furthermore, science can never answer the "why" questions. Why does life exist? Why is the earth in the perfect position to sustain life?

> " Before you accept science as your source of ultimate reality (in essence - your God) make sure you clearly understand how truly limited science is. "

Why can't people just get along? Why does evil exist? All of these questions are part of reality, yet science has no answer.

Science Can't Prove the Past

There are vast differences in opinion between equally qualified scientists over what happened in the distant past. For instance, dozens of theories exist about what caused the extinction of the dinosaurs and all of them are unprovable. Scientists can view the exact same data and come to completely different conclusions because all scientists approach the past with a bias. Equally intelligent and well-trained creationists and evolutionists differ profoundly on the history of life's development, the cause of the fossil record, and the age of the universe. All of these subjects deal with events of the past which can never be proven by scientific experimentation because the past cannot be repeated. Wise scientists from both viewpoints admit that science cannot prove what has happened in the past.

Science Can't Predict the Future with Certainty

The wiser the scientist, the more tentatively he draws his conclusions and the more carefully he extrapolates his data. Science can predict what may happen if all the variables are known, but seldom are all the variables known. This is very basis for new scientific discoveries and frequently changing theories. Furthermore, if God does exist, He is fully capable of changing the future course of events just as He seems to have done repeatedly in the past.

Science Can't Show How Things Should Be

Science merely observes and makes tentative predictions. It can make no comment on happiness, purpose, or fulfillment. It knows nothing of love, hate, faith, honor, or virtue. Science is totally silent on these important human characteristics and can provide no guidance concerning the existence of right and wrong. However, each person has an overwhelming inborn sense of how things "ought to be". Most of us also realize that things are not as they should be. Science simply cannot explain why there seems to be so much wrong with this universe in which we live.

1. David Barton, *The Myth of Separation, A revealing look at what the Founders and early courts really said*, Wallbuilders Press, 1992.

Inherit the Lie

By Bruce Malone

The key historical event leading to the general acceptance of evolution in America was not the publication of Darwin's book in 1859. The defining moment for evolution was the publicity surrounding the Scopes Monkey Trial in 1925. What most people know about creation is tainted by the distorted historical presentation of the trial called *Inherit the Wind*.

This Broadway play was first released in 1955 and a movie of the same name was released in 1960. Both the movie and the play are pure propaganda for an atheist worldview and grossly distort true historical events.

The one-sided publicity surrounding the Scopes Monkey Trial makes the truth of the trial relatively unknown. In 1925, Tennessee had an unenforced law which outlawed the teaching of evolution using public funds. The purpose of this law was to gain public support for science education by assuring citizens that public education would not be used to undermine religious beliefs. Sadly, educators today have little concern about undermining religious faith as they work to replace the Christian belief in the absolute truth with the religious relativism of Darwinism.

The ACLU advertised for a defendant willing to contest this law and John Scopes accepted the offer. Scopes had briefly taught biology as a substitute teacher and was willing to serve as defendant in the case (although he later admitted that he had never taught evolution). The town welcomed both the famous defense attorney, Clarence

Darrow (to defend evolution), and the great orator and three time presidential candidate, William Jennings Bryan, as prosecuting attorney (to defend the Biblical record of history). John Scopes

> The incredible irony of *Inherit the Wind* is mind-boggling. This piece of propaganda, which is suppose to encourage freedom of thought, is used to form public opinion in such a way as to exclude the possibility of allowing evidence for creation into schools - thus limiting "free thinking".

was neither ridiculed nor did he spend a single hour in jail. Clarence Darrow's goal, like the modern ACLU, was to rid public education of the evidence for a Creator and the acknowledgment of God's existence.

William Jennings Byran had limited ability to cross examine the experts brought in to defend evolution so their statements were broadcast unchallenged across the nation. Therefore, Bryan agreed to take the stand in defense of Biblical truth in exchange for the opportunity to put Darrow on the stand in defense of evolution. After ridiculing the inconsistencies of Bryan's limited knowledge of the Bible, Darrow ended the trial in a clever legal maneuver before the evidence for evolution could be questioned. As a result, the media portrayed the creation position as foolishness without ever having the evolution position brought under close scrutiny.

In retrospect, those defending the evolution position were shown 100% wrong. Every piece of

evidence cited as proof of evolution has since been falsified. From the fraudulent Piltdown man to the single tooth of Nebraska man (it turned out to be a pig's tooth) all of the evidence for evolution has been debunked. However, the media decided that creation was religion and evolution was scientific truth. Therefore, that view continues to be endlessly parroted to the public.

In the drama, *Inherit the Wind*, Christians are portrayed as narrow-minded religious bigots and Scopes is portrayed as an open-minded defender of truth and freedom. The drama itself is bigoted propaganda; although it is so skillfully presented that most people simply accept this distorted portrayal of the historic trial.

Although *Inherit the Wind* seems to be a drama about the freedom to think; it paints Christians as hypocrites in order to discredit the creation position. This type of evolution propaganda does not promote free thinking, but actually limits it. Scientific evidence for creation is not allowed in public school classrooms while fabrications such as *Inherit the Wind* are welcomed.

The irony of *Inherit the Wind* is profound. The drama which is supposed to encourage freedom of thought is used to form public opinion in such a way as to exclude the possibility of allowing evidence for creation in schools -- thus limiting student's access to the information they need in order to discover the truth.

Creation Viewpoint Heavily Censored

By Bruce Malone

Censorship is a word which evokes a strong response because it conflicts with our inherent sense of fairness. Each year, the humanist organization, ***Citizens for an American Way***, publish a report of supposed "censorship" incidents in which "fundamentalists" attempt to keep books out of libraries. Yet, a far more dangerous type of censorship is largely ignored.

Censorship is the banning of ideas so that people do not even have the opportunity to hear them. The reason this is so dangerous is that the human mind tends to work by paradigms. A paradigm is a framework which all people develop concerning what is right or wrong, true or false. The human mind often finds it very difficult to even consider ideas outside an accepted paradigm. Increasing exposure to the truth improves the probability that it will be embraced. Exclusive exposure to a false belief, no matter how outrageous, insures its eventual acceptance. This is the essence of brainwashing.

In an extensive search of 2.2 million mainstream magazine and journal articles (scanned by SCISEARCH), only 18 items were found which dealt with creation. When another computer search was done to find articles written by well-known creationist authors, not one creation-related article was found. Subsequent interviews revealed that whenever these authors had submitted articles showing specific scientific evidence supporting

creation, their work was rejected.[1]

The situation is no better in school, university, or public libraries where censorship leads to a scarcity of creation materials. Libraries typically purchase materials from a relatively small number of publishers. Creation publications are not selected, no matter how well their work has been researched and presented, because these publishers use reviewers who won't accept any material critical of evolution. For example, ***Biology: A Search for Order in Complexity*** is a well documented high school biology book written by a dozen Ph.D. level creationists. Yet, not one of 15 different textbook publishers WOULD EVEN LOOK AT THE MANUSCRIPT! The textbook finally had to be published by Zondervan (a Christian publishing house) effectively eliminating it from consideration in any public school. The authors of ***The Mystery of Life's Origin*** also had difficulty getting their book published because it critically exposed the enormous problems with chemical evolution. This exclusively scientific treatment of the subject was rejected by 100 agencies before being published by Philosophic Press. Phillip Johnson, law professor at U.C. Berkeley, had similar problems publishing his book,

Darwin on Trial, which deals with the fallacies of evolution. He finally settled on a Christian publishing house. Most creationist writers and researchers realize that this creation censorship exists so do not waste their time trying to publish their material with mainstream journals or publishers.

The late Dr. A.E. Wilde-Smith was an Oxford professor with 3 earned doctorates. Yet, an OCLC computer search of 1000 libraries showed that only 18 carried any of his classic works supporting creation while almost all of the libraries carried books critical of creation. Library journals publish book reviews and out of 100,000 book reviews, several hundred anti-creation books were favorably reviewed; yet, only one creation work was reviewed at all and the review was extremely negative.

There are hundreds of excellent books documenting the scientific evidence for creation, yet almost none can be found in any public, school, or university library. The ***Citizens for an American Way*** are correct - censorship is alive and well in America's libraries.

1. All of these examples of censorship (and many more) are documented in an article called the *Censorship of Information on Origins*, Jerry Bergman, ***Creation ex Nilhilo Technical Journal***, Vol. 10, no. 3, (1996). However, it is extremely unlikely you will find this well-written and peer reviewed research journal in libraries.

Chinese Language Reveals Creation

By Bruce Malone

One of the primary characteristics that separate human behavior from animals' is the ability to transfer abstract concepts to another human via written language. The Bible teaches that this ability came directly from our Creator. It also teaches that the vastly different languages of the world are a result of the confusion of one original language during an event known as the tower of Babel. Our English word babble (meaning gibberish, chatter, nonsense) has it roots in this event. Modern scientific studies really have no better explanation because it is still a mystery how totally different languages could have developed by any natural process.

There should be accounts in ancient cultures for Biblical events such as the creation of man, the fall of man, the existence of a single creator (God), the world wide flood, and the tower of Babel; if these were actual happenings in time and space. Knowledge of all these events can be found not just in the Bible, but in the ancient writings of people throughout the world.

One of the more interesting collaborations can be found within the very characters of ancient Chinese letter symbols. Ancient Chinese writing consisted of a series of word pictures or pictographs which combined separate features to express an idea or concept. Buddhism, Taoism, and Confucianism dominate the religious beliefs of China today. However, 2000 years before the appearance of any of these religious beliefs, the ancient Chinese served a single creator god known as "Shang Ti". The symbol for Shang Ti (God) is a combination of the symbol for emperor and the symbol for heaven (or above).

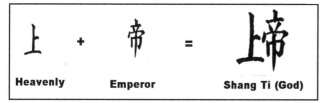

Thus, the original God worshiped by the Chinese was a single heavenly emperor (not many gods).

The Bible states that God created man from the dust of the ground and breathed into him the breath of life. This is presented as a factual event and the original Biblical language is not poetry, but a narrative description of a literal event. We even read in Matthew that Jesus Christ referred to this event as a true happening rather than a symbolic concept, *"Have you not read that in the beginning He made them man and women."* The

ancient Chinese symbol for create is a combination of person (or breath), dust, walking, and alive.

Thus, to create, is to have dust walk, breathe, and live.

The Bible further describes a world wide flood catastrophe in which all human life with the exception of eight individuals on a floating vessel were destroyed. The ancient Chinese symbol for 'boat' is vessel, eight, and people.

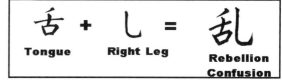

Thus, a boat is eight people on board of a vessel!

The Bible again states that man was told to spread out over the earth after the worldwide flood. Yet, he rebelled and built a tower to his own glory. God ended this rebellion by confusing man's language so that the people set out and journeyed across the globe in different language groups. Interestingly, the ancient Chinese chose to use the identical symbol for confusion and rebellion ... a combination of tongue and right leg (or journey).

Thus, to confuse is to set out on a journey with a new tongue (or language).

These are just a few of the many examples of the historical knowledge of the Bible that the ancient Chinese people must have had as they developed their written language. Many more examples can be found in an excellent book by C.H. Kang and Ethel Nelson called ***The Discovery of Genesis***.

Turn on Your Baloney Detector

By Bruce Malone

Carl Sagan was the unofficial voice for naturalistic atheism for many years until his death in 1997. In one of his last books, *The Demon-Haunted World*, Sagan lamented that in spite of monumental public education efforts to teach that random chance processes had produced all life, only 9% of American citizens accepted this as true. Sagan's solution was for people to learn critical thinking skills. However, Dr. Sagan never applied these same critical thinking skills to his own unshakable faith in naturalistic evolution. Professor Phillip Johnson does an excellent job of doing just that in his book, *Defeating Darwinism by Opening Minds.* Here is a summary of some classic distortion techniques used all too often to defend evolutionism.

BLIND APPEAL TO AUTHORITY

This is often the first resort used to discredit those who do not cower to the opinion of the majority. Yet every major breakthrough in science has happened because some researcher looked beyond the prevailing opinion. An authority stating that something is true does not make it true. When searching for the truth, rely on the quality and quantity of evidence rather than on empty claims. In science, experimental evidence must reign supreme - not opinions or appeals to authority.

SELECTIVE USE OF EVIDENCE

Evidence can be found to support any point of view - no matter how absurd it is. Truth is usually found by examining what most of the evidence supports. For example, lots of animals have similar appearances and features.

Is it any surprise that some fossils can be found that combine intermediate features between the features of two different animals? Just because a bicycle and a motorcycle both have two wheels does not mean random changes in a bike can turn it into a motorcycle. What does the bulk of fossil evidence reveal? An honest viewing of the fossil record reveals distinctly different types of animals without intermediate transitions.

AD HOMINEM ARGUMENTS

Ad hominem is Latin for "to the man". Those who publicly defend the scientific evidence for creation are often greeted with personal insults and attacks which have nothing to do with the evidence. The weaker the evidence for evolution, the more vehement the attacks. The essence of the attacks are, "Creationists believe in God. Therefore they are biased and anything they say on the subject of origins cannot be trusted." Everyone is biased. Believers in evolution whose jobs and funding depend upon agreement with naturalistic interpretations are also highly biased. It is the quality and testability of the scientific evidence which must determine a theory's validity.

TESTABLE CONCLUSIONS

One must learn to distinguish between interpretations and facts. Carl Sagan stated, *"The Cosmos is all there is, or ever was, or ever will be."* This is opinion... not science. How could statements such as this ever be tested? On the other hand, creationists make the following type of claims:

- There has been a worldwide flood in the past.

- Random information cannot produce ordered complexity by natural processes.
- One type of life has never changed into a distinctly different type with new functioning features not originally programmed into the creature's DNA code.
- Mutations destroy rather than create useful functioning features.

These statements are scientifically testable and there is enormous evidence to support each.

STRAW MAN ARGUMENT

A straw man argument is when a position is distorted and the distortion is then attacked. This is repeatedly done by evolutionists. The creation/evolution debate is about determining the truth of the past. Yet, believers in evolution constantly set up a straw man attack by trying to make this an issue of religion vs. science.

BEGGING THE QUESTION

Begging the question is asking a question to which you have already assumed an answer. Evolutionists start with the assumption that creation is a myth, there has never been a worldwide flood, and all animal life has evolved from a common source. By defining science to exclude supernatural intervention, evolutionists have begged the question by eliminating the truth before starting the debate. No honest debate is even possible under such circumstances.

Defeating Darwinism by Opening Minds is an excellent book which should be read by every high school and college student who hopes to resist the pressure to conform to the fuzzy reasoning and faulty logic which surrounds evolution.

Good Morning Students

By Bruce Malone

The debate over evolution vs. creation is not just a dry technical argument concerning isotopic dating methods, dinosaur bones, or even whether mutations can turn pond scum into people. What we believe about where we came from determines how we view life, and ultimately, our actions. Answers to such basic questions as "Where did we come from?", "What is the purpose of life?", and "How do we determine right from wrong?", are derived directly from our beliefs about our origin. If we are just the result of random chance changes that turned swamp gas into people; then life has no ultimate purpose or meaning... Each person must determine for themselves what is right or wrong... and any ultimate meaning and purpose for life, really does not exist.

This is the essence of what is being taught to your children each day in public schools:

"Good morning students and welcome to high school. Our first lesson today will be to teach you where you came from. Many of you have been taught that God created you. However, that is a religious concept and must be reserved for Sunday mornings. You may keep that belief, if you wish, but we will now teach you more important things like science and reality."

"You see, Johnny and Suzy, you are here as a result of cosmic accidents and random chance.

" I WISH THEY'D TEACH CREATIONISM TOO... I NEVER DID BELIEVE IN THE LITERAL INTERPRETATION OF DARWIN! "

Billions of years ago, "nothing" exploded and turned into gas molecules. These gas molecules bounced around until they became stars. The stars then changed simple atoms into bigger atoms. After lots and lots and lots of time passed, these larger atoms and molecules formed a big rock that we call Earth. Parts of this rock dissolved into water and came alive. After billions more years, little critters in the water climbed onto land and started walking around. Over time, birth defects happened (which we call mutations) and these critters turned into other kinds of critters. More often than not these critters wiped out the previous critters. Finally apes turned into people. And here we are. We were not there to see any of this happen, and we cannot really prove how it could have happened, but we are absolutely sure this is what happened. That's why we call this science. You see now Johnny and Suzy, why science and reality can teach you so much more than religion."

"One more thing, Johnny, because you are just a cosmic accident, you really have no basis for judging other people. You must be tolerant. Homosexuality is just a choice. Abortion is just a choice. Sex with anyone or anything at anytime is just a choice (but please be careful.) Anything you choose to believe is OK as long as it is good for you. And you get to define what is "good"! After all, you are really just a cosmic accident, and after a few more billion years the universe will collapse back into nothingness anyway."

"That's all the time we have for biology and history today. Now, it is time to go to your new class on self-esteem and good behavior where we will try to define good behavior for you. Have a good day, Suzy and Johnny, and be the best little well behaved accidents you can be"

Is it any wonder that lying and cheating are widespread in both schools and governments? Is it really surprising that despondent students resort to violence and suicide?

Let's return to true education where students have the freedom to view the scientific evidence for creation. Then, they will once again have a factual basis for understanding that their lives have meaning and value, because they are made in the image of a personal Creator. Only then will morality have an immovable foundation -- because it will be the reflection of that Creator.

Watch Out for the Snow Job

By Bruce Malone

Phillip Johnson in his book, **Defeating Darwinism by Opening Minds,** suggests that whenever the word evolution appears in schools, textbooks, nature programs, or museums, a red light should go off in our heads flashing, **"SNOW JOB ALERT...SNOW JOB ALERT"**. This is because the same word, evolution, is used to convey completely different meanings and the definition shifts without notice.

The most general use of the word evolution is *"change."* No one can argue with this - things do change. The second meaning of the word is also agreed upon by everyone. This is when evolution is used to mean microevolution or minor variations within a type of animal. Examples of this are different breeds of dogs and cats. Microevolution also happens in nature to produce such relatively minor changes as different beaks on finches (which Darwin observed on the Galapagos Islands). Notice that dogs are still dogs and finches are still finches.

The switch occurs whenever evolution believers switch to the third definition without mentioning that they are shifting definitions. Macroevolution is the concept of one animal turning into a completely different type. Believers in evolution repeatedly use the same word (evolution) to mean both minor variations and major transformations. Can minor variations create completely new biological features or creatures? The information needed for microevolution is already present

within a creature's genetic code. Macro-evolutionary change requires new functioning information. Furthermore, the fossil record reveals no evidence that any creature has ever turned into a

completely different type of creature. In any other type of scientific endeavor or debate using the same word to mean completely different things and changing the definition without notice would be intolerable. Yet, this is exactly what public school science textbooks and evolution believers routinely do.

Many examples of this bait and switch can be sited:

- *Almost all high school biology texts use examples of micro-evolution such as finch beak variations as an example of evolution, yet nothing really new is ever created. How can breeding existing characteristics transform a bird or a dog into some completely different type of creature?*

- *In 1996, Danny Phillips, a high school student in Denver, Colorado, wrote a lengthy defense of creation after being required to watch a government funded Nova television series*

which presented evolution as fact and glossed over the problems. The response to his request that such propaganda for an atheistic worldview be removed from the classroom was that the "scientific establishment" came down on him like a ton of bricks. Bruce Alberts, president of the National Academy of Sciences, felt that he needed to personally respond to Danny in a Denver Post editorial. His primary evidence to prove that evolution is a fact...finch beaks show variations!

- *Francis Crick argued for evolution with these words, "Richard Dawkins (in **The Blind Watchmaker**) shows that man, by selection, has produced an enormous variety of dogs." [2] Lost to this brilliant scientist is the obvious fact that the dogs remained dogs - what is not already present in this animal's DNA, can never be produced by random changes.*

The next time you see the word **"evolution"**, examine how it is being used. Is it the modification of already existing features (which proves nothing about the origin of those features), or is it a bait and switch where microevolution is used as "proof" of macroevolution (for which there is no proof)?

1. Bruce Alberts, **The Denver Post**, September 10, 1996, p. B9.
2. Francis Crick, **What Mad Pursuit: A Personal View of Scientific Discovery**, 1988, p.29.

What about all the other Creation Stories?

By Bruce Malone

One of the frequent objections to allowing the teaching of creation in public schools is that if "creationism" is taught, all other different cultural stories concerning creation would have to be brought into a science classroom. This is a classic example of a "straw man" (distortion of the truth) argument. This strategy is used to discredit the scientific evidence for creation by denigrating it as a religious concept. Those opposed to exposing students to the evidence for creation hope to equate this evidence with ancient creation myths, such as the absurd idea that the universe came from the egg of a large bird. Yet modern evolutionists believe that the entire universe essentially came from nothing, as the "cosmic egg" (which contained all the matter and energy of the universe) somehow explosively expanded. Creation is based on the existence of a Creator so at least it has a cause for the universe. Which group of believers really have egg on their face?

The primary desire of creationists is to have science taught in science classrooms. Unfortunately, that is not what is happening today. The current situation is that minor changes in animals (variations which are already encoded onto the DNA of the creature) are being presented as proof that one type of creature turned into a completely different creature. This is a religious belief, not science. Science is based on testable observations, and the creation theory, unlike ancient mythologies or modern evolution, is very testable.

Creation theory states that

complex ordered information requires an intelligent source. This is exactly what we find in the DNA molecule, and if the same type of code were found coming from outer space; it would immediately be recognized as having had an intelligent source.

The creation model predicts that there is a limit to natural genetic variation. In other words, one type of creature does not turn into a completely different type with totally new functioning features. This has been experimentally confirmed as the mutation rate of fruit flies has been accelerated by millions of times. Furthermore, no links between major forms of animals have been found in the fossil record. This confirms that biological variation has always been limited.

The creation theory states that new forms of animals do not form via random changes to previous life forms and throughout known history this has been observed to be true. However, thousands of different types of creatures have become extinct over this same time period. New viruses and microbes result from the rearrangement of information already present in existing microbes. This does not tell us where these organisms came from or how they could turn into a completely different type of organism.

The creation theory states that a massive worldwide flood occurred which buried and fossilized creatures by the billions. This is exactly what we find and there is abundant geologic evidence supporting the reality of this relatively recent catastrophe.

Furthermore, every scientific experiment ever performed has shown that chemicals fail to react in ways which result in the formation of living organisms. This is what the creation model predicts. Unlike the creation myths, such as the modern big bang *theory* and microbes-to-man evolution, the Biblical creation account and the worldwide flood described in Genesis is full of testable, observable predictions which can be explored in science classrooms.

Unfortunately, believers in evolution hold a firm grip upon most of the scientific community because science has been redefined to eliminate the consideration of an intelligent Creator. It's time to give students all the evidence and let them decide for themselves which theory holds up best under close scientific scrutiny.

Humanism only Allowed Public Religion

By Bruce Malone

Neither creation nor evolution can be proven by the scientific method. However, by examining which model best explains the observations of science, we can determine which is the correct explanation for our existence. However, how can students come to the correct conclusion if they are exposed to neither the scientific evidence for creation nor the scientific problems with evolution? The Supreme Court has repeatedly confirmed the rights of public school teachers to share the scientific evidence for creation.[1] Yet, any objective observer would have to admit that evolutionary presuppositions have almost total control over the public education system. This is typically not the teachers' fault because he or she is merely passing along the same one-sided information which they have been taught. They also put their career at risk when teaching creation in the current educational environment.

Instead of presenting evolution as a fact (which it is not), why not present the evidence which supports both positions and let the students make up their own minds which has the most validity? **If evolution is truly a fact of science and has overwhelming evidence supporting it, then there is nothing to fear from this approach and truth will triumph over fantasy.** This two-model approach was tried in a carefully controlled study with students in the Racine, Wisconsin, Unified School District. This was done before the death grip of evolutionary thinking became so strong in our school systems. At the time of the study, this district consisted of four high

schools and seven junior high schools. The biology classes were divided into two groups - one group was taught only the evidence for naturalistic evolution (the standard curriculum in most schools) while the other group was taught both the evidence for evolution and the evidence for the sudden appearance of life (creation). The result was that in standardized tests given to both groups, the group which had seen evidence for both viewpoints not only knew more about creation, but they also learned and retained more information about evolution![2] There are excellent two-model science curricula that present the evidence for both evolution and "sudden appearance" in a balanced manner with no reference to the Bible.[3]

Forcing high school science teachers to teach what they neither understand nor agree with would result in a caricature of the creation model. However, the current situation of only presenting the evidence for one of two possibilities is also unfair and unwise. The best option is for the school board and administration to encourage science teachers to present evidence for both creation and evolution. This allows students to make up their own minds as to which theory of origins has the most validity. However, this will ONLY happen if there is an outcry by concerned parents over the current indoctrination. By letting your child's teacher know that you would like the scientific evidence for creation to be presented, you may encourage some teachers to do so. You might start by giving them a copy of this book. There are dozens of technical supplemental texts available from the Institute for Creation Research (www.ICR.org) and qualified guest speakers could also be invited.

1. Edwards vs Aquillard, 1987, *The Supreme Court again confirmed that the scientific evidence for creation can be taught in public schools.*
2. Dr. Richard Bliss, ***Impact Article #36***, available from the Institute for Creation Research (619) 448-0900.
3. ***Origins: Creation or Evolution***, available from Master Books.

Creation Scientists are Abundant

By Bruce Malone

One of the many lies used to defend evolution is the statement that no real scientist believes in creation. Shown below are abbreviated biographies and quotes of just a few of the myriad of qualified scientists who reject evolution. Dr. Russell Humphreys estimates that in spite of heavy indoctrination from public education, "It's a conservative estimate that there are in the U.S.A. alone around 10,000 practicing scientists who are Biblical creationists."

<u>Scientist</u>	<u>Qualifications</u>	<u>Quote</u>
Dr. Russell Humphreys	Ph.D. Physics, retired physicist from Sandia National Lab. He is an expert on particle beam fusion and winner of several scientific awards.	"(The facts of science) support a recent creation and go strongly against the idea of billions of years which the theistic evolutionists uphold."[1]
Dr. Danny Faulkner	Ph.D. Astronomy, teaches physics and astronomy at Univ. of S. Carolina, has published several dozen papers in astronomy & astrophysics journals.	"(I believe) the universe is 6 to 8 thousand years old...we have a very clear indication from scripture that creation took place in six ordinary days."[2]
Dr. John Baumgardner	Ph.D. Geophysics, retired from Los Alamos Nat. Lab. - expert on modeling interior earth movement, winner of NASA's grand challenge project for high performance computing.	"To make sense of the world as the Bible lays it out, does not allow for millions of years, but does require that there be a catastrophe which destroyed all air-breathing land life except for that preserved in Noah's ark."[3]
Dr. Andrew Snelling	Ph.D. Geology, numerous published papers on a variety of geological topics, from coal formation to uranium deposits. mineral deposits, etc."[4]	"The flood was a global event, therefore we should expect to find global patterns of sedimentation, volcanic activity,
Dr. Eric Norman	Ph.D. Biochemistry, Asst. Professor of research and medicine at Univ. of Cinn., has published numerous scientific papers, pioneer in vitamin B12 research.	"Evolution is just plain unscientific. It violates the laws of chemistry including the second law of thermodynamics, the laws of probability, and information theory.[5]
Dr. Donald DeYoung	Ph.D. Physics, Chairman of Physical Science at Grace College, member of the Indiana Academy of Science; teaches physics, astronomy, electronics, and mathematics.	"...I would be very cautious about accepting the 'big bang' and trying to fit it into the book of Genesis...what encourages me in my science career (is) showing people that the creation view is not outdated - it's good science."[6]
Dr. Raymond Damadian	Inventor of the MRI, National Tech. Metal winner, National Inventors Hall of Fame inductee. Snubbed on Nobel Prize because of vocal stand on recent creation.	"Rejection of (the Bible's) account of creation... is basic to the spiritual, social, and economic sickness of our times."[7]
Dr. Jonathan Sarfati	Ph.D. Physical Chemistry with extensive training in mathematics, geology, physics. Co-authored papers on superconductors.	"Ninety percent of the methods used to estimate the age of the earth point to an age far less than the billions of years asserted by evolutionists."[8]
Dr. A.E. Wilder-Smith	Earned doctorates in three scientific disciplines including organic chemistry and biology. He has written 30 books, directed a pharmaceutical co., and taught extensively.	"[evolution's] influence has not been gained by displaying a knowledge of the fundamentals of modern science but by propaganda of a rather subtle sort." [9]

1. Creation Magazine, Vol.15, No.3, pp. 23.   *2. Ibid, Vol.19, No.4, pp. 20.*   *3. Ibid, Vol.19, No.3, pp. 42.*
4. Ibid, Vol.18, No.3, pp. 20.5. Ibid, Vol.17, No.   3, pp. 29.   *6. Ibid, Vol.17, No.2, pp. 28.*
7. Ibid, Vol.16, No.3, pp. 36.   *8. Refuting Evolution, pp. 112, 1999.*
9. The Scientific Alternative to Neo-Darwinian Evolutionary Theory, pp.131, 1987.

Science Foundation laid by Creationists

By Bruce Malone

Science is currently defined to exclude the possibility that a personal creator God exists. Those who dare to oppose this view are often insulted and censored. However, just because the majority believes something does not make it true. Science is neither a popularity contest nor a democratic endeavor. Science deals with observation of the physical world in order to understand its operation. Thus, the ultimate purpose of science is to understand reality. The great advances of modern science over the last 100 years have convinced many that because science can explain the operation of the universe, it also defines reality. However, there is a great difference between understanding how something operates and how it originated. It is revealing that many of the very scientists who laid the foundation for "modern" science saw no conflict between God's supernatural intervention and our ability to understand His creation. Below are quotes from just a few:

Scientist	Accomplishments	Christian Stance
Blaise Pascal (1623 - 1662)	Developer of first mechanical adding machine, developed mathematical basis for theory of probability, laid basis for hydrostatics and hydrodynamics.	"How can anyone lose who chooses to become a Christian? If, when he dies, there turns out to be no God he has lost nothing - in fact, he lived a happier life than non-believing friends. If, however, there is a God, he has gained heaven, while his skeptical friends will have lost everything in hell."
Sir Isaac Newton (1642 - 1727)	Discoverer of the universal law of gravity, three fundamental laws of motion; developed calculus into a mathematical science, developed the particle theory of light propagation, and made the first reflecting telescope.	Defended a young earth and wrote papers refuting atheism and defended creation and the Bible; believed in a worldwide flood as cause of geologic record, and believed in literal six day creation of universe.
Charles Babbage (1791 - 1871)	Father of modern computing. His design was the forerunner of modern computers. A prolific inventor of hundreds of items including the speedometer, cowcatcher, and ophthalmoscope.	Babbage believed that the scientific method pursued to its utmost limit was entirely compatible with the literal belief in the Bible.
James Joule (1818 - 1889)	Discovered the relationship between heat, electricity, and mechanical work. Founder of the science of thermodynamics. First measured velocity of gases and discovered Joule-Thompson effect (basis for modern refrigeration).	Joule stood firmly against those scientists of his day who were caught up in the increasing popularity of Darwinism. "The order maintained in the universe...works smoothly and harmoniously...the whole being is governed by the sovereign hand of God."
James Maxwell (1831 - 1879)	Developed the four equations which are the basis for modern electro-magnetic theory. His work ranks with Sir Isaac Newton and Albert Einstin in scientific significance.	Strongly opposed and demonstrated the fallacy of Darwinism. A prayer by Maxwell's says it all, "Almighty God, Who hast created man in Thine own image...teach us to study the works of Thy hand, that we may believe on Him Whom Thou has sent to give us a knowledge of salvation and the remission of our sins. All this we ask in the name of Jesus."
Louis Pasteur (1822 - 1895)	Proved that life comes only from pre-existing life. Developed the process of pasteurization which has saved countless lives. Developed the first vaccination (created the cure for rabies).	Pasteur strongly opposed Darwinism because the theory did not fit scientific evidence (it still doesn't). He believed, "Science brings men nearer to God." and he also said that, "The more I study nature, the more I stand amazed at the works of the Creator."
Werner Von Braun (1912 - 1977)	Led a team of scientists who developed modern rocketry and space flight. Director of NASA flight center from 1958 - 1971. Instrumental in the manned space program.	"I find it difficult...to understand a scientist who does not acknowledge the presence of a superior rationality behind the existence of the universe."

School Prayer Sets Tone for Society

By Bruce Malone

Since prayer was eliminated from public schools, the quality of education has shown a steady statistical decline. Is there a link between the two?

Humanism assumes that the supernatural does not exist and that reality must be discovered purely by man's reasoning. Our public school system has been operating on this foundation since prayer was removed in 1962. Returning prayer to school would be an affront to this philosophy because prayer acknowledges the existence of someone greater than mankind -- his Creator.

Allowing prayer in school sets an important standard. It tells students that they are more than just a collection of chemicals and energy that happen to be occupying space and time. Prayer is an action which proclaims that life is more than saving the environment or accumulating wealth. The fervency with which school prayer is opposed is not because the ACLU (an anti-Christian legal group) is trying to protect atheists from being indoctrinated by religion. It is opposed because it represents the antithesis to the beliefs of those who set policy for much of our public school system. Prayer is a frontal attack on the notion that mankind is in autonomous control of his own destiny and is an insult to those who believe that friends, possessions, or power can bring

lasting meaning or joy.

A primary purpose of public education is to shape good citizens. This involves more than just the memorization of facts. Most Americans are in favor of prayer in

Used by permission of Chuck Asay

public school because they realize something is to be gained from the open acknowledgment of God's existence. Morals can only be built on the basis that a moral source -- God -- exists. Once acknowledgment of God's existence is removed, there is no absolute basis for morals, and a free society drifts toward anarchy. Since prayer was removed from public school, we have had a sixfold increase in violent crime, our divorce rate has tripled, births to single mothers have increased fivefold, the teenage suicide rate has tripled, and SAT scores (standardized college entrance test) have dropped 80 points (10%).[1] The removal of prayer may not be the only cause of social ills, but the negative trends are certainly a symptom of the spiritual decline which is at their root.

What a hypocritical message we

send to our children when we allow laws to be passed which limit the free expression of speech in public by banning public prayer in classrooms. Federal and Supreme Court judges who undermine the very freedoms upon which America was founded, should be impeached. The situation has become so absurd that congressional prayers cannot be voluntarily read in a school building.[2]

Our nation was founded on the freedom to publicly acknowledge God's existence. Allowing prayer in schools will only improve, not detract from a student's understanding of the universe. Our experiment with replacing the affirmation of God's existence with atheistic humanism has been a dismal failure. Whenever the opportunity arises to support the public acknowledgment of God by prayer (or any other means), taking a vocal stand benefits all of society. As Edmund Burke, correctly noted in 1795, *"The only thing necessary for the triumph of evil is for good men to do nothing."* As with all truths, this is still applicable today.

1. Bill Bennett, *The Index of Leading Cultural Indicators*, published by the Heritage Foundation, 1993.
2. 1970 Supreme Court Case, *State Board of Education vs. Board of Education of Netcong.*

Creation as Comparative Religion

By Bruce Malone

Proverbs, an ancient book of wisdom, states that any story will sound true until the other side is heard. *"He that is first in his own cause seems just; until his neighbour comes and searches him."* (Proverbs 18:17) The primary strategy used to keep the evidence for creation out of public schools is to claim that teaching creation is introducing religion into schools. It is often suggested that the solution is to teach creation in a class on comparative religion.

Teaching the evidence for creation is not an issue of science vs. religion. The crux of the debate is whether students should be allowed to see all of the scientific data so that they can make up their own minds where we came from. Currently one religious belief (evolutionism) maintains such a monopoly over thought that students are only allowed to see literature favorable to it. *[Evolutionism is the belief that life formed itself and that a creature can transform itself into a completely different type of creature by some natural process.]*

Meanwhile, the scientific evidence supporting the other possible explanation for our existence (creationism) is suppressed. *[Creationism is the belief that the complexity of life requires an intelligent designer;*

that there is a natural limit to genetic variations; that one type of creature has never turned into a completely different kind, and that the vast majority of the fossil record is a result of an enormous worldwide flood.]

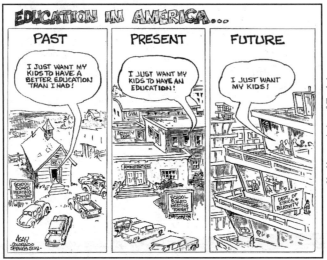

Neither evolutionism nor creationism can be proven because both deal with events of the past. Yet both provide models which can be tested by scientific observation.

There is no doubt that both natural selection and mutations occur. Small variations do occur as the result of random changes within a given type of animal. Yet dogs stay dogs and frogs stay frogs. Furthermore, there is an enormous amount of evidence supporting the creation model:

1. The fossil record shows a pattern of systematic gaps between vastly different types of animals.
2. Scientists have not come even remotely close to showing how non-living chemicals could form a living cell.
3. If the same type of code found on the DNA molecule were transmitted to earth from outer space, it would immediately be

recognized as having an intelligent designer.
4. The laws of thermodynamics show that matter and energy do not just appear and matter does not, by itself, increase in ordered complexity.
5. Accelerating the mutation rate of fruit flies by a million fold has not resulted in a new creature or any new functioning feature.
6. There is abundant geological evidence for a recent massive flood of worldwide extent.

These and many more evidences involving biology, geology, and physics, belong in a science class – not in a class on comparative religion. It is not the desire of creation scientists to indoctrinate students in religion. Creationists merely want students to have a chance to see all the data so they can decide for themselves whether creation or evolution is true. Currently, students are only given the selective evidence which supports a belief in evolutionism because that faith can only survive if evidence supporting creation continues to be censored.

A Barna poll conducted in 2004 showed that 68% of the people in the United States want the evidence for both creation and evolution taught in schools. The evolution/creation debate is not about whether teaching the scientific evidence for creation will bring religion into schools. Scientific evidence belongs in a science classroom, even if that evidence points to a Creator. Allowing the evidence for creation provides students with the opportunity to think and judge for themselves.

Biblical Creation vs. Intelligent Design

By Bruce Malone

Seldom does a year go by without a new controversy over the teaching of intelligent design in our public school system. When President Bush endorsed the teaching of intelligent design in 2005, the atheistic leaning educational establishment and media went ballistic. A federal court in Pennsylvania shot down the teaching of intelligent design in public schools in 2006. A sticker in the front of Georgia science books stating that evolution was "just a theory" was ordered removed in 2005. Just what is this thing called "intelligent design"?

In a nutshell, intelligent design is the acknowledgment of what almost everyone knows to be true -- that the intricate and interrelated design of living organisms require a Designer. Over 90% of American citizens already believe in the existence of God and 59% of American citizens want the evidence for creation taught in public schools. Even 30% of atheists/agnostics want this evidence taught in schools![1] Yet this evidence is systematically withheld from public school students all over America. Why is it being concealed? What is this evidence? And what is the difference between intelligent design and Biblical creation?

The evidence for intelligent design comes primarily from the science of statistics and biochemistry. Simply put, the information content of the DNA molecule could not possibly have arisen by mutational and natural selection processes because the rate of detrimental mutational changes in order of magnitude is higher than any yet to be defined beneficial mutational changes. This is widely acknowledged because there is a universal avoidance and fear of any such mutational change (i.e. birth defect) from radiation, drugs, or genetic diseases. Everyone instinctively knows that mutations result in a loss of functioning information and are to be feared, not welcomed as the source of an upward human evolutionary advancement. Furthermore, the incredible amount of information on the human genome can be statistically shown to have never arisen by chance mutational changes. Any similar code coming from outer space would immediately be acceptable as having come from an intelligent source. In short, the scientific case for an intelligent designer is overwhelming.

So why is this type of evidence not being shared with students? Because science and education have been defined as excluding any possibility of a Creator. When the Kansas State School Board voted to allow the critical examination of evolution in public schools in the late 1990's, (by allowing some of the evidence for intelligent design to be viewed by students) the national media overwhelmed the Kansas airwaves with a misinformation propaganda campaign which led to all of the school board members being replaced with pro-evolution candidates (who later overturned the decision). In a typical letter written by Dr. Scott Todd of Kansas State University, *"Even if all the data points to an intelligent designer, such a hypothesis is excluded because it is not naturalistic."*[1] Science has been defined to exclude the possibility of God's interaction. So no matter how strong or how scientific the evidence is, it will not be shown to students!

There is certainly nothing wrong with attempting to get the evidence for "intelligent design" into our schools and science classrooms, but in the end it will accomplish little. Over 90% of people already know we have an intelligent designer and in the 1800's, when Darwin first proposed that natural processes produced us, intelligent design (i.e. a watch must have a watch maker), was the primary argument used in favor of creation. Yet almost every European country eventually rejected the obvious and accepted evolution in its place. Why do we believe the result would be different in America?

What people in America really need to hear is the evidence for the Biblical creation model which involves evidence from geology, biology, paleontology, and cosmology. The overwhelming evidence for a worldwide flood explains the fossil record without the idea of slow transformation from one creature to another. The vast majority of dating methods indicate that the earth is far younger than the billions of years accepted by most intelligent design advocates. Furthermore, the fossil record clearly shows that one type of creature has never turned into a completely different type of creature. Once this type of model is openly discussed in our schools, then we will start to see a revival of faith in America.

1. Barna Group Poll, **www.Barna.org**, *Barna Update*, 7/26/05.
2. Dr. Scott Todd, *Nature Magazine* letter to editor, 9/30/99.

Questions to Ask

By Bruce Malone

As the relentless propaganda for an old earth and an evolutionary world view is piled upon your children, how should they respond? I Peter 3:17 should be our guide in these matters, "*Always be ready with an answer for the faith that is within you, but do so with gentleness and respect.*"

Directly challenging those in authority over you, either in a 'know-it-all-attitude' or with disrespect, will win neither hearts nor minds to the Truth. The best strategy is to understand the poor assumptions and presuppositions upon which evolution teeters (which even most teachers are unaware of) and ask these types of probing questions to reveal the fallacy of evolutionary presuppositions.

The Origin of Life:

Why do textbooks continue to imply that the Miller-Urey experiment shows how life could have developed when it actually uses an arbitrary and unrealistic set of conditions and produces amino acids which could not possibly lead to life? Only a few of the required amino acids have ever been produced and even those are an unusable mixture of stereotypes. Why was oxygen excluded, even though, rocks in the earth's crust indicate oxygen has always been present? Doesn't the origin of life remain a total mystery? (pp.13)

The Cambrian Explosion:

At the lowest rock layers containing life, why does every basic phylum (major animal group) suddenly appear with no transitions between very different forms of life? What better evidence for creation can be found and why is this not openly discussed in textbooks? Why isn't

this acknowledged as a direct contradiction to the idea that everything came from some unknown ancestor? (pp. 43)

Evolution Examples:

Why is archaeopteryx still used in textbooks as a link between dinosaurs and birds when modern birds fossils have been found in even lower (i.e. assumed to be older) rock layers? (pp. 50) Why are peppered moths still used as evidence for evolution, when it is now acknowledged that nothing new developed (just a shift in population), that the pictures were staged, and moths don't normally rest on tree trunks? (pp. 24) Why are accelerated mutational changes in fruit flies used as evidence for evolution, even though, mutated features have ALWAYS resulted in a nonfunctional rearrangement of already existing information? If these are the best examples that support evolutionary theory, isn't evolution really just a belief system and not science? (pp. 23)

The Age of the Earth:

Why are the majority of dating methods which indicate a young earth never shared with students? Radiometric decay assumes a constant decay rate extrapolated back billions of years. Yet, many decay processes produce helium which would VERY rapidly leave rock crystals. However, most of the helium decay product is still found in the rocks. Why is this strong evidence for recent, rapid radioactive decay not in our textbooks? (pp. 87)

The Worldwide Flood:

Why do textbooks never discuss the evidence for a worldwide flood? There is speculation that Mars experienced a global flood, even

though, there is currently no free water on the planet. Yet, on earth, where there is enough water to cover the entire globe with water 5000 feet deep, the evidence that we have experienced a recent global flood is ignored. Why do most cultures in the world have a cultural story involving a universal flood? Why did advanced cultures suddenly pop into existence, around the globe, almost simultaneously within the last 10,000 years? Why do many Ph.D. geologists believe that the flood explains the fossil and sedimentary rock record better than huge time periods yet the evidence for this interpretation is not shared with students? (pp. 40, 41, 42)

Apeman:

Why are artist drawings of apeman presented as a fact to students when fossil experts cannot even agree on where our ancestors came from or what they looked like? Why are the countless misinterpretations of the human to ape links not shared with students in order to put the "latest finds" into proper perspective?

Origin of Information:

Where did the information content of DNA come from? Why are students not told that undetectable mutational mistakes on our DNA code are building up hundreds of times faster than natural selection can remove them? Therefore, natural selection and mutations could not possibly have produced this information. (pp. 25) Why is the search on for the same criteria for intelligent design coming from outer space (a sequence of information such as is found on the DNA molecule) not acknowledged as evidence for intelligent design when already found in every biological organism? (pp. 16, 18)

Section IV:
Evidence for Creation from Physics, Cosmology and the Age of the Earth

Dear Bruce,

Thank you for your books. You do not know how much you have affected my life. Because of *Search for the Truth*, mine and my family's faith in the Bible was strengthened. My children and I now have interesting discussions whenever a new story comes out about the origin of life.

My wife and I were recently called to a new church very close to our house. We are part of the youth ministry there. I have no doubt I will start teaching more in the area of "Search for the Truth." Your materials are definitely unique and can appeal to the short attention span of today's teens. Trying to get them to read a book like *Darwin's Black Box* is like pulling teeth. I know from experience that kids will read your books. Both my boys have read your book from cover to cover.

Thanks again,

- Randy Yach

Dear "Friends that Awaken Us",

Thank you so much for the books you have written. I am 91 years old but still healthy (and no cavities yet!) As long as the Lord gives me life, I want to help my church stand strong on the Bible - the WHOLE BIBLE!

My pastor husband and I were missionaries in Bolivia and Ecuador, and after his death I went to Hungary under Campus Crusade. Now I'm in an assisted care home and trying to make my life count for the Lord. I'll be sharing your book with others.

With love and blessings,

- Elizabeth R. Rice

78

Chapter 4

"If I profess every portion of the truth except that little point which the devil and the world are at that moment attacking, I am not professing Christ. Where the battle rages, there the loyalty of the soldier is proved. To be steady on all the battlefield besides, is mere flight and disgrace if he flinches at the point of attack."

- Martin Luther

The primary objective of these individual **Search for the Truth** articles is to present the evidence for creation in an interesting, appealing, and an easy to read format. This book has the same goal. These articles are meant to be widely distributed and I have given away hundreds of copies over the years. Furthermore, readers of this book are encouraged to copy any part without compensation to the author in order to share the information with others. It would be appreciated, though, if you would E-mail or write to **Search for the Truth Ministries** to let us know how you are putting the articles to use. Our E-mail is truth@searchforthetruth.net and the address is 3275 Monroe Rd., Midland, MI 48642. In order to be most effective, each article is written on one specific subject so it does not require the reading of other articles in a given topic area. They are written in a variety of styles by several authors also to avoid becoming a sterile presentation of facts. In addition, all of the articles contain an illustration, cartoon, or quote in order to attract the attention of the reader and pull them into the body of the text. The CD at the back of the book contains both the text and the illustrations from all of the articles in this book, along with a audio lecture on why this issue is so important. Also a 15 minute radio talk is included on some of the latest scientific research findings which support Biblical reality.

The first time that these articles ran in public newspapers, it generated more than 60 letters to the editor. In the process, I was also insulted, lied about, and accused of undermining the Constitution of the United States -- all because I was presenting the evidence for creation in a public newspaper and recommending that students be allowed to view all of the evidence concerning their origin. There can be no doubt that this is a critcal battle front for our culture; if for no other reason than because creation is opposed venomously.

Should you decide to make this book or these articles available to others, be prepared for a spiritual battle. It was a spiritual revelation rather than an intellectual argument that first convinced me of the truth of creation. Putting this material to use will only have a lasting impact if it is accompanied by prayer. Before starting the first time, I sought the encouragement and approval of my pastor and close friends. After explaining what I hoped to accomplish with the series, I asked for help proof reading the articles, ongoing prayer support, and help paying for the column space. The response was overwhelming. There were many people praying for each article and $3000 was raised to pay for the cost of publishing the series over a six month period. Many of these articles have since been updated and were seen in the Granville Booster, a free countywide newspaper with a distribution of 20,000.

In addition to the letters to the editor, over 100 people wrote during the first year asking for copies of the articles. They also enclosed encouraging comments on how the series had helped their faith. I recieved feedback from college students, pastors, and people from all walks of life thanking me for putting this information in a weekly column. Before this first outreach ended, articles on creation had been sent to Christians on five continents; I had been invited to talk to two different college classes; and I had the opportunity to debate one of the country's top defenders of evolution on a live public radio broadcast. It is truly amazing what the Lord can do with a willing believer who steps out in faith and obedience. In many ways, the original outreach via public newspapers is still continuing because it led to other outreaches, books, and hundreds of speaking opportunities. Further to all this, the truth is continuing to spread in ways I could never have anticipated or imagined.

Time, Computers, and Eternity

By Bruce Malone

One of the most startling discoveries of the twentieth century was Einstein's theory of relativity, which shows that time, space, and matter are all interrelated. For instance, it has been demonstrated that time does not move at the same speed everywhere, but varies with the mass, acceleration, and gravity in its immediate vicinity. Modern physics has also shown that without mass, there is no time. In other words that which is without weight is eternal.

One of the technological marvels of our modern age is the computer. Computers can store enormous amounts of information, perform calculations at incredible speeds, and operate complex video games. But what is a computer? If we tore it apart and examined every physical component in minute detail, we would learn nothing about how the programs work or their origin. This is because the real value of a computer is not the hardware. The real value of a computer is in the software. The hardware is just the means by which a computer communicates what it is programmed to do.

So what is this mysterious thing we call *"software"*? It can be transferred from machine to machine. It can be transmitted by electromagnetic waves through phone lines or across the universe. It can be loaded into another machine which would then operate in the same way as the original. The entire software from a computer can be loaded onto memory cards and the weight of the card will not change. Software is

weightless, and therefore, eternal. As long as it is *"remembered,"* it can never disappear. In essence, it is a creation from the mind of a creator.

"The guy at the door wants to know if we've all been saved...?"

Now let's combine these two observations from computers and relativity to derive some practical implications. Some day, each of us will die. These biological machines that we call our bodies will return to dust, as it is dust from which we are composed. But what about the programming? What about the soul and mind which inhabit this hardware, we call our bodies? Since our souls, our minds, and our thoughts are without weight, they are eternal and will last forever. This is who we really are. Our bodies are just the "hardware." Furthermore, just as the software from an old 300 MHz computer can be moved into a machine which operates 10 times faster, the Bible states that we will some day be given far superior bodies. Given what we know about information and software, this concept is not all that strange.

One of the greatest practical scientists of the last century, George Washington Carver said it best, *"I*

have found nature to be a conserver. Nothing is wasted or permanently lost in nature. Things change their form, but they do not cease to exist. After I leave this world I do not believe I am through. God would be a bigger fool than even a man if he did not conserve what seems to be the most important thing he has yet done in the universe."[1]

Long before we understood anything about relativity or computers, the Bible stated that we would live forever and be given new bodies. Given the discoveries of modern physics, this is quite reasonable, but there is a catch. We don't deserve to live forever in the presence of a perfect and Holy Creator because we are rebellious and sinful creatures. Anyone looking at the mess that humans have made of this world has to admit this. The One who created us would not be righteous; if He allowed sin to go unpunished. Furthermore, it is an insult to God to believe that our puny attempts to be "good" can pay the price required for **our** shortcomings. Fortunately, there is a solution to this dilemma.

You might want to take some of your limited time, while you are still inhabiting this very fragile piece of hardware that we call bodies, to check the solution for how God can be totally merciful and totally just. The Bible, from cover to cover, is about that solution. He's called Jesus.

1. George Washington Carver. 1928, Tuskegee Institute. Ethel Edwards, ***Carver on Tuskegee***, pp. 157 - 160.

Can Time Plus Chance Create Life?

By Bruce Malone

Have you ever wondered why a car doesn't get shinier and more trouble free with each passing year? As obvious as the answer seems, it took scientists centuries to formally define the cause as the action of the second law of thermodynamics. It is why houses, machinery, and even our bodies wear out, run down, and fall apart. Stated in simple terms, the second law of thermodynamics means that everything eventually breaks! If no maintenance is done, things become dirty and disorganized and are eventually reduced to dust. Every person, every machine, every reaction, and every molecule is subject to this law of nature.

Try the following experiment to see this law in action. Find a detailed picture of an animal (such as a frog) and make a photocopy of it. Now take the copy and use it to make another copy. Continue this process while observing the change with each copy. This Second Law predicts that something will get lost with each copy. It would violate this law of science for the process to produce a picture of greater clarity, new features, or be slowly transformed into another creature of more ordered complexity. By the thousandth "generation", not only will nothing new have developed, but the picture will have degenerated to the point that the frog will be hard to recognize as a frog. We observe similar degeneration (loss of information) occurring as biological life makes copies of itself. This loss of information (degeneration) never results in creatures with completely new features.

For something to increase in complexity, there must be an ordering mechanism already in

The odds of life forming by chance are like believing that "a tornado sweeping through a junkyard might assemble a Boeing 747 from the materials therein."[1]

Used by permission of Master Books

place. For instance, a seed becoming a full grown tree can be considered an example of increasing complexity. However, the seed starts with the necessary characteristics (or inherent information) to make this transformation. This example does not begin to explain how the seed developed. Without an ordering mechanism, energy destroys order not unlike a tornado's sweeping through an airplane factory -- there would be abundant available energy and the tornado could be even carrying sufficient raw materials. Why is the end result not a fully operational airplanes? It takes intelligent design and controlled energy to create ordered complexity.

Let's return our focus to the supposed evolutionary origin of life. What is the ordering mechanism that caused chemicals to come together to form the first complex living cell? Natural selection and mutations are of no effect before life exists. Even with living organisms, neither natural selection nor mutations provide a plausible ordering or energy conversion mechanism. Furthermore, how can the mechanisms of evolution explain the increasing complexity which supposedly happened in the biological world. Mutations are random mistakes (causing increasing disorder) and natural selection can only select that which is advantageous within an organism. The entire concept of macro-evolution is based on tenacious faith because no evolutionary mechanism can adequately explain the increase in complexity which happened as the universe and life formed. The 'big bang' model of cosmic origins can only be true, if some yet to be defined ordering mechanism is found (*other than God...of course*). How much more intellectually honest it is to accept intelligent design as the guiding force which created both our complex universe and all of life.

As you search for the truth, consider which explanation of life's origin is most logical. Is it evolution, which starts with basic assumptions that eliminates the consideration of outside intelligence? Or is it creation, which acknowledges the possibility of supernatural intelligence and provides the ordering and energy conversion mechanism required?

1. Sir Fred Hoyle, "Hoyle on Evolution", *Nature*, 11/81, p. 105.

Physics Show Six Day Creation Possible

By Bruce Malone

Exodus 20:11 makes one of the most unbelievable statements of the Bible: *"In six days the Lord made heaven and earth, the sea and all that is in them, and rested the seventh day."* It is hard to imagine a clearer statement defining how long God took to create the entire universe. However, this simple statement has presented a seemingly impossible dilemma for Christians. On the one hand, modern cosmology teaches that the universe has taken billions of years to form. On the other hand, **if** this clear and straightforward statement of the Bible cannot be trusted to mean what it says; how can we know that any statement of the Bible can be trusted to mean what it says?

This was the dilemma that Dr. Russell Humphreys (recently retired physicist from Sandia National Laboratory) set out to solve as he studied what the Bible had to say about the formation of our universe. Most people have been taught that the universe is the result of a gigantic explosion called the "Big Bang". During this explosive expansion, all of the matter of the universe supposedly expanded outward from a tiny pinpoint. All modern cosmological models start with the assumption that the universe has neither a center nor an edge. When these assumptions are plugged into Einstein's general theory of relativity, the result is an expanding universe which is billions of years old at every location.

Rather than start with these arbitrary assumptions (a universe having no center and no edge), Dr. Humphreys decided to take the most apparent meaning of the Biblical text

> **"How ironic that the most ridiculed Biblical account (about a recent, literal, six day creation of the universe) is exactly the story which Albert Einstein's work has shown to be entirely possible."**

and see what model of the universe developed. He reasoned that, if the Bible was inspired by God, as it claims to be, it should not have to be twisted to be understood. It should have the same straight forward meaning for a "man on the street", a brilliant physicist, or a theologian.

The Bible clearly indicates three things about God's formation of the universe: first, the earth is the center of God's attention in the universe; By implication, the earth may also be located near the center -- perhaps so man can see the glory of God's creation in every direction. Second, the universe (both matter and space itself) has been "stretched out"[1]. Third, the universe has a boundary, and therefore it must have a center. If these three assumptions are plugged into the currently accepted formulas of physics, and the mathematical crank is turned; we find that we live in a universe in which clocks tick at different rates depending on your location.

Furthermore, this *"time dilation"* effect would have been magnified tremendously as the universe originally expanded. There would have been a point at which time was moving very rapidly at the outer areas and essentially stopped near the center. In other words, only days were passing near the center, while billions of years were passing in the heavens. This is the inevitable conclusion based on our current knowledge of physics and starting with Biblical assumptions instead of arbitrary ones.

Albert Einstein rejected the idea that the Bible could be literally true. He wrote that, *"Through the reading of popular scientific books, I soon reached the conviction that many of the stories in the Bible could not be true."*[2] How ironic that the most ridiculed Biblical text (the account of the recent, literal, six day creation of the universe) is exactly the account which Albert Einstein's work showed to be entirely possible. A comprehensive explanation of Dr. Humphreys work, can be found in his popular book, ***Starlight and Time***.[3]

1. Job 9:8, Psalm 104:2, Isaiah 40:22, Jeremiah 10:12, Zechariah 12:1, 2 Sam. 22:10, Psalm 144:5, Ezekiel 1:22, Isaiah 48:13, Job 26:7, Isaiah 42:5, Isaiah 51:13, Job 37:18, Isaiah 44:24, Jer. 51:15, Psalm 18:9, Isaiah 45:12.
2. Joseph Schwartz, ***Einstein for Beginners***, Pantheon Books, New York, p.31.
3. Russell Humphreys, ***Starlight and Time***, Master Books, 1994.

The Odds are on God's Side

By Bruce Malone

Statistics is science. This is why Las Vegas is filled with multi-billion dollar casinos. Casino owners know the statistical odds are in their favor; even if they occasionally lose, in the long run they will make enormous amounts of money. So what are the odds that our current universe could have formed via random chance processes? In actuality the statistical odds of this are totally, impossibly, essentially infinitely, negligible.

Our universe is "fine tuned" to make life possible. There are over 25 precisely tuned scientific constants, which if changed, even the slightest amount would make life impossible anywhere in the universe. For instance, there are four known forces which hold the entire universe in place. If gravity (which draws any two objects together) is given a relative strength of 1, the **weak** nuclear force which holds neutrons from flying apart is 10,000,000,000,000,000,000,000,000,000,000 times stronger! Electromagnetism is 1000 times stronger than this "weak" nuclear force, and the strong nuclear force (which keeps positively charged protons in close proximity on a nucleus) is 100 times stronger than electromagnetic forces. If ANY of these forces were varied even slightly; every atom in the universe would either fly apart or fail to allow the existence of most elements. Where did this fine tuning come from?

There are dozens of factors that determine if any planet could be habitable for life: the size and type of the nearest star, distance from the star, position within the galaxy, presence of water, presence and characteristics of any moons, rotational rate, size of the planet, magnetic field of the planet, presence of the right concentration of O_2, etc. By attaching a reasonable probability to each required condition and to each of the required characteristics, a conclusion can be drawn that less than 1 in 10^{69} (1 with 69 zero's after it) potential planets in the entire universe could harbor life. This is a number trillions times trillions greater than all of the stars in the entire universe.

If you combine this infinitesimally small probability, with all of the known constants that "just happen" to have exactly the value they need to sustain life; you will find that the odds of this happening is 10,000,000,000[123]. This is a line of zeros reaching beyond the edge of our 15 billion light year universe and it represents a number far beyond the total number of subatomic particles in the entire universe. Thus the probability of our universe happening by random natural processes is so far beyond plausibility as to be the closest definition to an impossibility as could exist.[1]

The entire universe gives the distinct appearance of having been designed to allow for life on earth. Furthermore, although we can describe the strength of the forces which hold the universe together and observe the incredible number and variety of stars within our universe: we really do not have any idea what these forces are, nor do we know how EVEN ONE of the hundred billion stars in a hundred billion galaxies could have ever formed by any natural process.

All this by Random Chance?

How do believers in cosmic evolution respond to this obvious evidence for a creator? Since their *prime directive* (see pp.14) is to explain everything without a designer, no matter how strong the evidence for that Designer, they are incapable of seeing the evidence. The most common response is that the design of the universe is only an "appearance of a design", but is not really a design. The irony of this intellectual blindness is no more apparent than in the writings of one of the most brilliant theoretical astrophysicists of our time.

Stephen Hawkings, in his book, *Brief History of Time*, claimed that the big-bang theory is *"in agreement with all the observational evidence that we have today."* Yet a few sentences later, he admits that *"the origin of both stars and galaxies is yet to be explained."* Without stars and galaxies, there is no universe. So how does the big bang theory explain all observational evidence?[2]

If you want to gamble on your eternal destiny put your bets on the God of the Bible, not the fruitless speculations of modern scientists who start with an assumption that God did not design the universe.

1. Charles White, ***God by the Numbers***, *Christianity Today*, 3/06, Vol.50:3, p.44
2. Alex Williams & John Hartnett, ***Dismantling the Big Bang***, Master Books, 2005, p. 59

An Alternative to the Big Bang

By Bruce Malone

It has been demonstrated both mathematically and experimentally that time is not a constant, but is dependent on the gravitational pull at the location where time is being measured. This concept was first proposed by Albert Einstein and is called gravitational time dilation.

Numerous experiments seem to indicate that this strange concept is true. For instance, time moves five microseconds per year slower at the Royal Greenwich Observatory (which is located at sea level) than it does at the National Bureau of Standards in Boulder, Colorado (which is 1 mile above sea level). Atomic clocks flown around the world in different directions seem to vary by the amount predicted by Einstein's equations. The direct result of this gravitational time dilation is that seemingly strange things happen to time near areas of space known as black holes.

A black hole is an area where matter is so concentrated that its gravity prevents even light from escaping. Indirect observations seem to indicate that many areas of our universe do indeed contain black holes. Black holes are so dense that they actually "bend" the fabric of space. In addition, time moves exceedingly slowly at the boundary of the black hole. Thus, if you could move from the center of a black hole outward, while

observing what was happening far away, it would appear that clocks and all natural processes were proceeding in a rapid fast-forward

All the Matter in the Universe Rapidly Expanding Outward

motion. Although one has never been observed, Einstein's equations also allow the existence of "white holes". Instead of collapsing inward, matter (and space itself) would expand outward from a "white hole". When matter inside the white hole moves past the boundary, the boundary begins to shrink inward. Eventually, the radius shrinks to zero and the white hole disappears, leaving behind all of the matter which it originally contained. However, the first material out would have aged millions or billions of years while the last material out may only have aged a matter of days.

Dr. Russell Humphreys[1,2] has proposed that this expansion of a "white hole" rather than the standard "big bang" theory is the method God used to create the universe we live in. Three effects should be apparent, if this is how

our universe formed. First, the expansion of space would have left a very uniform background radiation throughout the universe.

Second, as space itself expanded, the light coming from stars (which formed as the matter moved out of the white hole) would be shifted toward the red end of the spectrum. Third, if the earth was close to the center of our universe, it would have been one of the last things to have emerged from the white hole. Billions of years would have elapsed for distant stars giving plenty of time for light from those stars to have reached the earth. These three observations are exactly what we find as we observe our universe.

From the moment that all of the matter of the universe was created (day one of creation), until the earth emerged from near the center of the white hole (at which point stars would have appeared), it is quite mathematically feasible that only four 24-hour-days had passed on earth. Although this theory is quite controversial (and rejected out of hand by those who are committed to evolutionary development theories), this type of work demonstrates that there is not necessarily a contradiction between a six day creation and modern science.

1. Russell Humphreys, ***Starlight and Time***, Master Books, 1994.
2. Alex Williams & John Hartnett, ***Dismantling the Big Bang***, Master Books, 2005.

Wrong Assumptions Yield Wrong Answers

By Bruce Malone

It is hard to open a newspaper, book, or magazine without finding some implication to the earth being billions of years old. Given the overwhelming barrage of these statements, it is understandable why so many people have trouble considering the possibility that the earth might be only thousands of years old. Yet there is actually an overwhelming amount of data that indicates that the earth is indeed much younger than the billions of years needed for evolutionary theories.

Despite what people have been led to believe, there are no dating methods which give an absolute date for the formation of the earth. All dating methods are based on non-provable assumptions about some event in the distant past. Furthermore, there is a strong bias to reject any dating method which does not allow enough time for evolution to have happened. To understand the validity of any date, the reader must gain an understanding of how all dating methods work. The following illustration should help:

Suppose you were up at 6:00 a.m. and happened to see a friend who lives in a nearby town. You observe that he is walking along at 2 miles an hour and you know that he lives 16 miles away. You can easily use the formula at the top of the illustration to calculate that your friend left home 8 hours earlier.

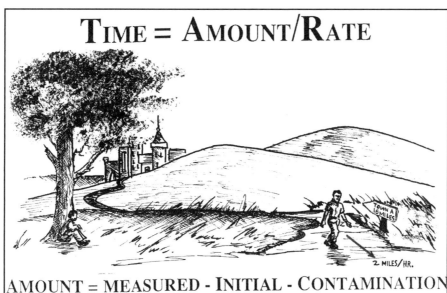

TIME = AMOUNT/RATE

2 MILES/HR.

TOWN A 16 MILES

AMOUNT = MEASURED - INITIAL - CONTAMINATION
RATE = AVERAGE RATE OVER THE WHOLE TIME

Used by permission of Russ Bradshaw

You have just performed a dating method of how long your friend has been on the road. However, something doesn't make sense. Why would your friend be up all night walking? Although you used the correct formula, your assumptions may not have been correct. Perhaps your friend stayed with someone in town and woke up minutes before for a morning stroll. In this case, you have used the 'WRONG INITIAL AMOUNT' in your calculation. Perhaps he took a shortcut which cut 12 miles off his walk. In this case there was 'CONTAMINATION' of the total amount. Perhaps since you last saw your friend, he has taken up marathon running and averaged 8 miles an hour (only having slowed down just before you saw him). In this case, you have used the wrong 'AVERAGE RATE'. The point is, wrong assumptions lead to wrong answers.

In all dating methods, the initial amount is an assumption, the estimate of contamination is an assumption, and the overall rate is an assumption. The only things which can be known for sure are the present amount and the present rate.

Unless you estimate the initial amount correctly, the average rate correctly, and the amount of contamination correctly, your answer will be wrong. Furthermore, depending on your assumptions, it could be very, very wrong.

There are actually very few dating methods which seem to indicate that the earth is extremely old. On the other hand, nine out of ten dating methods indicate that the earth is quite young. If the earth is relatively young; then evolution is obviously a myth and creation becomes the only logical alternative. Could this be the primary reason that only those methods which seem to indicate the earth's very old age are shown to students?

Science Indicates the Earth is Young

By Bruce Malone

Rivers are carrying salt into the world's oceans at a known rate, yet the sodium (salt) level in the oceans is far below saturation. Oceanographers have determined that, at most, 27% of this sodium flowing into the ocean, manages to get out of the ocean each year. Therefore, every year the concentration of salt should be a featureless smear instead of a distinct spiral. For 50 years. this problem has been known, but no plausible explanation has been found.[4] The best current explanation for how stars could have formed involves "density waves" from supernovas. Yet, how could there have been supernovas limit of the age of the earth is approximately 6000 years because this is when historical records began. All other methods are based on unprovable assumptions. The graph below shows the maximum age from a few of the hundreds of possible ways to date the earth or various geological features. Notice

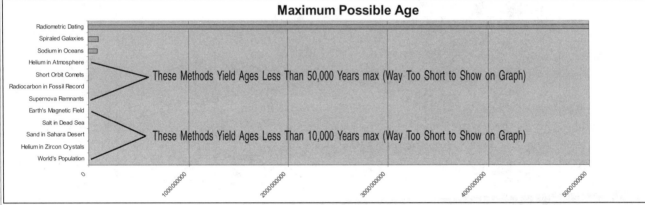

Maximum Possible Age

These Methods Yield Ages Less Than 50,000 Years max (Way Too Short to Show on Graph)

These Methods Yield Ages Less Than 10,000 Years max (Way Too Short to Show on Graph)

(Categories listed: Radiometric Dating, Spiraled Galaxies, Sodium in Oceans, Helium in Atmosphere, Short Orbit Comets, Radiocarbon in Fossil Record, Supernova Remnants, Earth's Magnetic Field, Salt in Dead Sea, Sand in Sahara Desert, Helium in Zircon Crystals, World's Population)

in the oceans increases slightly. All of the salt in the world's oceans can be accounted for in just 1/50 the time assumed available by evolution[1].

Helium is being released into our atmosphere by radioactive decay at a known rate, yet all of the helium in the atmosphere can be accounted for in 1/2500 of the time assumed by evolution. This dating method accounts for all of the helium escaping into space and assumes no starting helium.[2]

Measurements indicate that the total energy of the earth's magnetic field has decreased by a factor of 2.7 in the last 1000 years. This sets an upper limit to the age of the earth's magnetic field at 10,000 years. Were the earth older than this, the magnetic field would be impossibly strong.[3]

The inner stars of galaxies rotate faster than the outer stars. If spiral galaxies were more than a few hundred million years old, they to create the stars when there weren't any stars to begin with?

These young age indicators are not based on just one technique, but cover a wide range of scientific disciplines. They are just a few of the hundreds of dating methods, which give a wide variety of possible ages. The vast majority of methods yield dates far too short for evolution to have taken place. This leaves those scientists who are intent on maintaining extreme ages for the earth in the unenviable position of trying to explain away the majority of the data while basing their position on the minority of the data.

No dating method provides an absolute date for the age of the earth. With each method, the lower limit can be zero (for instance, salt could have started out at current levels in the ocean, air may have started containing current levels of helium, etc.), but each sets an maximum possible limit. The lower that many of methods give an age which agree with the Bible (less than 10,000 years) whereas the evolution assumption that radiometric methods give the correct age of the earth (5 billion years) is completely out of touch with all other methods. Problems with radiometric dating are discussed on pages 87, 91, 94.

1. Austin, S.A., Humphreys, R.D., *"The Sea's missing Salt: A Dilemma for Evolutionists"*, **Proceedings of the Second International Conference on Creationism**, Vol II, 1991.
2. Vardiman, L., **The Age of the Earth's Atmosphere: a study of the helium flux**, ICR (1990).
3. Humphreys, R.D., *"Physical mechanism for reversals of the earth's magnetic field during the flood"*, **Proceedings of the Second International Conference on Creationism**, Vol. II, 1991.
4. Scheffler, H., Elsasser, H., **Physics of the Galaxy and Interstellar Matter**, Springer-Verlag Berlin p. 352-353, 401-413, 1987.

Accelerated Radiometric Decay

By Bruce Malone

Radioactive elements decay like a set of racked billiard balls struck by the cue ball. The decaying element fragments into pieces, among which are *alpha particles.* These are pieces of the nucleus of an atom which consists of two protons and two neutrons. These particles rapidly grab two electrons to become a very stable helium molecule. Since the original location of the radioactive elements is often within cooled rock layers (such as granite) the helium which forms from this radioactive decay is also trapped inside these rock layers. Many of these granite layers are assumed to have been formed billions of years ago so the radioactive decay would have happened shortly after the formation and cooling of the granite. Thus, if the rock layers are millions of years old, any helium found within these rock layers would have had to have been trapped for millions of years.

The reason why helium balloons float is because helium is an energetic molecule which is lighter than air due to the low density (weight) of the gas. Helium balloons do not float indefinitely because the helium molecule is so small that it slips right through the wall of the balloon and escapes to an area where the concentration of helium is lower. This is why helium filled latex balloons sink within hours and even aluminum coated mylar balloons stop floating within weeks. Helium is such a small energetic molecule that it can escape at a measurable rate through solid stainless steel (i.e. it

has a high permeation rate). This allows helium to be routinely used to measure the leakage rate through other materials. If you found a

> **The radioactive decay which created the helium in the rock layers of the earth had to have happened within the last 6000 years... not over billions of years.**

helium balloon floating on the ceiling of an ancient Egyptian tomb; you would know that someone had recently been in that room. If your guide told you that no one else had been inside the tomb in the last 4000 years, you would know that they were either ignorant or lying. This brings us back to the helium found in granite across our planet.

The amount of radiometric decay that has happened within any granite containing zircon crystal can be calculated by measuring the amount of original uranium-238 and the final amount of stable lead-206 within a given crystal. The decay sequence from uranium to lead actually creates eight helium molecules which are then trapped within the zircon crystal. What has not been measured until recently is the rate at which the resulting helium diffuses out of the zircon crystals.

In 1974, a project by Los Alamos National Laboratories collected core samples of granite drilled down 2.6 miles into the earth's crust at Fenton Hill, New Mexico. The permeation rate of helium through this granite was then measured at an internationally renowned laboratory. Samples of these rocks were obtained at a wide variety of depths, corresponding to different

temperatures, and the permeation rate vs. temperature equation was developed. By dividing the amount of helium left in the rock with the measured permeation rate of helium through the zircon crystals, it is possible to measure how long ago the radioactive decay happened. This is the same concept as measuring the age of a helium balloon by knowing the amount of helium left in it and dividing by the rate at which the helium left the balloon. The result was the astounding discovery that the radiometric decay which created the helium within these zircon crystals had to have happened within the last 6000 +/-2000 years. There is no known mechanism which could have allowed the helium to remain within these rocks for a longer period of time. However, conventional dating techniques place these rocks at over a billion years old. This is incredibly strong evidence for both the recent creation of the rock layers of our planet and the accelerated nuclear decay which must have happened either at the time of creation (when the heavens were being "stretched out") or possibly during the year of the worldwide flood.[1]

This evidence for our recent creation is no different than finding a helium balloon still floating in a tomb. It is unmistakable proof that the balloon had to have been filled recently. In a similar way the granite (foundational) layers of our planet had to have also been created quite recently.

1. DeYoung, Don, ***Thousands...not Billions***, Master Books, 2005.

More Young Earth Indicators

By Bruce Malone

Evolutionists assume that man dropped out of the trees 1 to 5 million years ago and became fully human about 100,000 years ago. Archeological records show that civilizations appeared around 5000 years ago. It has been said that the ability to raise food (farming) drove the advancement of modern civilization. In other words, by evolutionary reasoning, it took mankind 95,000 years (after becoming fully human) to figure out that food could be produced by dropping a seed into the ground. Even many animals and insects seem to know this.

It has been estimated by evolutionary anthropologists that the earth could have easily supported 10 million hunter/gatherer type humans[1]. To maintain an average of 10 million people, spread over the entire planet, with an average life span of 25 years, for the last 100,000 years...would mean that **40 billion people** lived and died. Archeological evidence clearly shows that these "stone age" people buried their dead. Forty billion graves should be rather easy to find. Yet only a few thousand exist. The obvious implication is that people have been around far less than 100,000 years.

Another indication of both a young earth and a confirmation of the worldwide flood is the scarcity of meteors in sedimentary rock layers. If most of the rock layers were laid down rapidly during the one year period of a worldwide flood; you would not expect to find many meteorites buried in only one year. However, if the sediment was laid down over billions of years, there should be billions buried within this sediment. Meteorites have a distinct composition which is easy to identify. The fact that we find so few is confirmation of the rapid accumulation of Earth's sedimentary layers.

Used by permission of AIG

God declared that creation was "very good" at the end of the sixth day of creation. Evolution requires that mankind is the result of billions of years of death and survival of the fittest. Both cannot be true.

Suppose you walked into an empty room and found a smoking cigar. You **could** assume that the cigar was very old and that it had only recently burst into flames, but the more logical conclusion would be that someone had recently lit it. The universe is full of similar "smoking cigars":

- All planetary rings still exhibit intricacies which **should have** long ago disappeared.
- All known comets burn up their material with each pass around the sun and **should have** a maximum life expectancy of 100,000 years.[2]
- The outer planets in our solar system **should have** long ago cooled off.

Scientists working from the preconception that the universe is 10 - 20 billion years old have suggested controversial and complicated possibilities as to how these types of transient phenomena could still exist. However, their explanations are based on faith, not science. The simpler explanation is that these "smoking cigars" are still smoking because they are young.

What about dating methods which seem to indicate that things are very old? As seen in the first article on dating methods, assumptions are everything. Carbon-14 dating, for instance, assumes that there never was a worldwide flood. This is the main method cited as proof for the existence of mankind tens of thousands of years before the Bible states that we were created. A recent worldwide catastrophe would have caused an enormous change in the total amount of carbon in earth's biosphere. This shift in the total amount of carbon in the biosphere completely invalidates one of the starting assumptions of the carbon-14 dating method (a known carbon-14 to carbon-12 ratio throughout the measurement period). This is why the method results in erroneously old dates for organisms alive shortly after this flood. Similar faulty assumptions exist for all old age dating methods.

The vast majority of methods indicate a young earth. Why would God use billions of years of death and dead ends before making mankind and then deceive us by telling us that he created us recently (Genesis chapter 5)?

1. E.S. Deevy, *"The Human Population"*, **Scientific America,** (9/60) 194-204.
2. William Stillman, *"The Lifetime and Renewal of Comets"*, **Proceedings of 2rd International Conference on Creation,** 1990.

Only a Personal Test Matters

By Bruce Malone

In another universe and another time, lived a civilization of two-dimensional people, which we will call the "Flats." For them, two dimensions (a flat plane) was reality and they could not conceive of beings which inhabited more than these two-dimensions. One day, a three-dimensional being visited the universe of the Flats. Since they were two-dimensional, they could only see, touch, and feel the two-dimensional outline of the creature as it passed through their plane of existence. Even more mysterious was that this outline would disappear from their plane of reality without a trace... only to reappear in another location. This happened each time the three-dimensional creature stepped in and out of their two-dimensional plane. Some of the Flats proposed that there existed a reality which was outside their known science. Therefore, it was deemed supernatural. They proposed that this universe was inhabited by creatures possessing more than just two-dimensions. They also reasoned that an entity possessing one more dimension could move in and out of a universe which possessed one less dimension. Although this explanation of the mystery explained the observations, it was rejected because it could not be scientifically tested. It relied upon *the supernatural.*[1]

It is impossible to observe what happens at the point of singularity inside an area known as a *black*

Used by permission of Len Boro

hole. A black hole is an area in space where it is believed that matter is so concentrated that the gravitational pull prevents even electromagnetic waves, such as light, from escaping. When any particle approaches a black hole, it disappears at what is known as the "event horizon." Anything that comes closer than the event horizon is sucked into the black hole and cannot escape. At the center of the black hole is a point of singularity where (supposedly) matter accelerates to the speed of light, time stops, and mass becomes infinite. This is an area in our own universe about which we can only speculate. Experimentation is absolutely impossible. Yet scientists accept its existence.

These illustrations show that just because you cannot see, touch, feel or falsify the existence of something; does not mean that it is not *scientific.* The miracles of the Bible demonstrate that the One who created the known universe has control over time and creation. The accounts of Jesus walking on water, appearing in locked rooms, healing the sick, changing water into wine, bringing food into existence from

nothing, coming back from death, and ascending into heaven are easily explained by the acknowledgement that He was this Creator. Therefore, He had the ability to take on extra "dimensions" in time and space. Thus, just as in the first illustration the three-dimensional entity could step in and out of two-dimensional space, Jesus has the ability to step in and out of four dimensional time/space and at present abides outside of time as we know it. (See pp. 131.) The Bible is not unscientific because it cannot be tested in a laboratory anymore than a black hole is unscientific because we cannot go inside one.

Christianity is based upon personally accepting the death and sacrifice of Jesus Christ as payment for our own wrongdoing. This payment is only necessary because of the literal rebellion of the first man against His Creator. The historical events described in the Bible *are* testable and verifiable by archeology, historical documentation, and scientific study. However, ultimately the only test of Christianity which matters is a personal one. Until you are willing to submit to His authority and accept His payment for your sin, you cannot know whether Christianity is true. Only by personally testing the promises of God can you know the Truth.

1. This illustration is used by Dr. A. E. Wilder-Smith in his book, *__A Scientific Alternative to Neo-Darwinian Evolution.__*

Why Radiocarbon Gives the Wrong Dates

By Bruce Malone

In order to understand why carbon-14 (^{14}C) dating gives erroneously ancient dates, we must understand how this dating method works and the assumptions used for interpreting the results.

When one of the sun's high energy particles hits a nitrogen nucleus, neutrons are released which react with ^{14}N to form ^{14}C. This ^{14}C atom rapidly reacts with oxygen to form a $^{14}CO_2$ molecule. Plants take in the $^{14}CO_2$, animals eat the plants, and a uniform dispersion of radioactive carbon throughout the biosphere (all living organisms) results. The current ratio of radioactive ^{14}C to normal ^{12}C is one atom of ^{14}C per trillion atoms of ^{12}C. As long as an organism is alive, it continues to take in both ^{14}C and ^{12}C in this ratio. However, after it dies the radioactive carbon begins to decay and the ratio of ^{14}C to ^{12}C decreases. It takes 5,730 years for 1/2 of the original ^{14}C to decay. Thus, if something has a ^{14}C to ^{12}C ratio of 1:2 trillion, instead of the current 1:1 trillion, it is assumed to be 5730 years old. A ratio of 1:4 trillion would be interpreted as 11,460 years old, 1:8 trillion would be 17,190 years old, etc. Highly sensitive accelerator mass spectrometer methods have improved the ability to measure the amount of ^{14}C so that 0.001% of modern amounts can be measured. If the ^{14}C generation level was always constant, this would correspond to an organism about 100,000 years old. The decay rate of ^{14}C is such that after 250,000 years, starting with modern concentrations, every molecule of ^{14}C should be gone. Astonishingly,

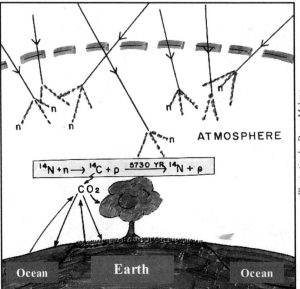

Illustration by Bruce Malone

over the last twenty years, samples from every carbon containing substance (supposed to be up to 300 million years old) has been shown to contain measurable levels of ^{14}C, averaging 0.3% modern of ^{14}C levels.[1] This is 300 times above the detection limit and has never been explained as contamination. The presence of this radiocarbon is strong evidence for a recent worldwide flood (see pp. 91).

The level of ^{14}C is significantly lower than expected for creatures alive 5000 years ago because of the much greater amount of vegetation alive on the planet before the worldwide flood (as attested by the massive worldwide coal fields). This resulted in much less ^{14}C in all organisms alive before and shortly after the flood than there is in modern organisms. During this global flood, enormous quantities of plants and animals were buried and massive amounts of carbon dioxide precipitated out of the oceans as calcium carbonate. The world rapidly readjusted after the flood,

but the total carbon in the biosphere and oceans would have been much greater before the flood - making the concentration of ^{14}C in all living things significantly less. The assumption that there has always been the same amount of vegetation on earth leads to the belief in a uniform ^{14}C to ^{12}C ratio throughout history. This is simply a wrong assumption that causes vastly overstated ages when dating those organisms which were alive before or immediately following the flood. You cannot accept both the reality of a worldwide flood and radiocarbon dates of great age. The flood would have caused an enormous shift in the ^{14}C level of all creatures. Many scientists believe this flood happened as recently as approximately 5000 years ago, making any organism dated older than this totally inaccurate. Such an artifact simply contains a lower concentration of ^{14}C, because at the time it was alive, the available ^{14}C was spread throughout more living organisms.

The real challenge to evolution believers is to explain why there is ANY radiocarbon left in coal, wood, gas, bones, and shells which are supposedly millions of years too old. Absolutely no ^{14}C should remain. Yet it does....

1. "Measurable Radiocarbon in Fossilized Organic Materials", Baumgardner, John, et. al, ***Proc. of the Inter. Conf. on Creationism***, 2003, p.127-142.

Scoffers and an Old Earth

By Bruce Malone

Almost 2000 years ago, an astounding statement was made, *"...scoffers will come in the last days, walking according to their own lusts, and saying, 'Where is the promise of His coming? For since the fathers fell asleep, all things have continued as they were from the beginning of creation.'* **(belief in uniformitarianism)** *For this they will willfully forget: that by the Word of God the heavens were of old, and the earth standing out of water* **(denial of creation)**...*and the world that then existed perished, being flooded by water* **(denial of a global flood)."** (2 Peter 3:3-6)

Hundreds of methods exist for dating the age of the earth, yet no dating method can absolutely prove the age of the earth. Scoffers intent on explaining everything without God, simply invent excuses to ignore the obvious. They will define science to exclude God, suppress the evidence for creation and the worldwide flood, and ignore the overwhelming majority of straightforward dating methods that indicate a young earth. What do evolution believers say about the many young earth indicators mentioned throughout this book?

1. Galaxies wind up too quickly - *They rely on some unknown mechanism to wind them up - i.e. faith that God's word is wrong. Shockwaves from exploding stars (where did they come from) somehow compress gas to form new stars.*

2. Short lived comets would not be around if the solar system were billions of years old - *The response is the belief in a unseen Oort cloud full of comets. Not mentioned is that this is based on faith, not observations, and it is statistically improbable at best.*

3. The amount of sediment in the oceans indicates that they are quite young -- *The response is an assumption of old age, an assumption that there was never a worldwide flood depositing sediment at rates greater than today, and an assumption that geological processes do things that we don't observe them doing today. Again faith in an old age is not based on data, but on a distrust in God's Word.*

4. Not enough salt in the sea -- *Scoffers totally ignore the scientific studies and papers that document the criteria for this conclusion. They simply ignore the mathematics and have faith that unmeasured natural processes can explain the relatively low salinity of the ocean.*

5. The rapid decay of the total strength of the earth's magnetic field - *An indication of how damaging this evidence is to old earth believers is their need to distort Dr. Humphreys work. He has conclusively shown that there really has been a systematic decrease over time and field reversals would make this problem even worse. Scoffers simply have faith this isn't true and have not even tried to rebut the mathematics.*

As one examines the objections to each of the straightforward young earth dating methods, it becomes apparent that the objections are based on faith rather than on good science. Yet, these same scoffers sound authoritative because their claims are repeated everywhere and few people take the time to check out the validity of their claims.

The Bible, read in the same straightforward way that any other book would be read, clearly indicates that the world and the universe were created quite recently -- in six literal days. Genesis is a narrative passage and is not intended to be poetic or figurative. Genesis chapter five lists a geneaology from Adam (the first man) to Abraham which spans about 2000 years. Abraham to the present day spans only another 4000 years. Then, in Exodus 20:11 God gives us the only one of the ten commandments with a justification, *"...For in six days the LORD made the heavens and the earth, the sea, and all that is in them, and rested on the seventh day..."* This statement makes absolutely no sense unless it means six literal days.

The reader really only has two choices when approaching the subject of the age of the earth:

A. Join the ranks of the scoffers, who, as predicted would deny a literal creation, literal worldwide flood, and by implication deny a young earth -- in the "last days".

B. Accept the vast majority of very straightforward dating methods that indicate this earth really is quite young so, therefore, God's Word can be trusted to mean what it says.

The strategy of Satan has really not changed in 6000 years of human history. Remember what Satan first said to Eve in the garden of Eden, *"Has God indeed said..."* He is asking each of us the same question today. What is your answer?

Where Have all the Remnants Gone?

By Bruce Malone

Stars are large spheres of highly compressed gas millions of times larger than the earth. Like everything else in our universe, they eventually wear out. At a certain point in the lifetime of a very massive star, it implodes upon itself releasing energy that exceeds the output from an entire galaxy. This of the universe near Earth's location.

Theoretical models suggest that the expanding debris from a supernova would go through several stages as the matter and energy dispersed. During the first few hundred years after a supernova, material is hurtled outward at supernova should occur within our Milky Way galaxy approximately every 25 years, if the remnants last an average of 55,000 years, there should be 55,000 years divided by 25 supernova/year = 2200 second stage supernova remnants detectable. Even if we can only detect 1/2 of those remnants, there

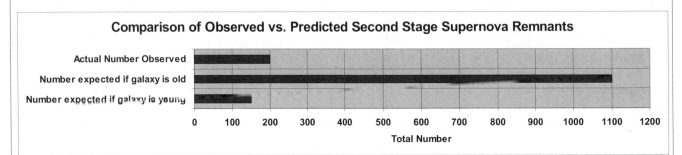

Comparison of Observed vs. Predicted Second Stage Supernova Remnants

is called a supernova and results in a center that is so dense that it cannot collapse further. The rest of the stellar debris spreads outwards.

These supernova remnants (the collapsed center and the spreading debris) should be detectable for millions of years after the initial implosion. Based on what we currently know about stars, scientists estimate that a galaxy the size of the Milky Way (our galaxy) should have one supernova approximately every 25 years. This estimation is based on historical observations over the last 2000 years. If our galaxy is 10 to 20 billion years old; millions of supernovas should have occurred since it first formed. Thus, the number of supernova remnants actually observed could indicate the age of our galaxy. However, if Dr. Humphreys is correct (that time has moved in fast forward for distant galaxies during the formation of the universe - pp. 82)[1], then only those remnants within our own galaxy are of significance in revealing the age

thousands of kilometers per second. Later a blast wave forms, emitting powerful radio waves for 10,000 to 100,000 years (an average expected detectability of 55,000 years). During the final stage, the material becomes so spread out that only heat energy is emitted.

Although opinions vary, scientists have estimated approximately how many supernovas should be visible from each stage of development[2]. Even if supernova remnants last for an average of only 55,000 years; we should be able to detect most of the ones which have exploded in our galaxy. First stage supernovas are hard to see because of the massive number of stars within our galaxy which blocks the view. However, second stage supernovas are more detectable because of the radio signals they emit. Statistical estimates indicate that we should be able to detect at least 50% of the second stage supernovas which have occurred in the last 55,000 years.

Using the estimate that one

should still be 1100 detectable remnants in our galaxy if that much time has passed. However, if our galaxy is only 10,000 years old, the number of second stage remnants would be (10,000/25) x 1/2 = 150. So the number of second stage supernova remnants actually detected reveals the actual age of our galaxy. **Only around 200 have been found.** The chart above graphically illustrates which theory best explains the observable data.

This is one more piece of evidence that indicates that the earth and the universe are far younger than commonly thought. Indeed, the vast majority of dating methods indicate a young earth.

1. Russell Humphreys, ***Starlight and Time***, Master Books, 1994.
2. This article is a condensed version of a technical paper given by Keith Davies, 'The Distribution of Supernova Remnants in the Galaxy', ***Proceedings of the Third International Conference on Creationism***, 1994, p.175-184.

The One and Only Ice Age

By Bruce Malone

On the morning of July 15, 1942, six brand new P-38 Lightnings and two B-17 Flying Fortresses took off from a secret airfield in Greenland, heading for bombing missions in Germany. The squadron became lost in a blizzard and ran out of fuel. The pilots were forced to land on a glacier. One made a crash landing and the other seven made perfect belly landings. The crewmen were rescued nine days later, but the planes were abandoned to the relentless snows and remained on the glacier for half a century.

In 1980, Richard Taylor and Patrick Epps, two Atlanta businessmen, decided to find the airplanes. Patrick Epps joked that *"All we'd have to do is shovel the snow off the wings, fill them with gas, crank them up, and fly them off into the sunset."* After twelve years of obsessive effort, extensive searching, back breaking labor, and millions of dollars spent; the persistent partners finally succeeded in locating and retrieving one of the eight airplanes. It was awhile before that P-38 was "flown into the sunset" because it had to be recovered from underneath 250 feet of solid ice and then dismantled piece-by-piece. The story of this discovery can be found in the December 1992 issue of Life Magazine, "The Lost Squadron".

This event calls into question the standard interpretation of ice cores that have been drilled in the ice at the polar caps. These cores supposedly show hundreds of thousands of years of accumulation and multiple ice ages on our planet. The fact that 250 feet of solid ice can accumulate in only 50 years clearly illustrates that hundreds of thousands of years are not required

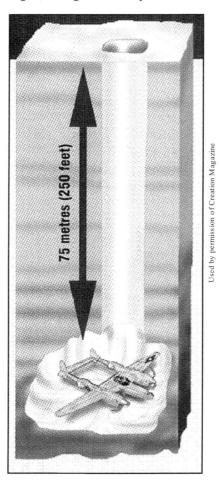

75 metres (250 feet)

Used by permission of Creation Magazine

for the formation of the polar ice caps. Instead of hundreds of thousands of years and multiple ice ages, a single catastrophic event that caused an incredible shift in climatic conditions, could explain the depth of ice at the polar caps.[1]

Both evolutionists and creationists alike recognize the ice age as the last major geologic event to have drastically affected our planet. Most evolutionists believe there have been dozens of ice ages, but this belief is based on secondary evidence, such as changes in the oxygen concentrations in ice cores, rather than direct evidence. Most creationists believe that the earth has experienced only one great ice age which lasted several centuries

before the ice receded to present levels. The evidence for this ice age, and for a dramatically different climate in the not so distant past, is undeniable. Furthermore, evidence is rapidly accumulating to indicate that there has been just one ice age.[2,3]

The creation model of history shows that the great ice age was an inevitable outcome of the worldwide flood. The massive land movements and volcanism which accompanied the flood would have left the oceans considerably warmer than they were before the flood or following the ice age. Solar radiation would have been reduced by volcanic ash high in the sky following the flood, resulting in colder terrestrial temperatures. The inevitable result of warmer oceans would be increased water evaporation. In combination with less solar radiation reaching the earth's surface, massive snow storms would be caused in the northern and southern latitudes. These snow storms would have continued for centuries until the oceans cooled off and the atmosphere cleared up. Thus, the great ice age is not only explained by the worldwide flood but would have been an unstoppable consequence of this flood.

1. Larry Vardiman, ***Ice Cores and the Age of the Earth,*** ICR, 1993.
2. Michael Oard, ***The Evidence for only One Ice Age***, *Proceedings of 2nd International Conf. on Creationism,* 1990.
3. *Michael Oard, **Submarine Mass Flow Deposition of Pre-Pleistocene Ice-age Deposits**, Proceedings of 3rd International Conference on Creationism,* 1994.

Will the Real Date Please Step Up

By Bruce Malone

The Institute for Creation Research recently concluded an eight year research project aimed at understanding variability in radiometric dating methods. Six Ph.D. experts from fields of geology, experimental physics, and geophysical modeling were chartered with understanding this type of dating on a fundamental level. As with any real scientific endeavor, the team did not know what the research results would reveal. They suspected, though, that many of the widely unreported problems with radiometric dating accuracy could be explained within the Biblical framework of a recent creation, followed by the curse and a global flood. One of the facets of this project was to compare several widely used radiometric dating techniques to determine how consistent different methods were when used to measure the age of the same rock sample.

Radiometric dating is based on the amount of decay of unstable isotopes of radioactive elements trapped in rocks as they form and cool. These elements fly apart over time leaving some of the original element in the rock while a portion is changed into a different element. It is similar to sand in the top of an hour glass. If you know the rate at which the sand is flowing into the bottom (turning into a different element) and the amount of sand in the top and bottom of the hour glass (the amount of the original and final elements); you can determine how much time has passed. Since the rate at which many radioactive elements decay is currently very slow, it would take millions of years (at today's decay rate) for any significant quantity of decay. If

large proportions of the final decay product is found in the rock; it is assumed that a huge amount of time has passed.

Since it cannot be known exactly how much of the original material was present, the analysis of several different minerals within a given rock sample increases the confidence that the correct starting amount can be found. This method, called an isochron, is believed to be extremely accurate; if it yields straight line results between the various ratios of mother and daughter elements in different minerals in the same rock sample. It is not uncommon to achieve a reported dating accuracy of +/- 1% using this widely accepted radiometric technique.

What has not been systematically studied is a comparison of completely different elemental dating methods on the same rock sample. If each specific radiometric dating method is so accurate (often stated as within +/- 1%); then using four completely different types of radiometric dating, on the same rock sample, should yield very similar ages. The RATE team chose four common dating techniques -- potassium-argon (K-Ar), lead-lead (Pb-Pb), rubidium-strontium (Rb-Sr), and samarium-neodymium (Sm-Nd). From 11 to 20 samples of each mineral from carefully documented rock samples were sent to world class radiometric dating laboratories for analysis of the mother and daughter elements. Isochron dating correlations were developed for each of the four different methods for the same rock sample. The results showed an astonishingly wide variation.

For instance, for the rock sample taken from the Bass Rapids Sill in the Grand Canyon the K-Ar date was 656 +/-15 million years. Rb-Sr yielded 1055 +/- 46 million years. Pb-Pb yielded 1250 +/- 130 million years. Sm-Nd yielded 1379 +/- 140 million years. This is a huge variation -- way outside the supposed accuracy of each individual method. So what is the real age of the rock? Believers in evolution will commonly use whichever method gives the date in agreement with the already established "geologic time table." Furthermore, all the methods ignore the reality that the radioactive decay rate has been faster in the past as proven by the presence of helium (a product of many radiometric decay processes) still trapped in rock crystals.[1]

One of the significant finds of the RATE project was that those elements which decay by alpha particle emission show statistically greater amounts of decay than those elements which decay by beta particle emission. This may be an important clue to exactly what happened to accelerate radiometric decay in the past.

These types of scientific research programs are, of course, being ignored by evolution believers who are blinded by their need to maintain a belief in huge time periods. Studying the universe from a creation perspective repeatedly yields discoveries not seen by those blinded by this evolutionary bias.

1. DeYoung, Donald, *Thousands...Not Billions*, Master Books, 2005.

How Prophecy Validates God's Word

By Bruce Malone

A very scientific method exists for confirming that the Bible is what it claims to be -- a document inspired by the Creator of the universe who is outside of time and space.[1] Only someone outside of time and space, who could, therefore, see the future in advance could inspire very specific predictions of future happenings to be documented. It is statistically possible to prove that the Bible is the inspired Word of this Creator by studying these predictions (prophecies). Over 300 predictions, of very specific events surrounding the birth, life, ministry, and death of Jesus are documented in the Old Testament. Copies of the Old Testament (the Jewish Torah) have been found which we know were written and sealed in containers over 300 years before the birth of Christ (The Dead Sea Scrolls).

Amazingly, these documents agree with modern versions of Hebrew Scriptures with a greater than 99% precision with differences only being minor spellings of names and some slight numerical deviations. This in itself is an astounding feat that testifies to God's ability to protect His inspired revelation to mankind. Within these documents are specific predictions of a coming Messiah who would save mankind from God's judgment of sin. Let's examine just eight of some 300 specific prophecies and place conservative probabilities that these predictions could be fulfilled by one specific person:

1. This Messiah would be born in Bethlehem (Micah 5:2). Perhaps 1:200,000 people born in the last 2000 years could fit this requirement.

2. This person would declare himself king while riding into a city on a donkey (Zechariah 9:9). Perhaps 1:100 kings throughout the last 3000 years have done this.

3. He would be betrayed in a house of God and the money would go to a potter (Zechariah 11:13). Perhaps this has happened to 1:100,000 people born.

4. The price of his betrayal would be exactly 30 pieces of silver (Zechariah 11:12). Pretty unlikely, but lets say it has happened in 1:1000 betrayals.

5. He would receive significant wounds on his arms (Zechariah 13:6). Maybe 1:100 received significant wounds on their hands, wrists, arms during their lifetime.

6. He would be an innocent man brought to trial, yet would make no attempt to defend himself (Isaiah 53:7). How many innocent men would not even try to defend their innocence? Perhaps 1:1000

7. He would die with the wicked, yet be buried with the rich (Isaiah 53:9). Surely this has happened to less than 1:1000 people throughout history.

8. He would be crucified (Psalm 22:16). Less than 1:10,000 people born in the last 2,300 years have died from crucifixion.

Now comes the fun part. The statistical odds of one person, of the 100,000,000,000 people born in the last 2300 years, fulfilling all of these predictions, is $1:10^{17}$. This is the same as randomly picking up one specific silver dollar, from an area the size of Texas, covered with silver dollars ten feet deep. It is actually far less likely than winning a lottery in which every person ever born has entered. And that is just 8 of these 300 very specific predictions! The odds of one person fulfilling 48 of these 300 very specific prophecies would be equivalent to randomly picking one specific atom out of a sphere packed with atoms -- the sphere being the size of our entire universe (15 billion lights-years across). However, you would need an atom filled sphere for every atom, and this many spheres created every second for 10 billion years to have enough atoms to choose from. The only scientifically valid conclusion is that these very specific prophecies of the Bible were inspired to be written by someone who could foresee the past, present, and future. Only an entity outside of time would be capable of so accurately seeing the future in advance. Only the Creator of the universe can fulfill this description.

Some people believe that, if they just saw God or a "miracle", they would then believe in God or trust the Bible. God has provided more than enough evidence for us to trust that the Bible is indeed His inspired revelation to man without having to physically appear before each of us. Prophecy is proof that the Bible can be trusted in every area of knowledge. We are without excuse for not believing His Word and turning our lives over to the one who died for our wrongdoing. The choice is left to each of us. Making no choice is choosing to live for ourselves and the result will be spending eternity separated from our Creator. It takes an act of our will to accept the price Christ paid for our sins, to repent for rejecting his authority over us, and to live for eternity forgiven.

1. Chuck Missler, *The E.T Senario*, 1994.

Why is There so Much Carbon-14 Left?

By Bruce Malone

Carbon-14 (^{14}C) dating has long been heralded as the definitive proof that the Bible is wrong when it speaks of a 6000 year old earth. ^{14}C is a radioactive element which disappears over time as an unstable carbon atom (which contains 8 instead of the normal 6 neutrons in the nucleus of the atom) breaks down to form other elements. At today's decay rate, one half of any ^{14}C disappears every 5730 years. ^{14}C is present in all living organisms in the proportion of 1 radioactive ^{14}C atom for every trillion regular ^{12}C atoms.

As long as any organism is alive, it is taking in radioactive carbon and making the very structure of its body from this radioactive material. However, as soon as it dies the radiocarbon starts to decay and within 5730 years 1/2 of the original material disappears. In 11,460 years 3/4 of the original ^{14}C is gone. In 17,190 years 7/8 of the original ^{14}C is gone, etc. Since the original amount of ^{14}C in living organisms is incredibly small, the measurable amount of ^{14}C relatively soon reaches immeasurable levels.

One of the amazing feats of modern science has been the development of instruments such as the accelerated mass spectrometer which is capable of measuring ^{14}C levels as low as 0.001% of the amount present in living creatures. This is equivalent to measuring one specific grain of sand on a beach 10 miles long! At the current decay rate of radioactive carbon, this corresponds to approximately 100,000 years of decay. However, the reality of a worldwide flood means that creatures alive before and relatively soon after this flood would have started out with much less ^{14}C even while still alive. Therefore, they would "date" as if tens of thousands of years old even while still alive.

A second important implication

Radiocarbon Levels in "old" Carbon Containing Materials		
Sample	**Assumed Age (millions of years)**	**% Modern Carbon**
Cenozoic Coal	30 - 50	0.2 - 0.3
Mesozoic Coal	65 - 145	0.10 - 0.35
Paleozoic Coal	300 - 311	0.13 - 0.46
Namibia diamonds	millions?	0.04 - 0.17

of radiocarbon dating is the speed with which radiocarbon disappears. ^{14}C decays so fast that not a single atom of ^{14}C could remain in a mere 250,000 years. Thus, if ^{14}C is still found in ancient organic matter, it is proof that this organism cannot possibly be millions of years old.

Note the table above. It is a little publicized fact of the radiocarbon industry that every carbon containing material still contains a measurable amount of ^{14}C in its structure. In a ten year effort to understand how this could be true, the radiocarbon industry went to extreme measures to eliminate every possible source of modern carbon contamination. Yet the labs involved still found significant amounts of undecayed ^{14}C in all samples tested.[1]

Careful research efforts by the RATE team at the Institute for Creation Research sent carefully collected and uncontaminated coal samples from a variety of locations to nationally certified radiocarbon labs and found an average of 0.25% modern ^{14}C left. These coal seams are thought to be 35 to 300 million years old so should not contain a single atom of ^{14}C. Even more amazing is that ^{14}C was found by the same research team in measurable quantities inside unflawed diamonds. Diamonds are the hardest natural substance known to man and are completely impervious to infiltration by modern carbon contamination. Diamonds form deep in the earth under tremendous temperature and pressure and are thought to be millions, if not billions, of years old. The presence of measurable amounts of ^{14}C inside diamonds is again proof that they could not possibly be this old.

The actual age of any ^{14}C containing sample older than Noah's flood is unknown because the starting concentration of ^{14}C is unknown and any acceleration of radiometric decay during this time also unknown. What is apparent is that these samples could not possibly be as old as commonly thought.

How do evolution believers deal with this anomaly? They sweep it under the proverbial rug by simply subtracting the existence of known amounts of ^{14}C in all carbon containing matter and calling it "background contamination". Once again the dogma of evolution does not allow the actual evidence to modify their belief system.

1. Vardiman, Larry, et.al. editors, *Radioisotopes and the Age of the Earth: results of a Young Earth Creationist Research Initiative*, El Cajon, CA, 2005.

Section V:
Creation, Absolute Truth & Society

Dear Mr. Malone,

Thank you so much for sending copies of your articles. There's a saying, "If the facts do not conform to the theory, they must be disposed of." It's great to finally see some of the facts that are being ignored by science, as it is taught.

I'm taking a physiology class this semester, and it astounds me that ANYONE can look at all the complexity that is necessary for a single cell to function and say that it is just a chemical reaction that happened to come together in the right way and get all the things it needed to exist and reproduce itself. Nobody ever mentions the odds against it, they are just too staggering to comprehend.

Some of the articles really struck a chord in me, like when you mention "relative morals" and the "worship of the creation." Last year, my best friend from high school, who also attends Case Western Reserve University, "gave up" Catholicism in favor of WICCA (witchcraft) and neo-paganism. Essentially, they are strongly influenced by the New Age worship of the Earth, and their fundamental belief is that whatever you choose to believe is your own personal reality and is "right." The quote on which WICCA is based is, "So long as it harms none, do as you will." It's a striking contrast to, "Trust the Lord with all thy heart and lean not upon thine own understanding," and "Love thy neighbor as thyself."

Facing the changes that occurred in his personality and eventually giving up his friendship altogether was one of the most difficult things I have had to deal with, but I do have to say the changes that took place in his personality made me realize that there IS an absolute right & an absolute wrong and that humans are not capable of making their own rules based on their own perceptions.

I want to say thank you again for the articles and the book. I plan to make copies of the articles and share them with my friends. I have already shown the articles from the Booster to one of my suitemates, who is a biology major and she asked me to let her read the rest of them when I receive them from you. I am enclosing a small donation to help you continue to publish the articles. Although it's not much, I hope it encourages you to know that your efforts in correcting the biased teachings of "science" are appreciated. I have learned a lot from your articles and the book and it really strengthens my faith to know that creationism cannot be dismissed as unscientific, especially as Christianity seems to becoming more and more politically incorrect. Thank you for taking the time to share your knowledge & faith.

                                    With His love,   Kristin Werner

Chapter 5

"But be doers of the word, and not hearers only, decieving yourselves. For if anyone is a hearer of the word and not a doer, he is like a man observing his natural face in a mirror; for he observes himself, goes away, and immediately forgets what kind of a man he was. But he who looks into the perfect law of liberty and continues in it, and is not a forgetful hearer, but a doer of the work, this one will be blessed in what he does."

- James 1:22-25

In order to explain what brought about the next development leading to this book, I need to elaborate on how the Lord was working in my life following the first publication of the **Search for the Truth** articles. After the publication of the first set of articles, I felt that my usefulness in this area had run its course so I moved on to other activities. Even though, belief in evolution was continuing to undermine the faith of believers and continuing to be a root cause of the moral decay in our society, God seemed to be leading me into other areas of ministry. I had an occasional opportunity to speak on creation, and sporadically someone would request a set of articles, but there did not seem to be much I could do about the situation.

Then Dow Chemical announced the closing of the research center where I had worked for over 15 years. I had the option of finding another job locally or moving with the company to Midland, Michigan (rumored to be a flat, barren land of ice and cold). Granville was the only home our family had known (we have 4 children) and our roots had grown deep. Furthermore, the Lord had blessed us greatly over the years and we had our home almost paid off. This meant that we could have stayed on in Granville, even if I had to take on a lower paying job. More than anything, though, I wanted to know God's will. Through my study of Creation, I had come to deeply trust God and greatly appreciate His guiding hand over every circumstance. Deep trust in God comes from being on the front lines of a spiritual battle and seeing God victorious.

After learning that the research center was closing, I applied for a job at a competitive research organization located within a mile of our home. I was a highly rated and prolific new product development leader who had worked on exactly the type of products that this company was involved with. Amazingly, in spite of the fact that they were hiring, I did not even get a job interview. Employees at the research center were given two months to decide whether or not they would move to Midland. Every morning, I was up early to pray. Nothing improves your prayer life like stressful situations. After a few weeks of seeking direction, I heard the Lord speak quietly to me. It came in the form of a thought that said, "You can enjoy this time, I am in control." Several more weeks passed and I was given the answer I had been seeking. As I was reading Luke 18:29 I came across a passage which said, *"...there is no man that has left house, or parents, or brothers...for the kingdom of God's sake, who shall not receive manifold more in this present time, and in the world to come -- life everlasting."* The words seemed to just jump off the page as if they had been written directly for me. The Lord had told me through His thoughts, through His Word, and through circumstances what I was to do. Yet, I still did not want to go to Midland (that flat, barren land of ice and cold). I held off signing my transfer commitment until the last possible day.

On the morning the decision was due, I walked out to the wildlife pond on the site and made one last appeal. It went something like, "Dear Lord, You know I don't really want to go to Midland (the flat, barren land of ice and cold). However, if that is where you want me, I would be foolish not to go. I know there are going to be times when I'll wish I'd stayed in Granville. I really need to know you want me to move. Jesus, you have repeatedly shown me that you are in control of everything, including the animals you created. If you really want me to move, bring a deer as a sign that I'm making the correct decision."

Perhaps not an elegant prayer and I certainly had no right to ask for further confirmation, but it was from the heart. I opened my eyes with the expectation of seeing "my" deer -- none appeared. So I waited... and waited...

and waited. I was getting both cold and disappointed. I even climbed up on the railing of the wildlife observation platform for a better view… still no deer.

I finally gave up and started back to D building where I worked, praying as I walked. As I prayed, that soft thought, which I am still learning to recognize, rebuked me, "I've already told you where I want you." Right after that I looked up and not 15 feet away from me a deer stood up in the tall grass. We looked at each other for a few moments, and as tears clouded my eyes, he bounded off into the woods. The God of this universe loves us dearly, and when we truly seek His will, with the intent to obey, He will not remain silent. Too often we do not hear because we already know the answer, don't want to obey, or are too distracted by our own thoughts to hear Him.

In hindsight, I can see the hand of God orchestrating our entire move. Our son was heartbroken that we would have to leave our home surrounded by acres of fourteen-foot tall pine trees that we had planted as saplings. We had spent many evenings singing around campfires or playing ball tag among the trees. So guess what the Lord provided in Midland? -- a home which had been on the market for over a year without a single offer (*the Lord had it reserved for us*) and had recently been marked down into the range we could afford (*He knew our limits*). It was built on a small rise with a hill in the back yard (*making Midland no longer flat.*) It came with a completely finished wood shop in the back (*He knows my hobbies),* and was surrounded by acres of mature pine trees (*just for my son*)! The Creator of the universe is a God who can orchestrate details.

Even after the Lord had provided our home, He was not done pouring out His blessings. We had been trying to sell our home in Granville for several months with no success. If our house did not sell; Dow Chemical would purchase it, but at a reduced price. I had been on a short trip to Midland and was driving home when the Lord again spoke a distinct thought into my mind. My wife had just called to tell me that the only prospect that we had for selling the house had fallen through. After months of keeping the house clean and holding open house showings, we were left without a single prospect. As I was thinking this over on the five-hour drive back to Granville, the Lord impressed His desire upon me, "You have not prayed with Robin." Sure enough, I realized that Robin and I had been praying about selling the house for months, but we had never brought our petition before the Lord as a couple. As soon as I walked in the door, I grabbed Robin's hand, pulled her into the living room, and said, "We've got to pray!" I don't remember the exact prayer, but the gist of it was, "Dear Lord Jesus, we would really like this house to be sold seven days from now. Thank you." We even told others in our Bible study group what I felt the Lord had said and how we had prayed. Three days later, the realtor called with a prospect. Four days later, the couple returned for a second look. Five days later, we had an offer and six days later the house was sold! I had asked for a week, but should have known the Lord only needs six days to complete any job.

Most significant of all was how the Lord used this move to affect others. I now know of dozens of people who accepted Jesus as their Savior as a direct result of our move to Midland and the events that followed. How wonderful to be used by the Maker of the universe and to see the fruits which develop out of faith and obedience.

The purpose of this digression was to lead into the subject at hand -- what happened after moving to Midland? The Lord led our family to a wonderful mission-minded church in Midland and during a Sunday night prayer meeting, the Lord once again spoke to my spirit. We were facing outward in the sanctuary praying for the city of Midland, when I felt as if the Lord was saying to me, "Satan is not going to flee just because you are praying." The implication was that we needed to follow prayer with action. I felt God was telling me to publish **Search** in the Midland paper. God has brought me a long way since that night 12 years earlier when I had sat alone on our couch and given Him my life. I didn't feel any different after I accepted Him as Savior, but my life had changed. I can see that my priorities changed for the better.

♦ *I have learned that God often uses us in ways we would least expect. God didn't send me off to the mission field (although I have travelled aound the world on short term mission trips), but He gave me dozens of new product ideas for my existing job. I have always wondered where an original idea comes from. Giving credit to God is not only a great cure for pride, but is a better explanation than humanists have to offer.*

♦ *God didn't wow me with chills up my spine, flashing lights, audible voices, or bowl me over. However, once Jesus became my Lord, I was able for the first time to resist sins which had controlled my life for the previous 15 years.*

♦ *God didn't send me off to Bible college, but used me to tell friends, family, and co-workers about Him through my life, actions, and words. Furthermore, He steadily transformed me from a shy introvert to a confident person whom He could use to reach others with the truth of His love and the reality of His existence. Perhaps, the greatest evidence of His sovereign hand was His taking someone who was petrified of speaking in front of people and ultimately bringing him to the point of being a public speaker for one of the greatest scientific organizations in the world -- The Institute for Creation Research.*

After moving to Midland, God seemed to be leading me to proclaim in the public newspaper of a highly scientific, highly educated town that the earth is young, that diverse forms of life instantaneously came into existence, and that much of what people were being taught about geology, anthropology, cosmology, biology, and biochemistry was wrong. This time, God didn't have to tell me twice...

First, the 50 original articles were significantly updated. Next, twenty new articles were added from ideas that I had put on hold as I thought my ministry in the area of Creation was over. The Lord had already provided the money to purchase the newspaper space via a moving bonus. Thus, all that remained was to make sure that I had the support of the pastor and the church. I would not have proceeded without this, so I presented the concept to Pastor Stocker. He was enthusiastic and set aside part of a Sunday night prayer meeting to launch the project. The next step was approaching the newspaper. I had written half a dozen editorial letters since arriving in Midland, so I asked the editor if there was any chance of the newspaper donating the space for a regular weekly column. As expected, the answer was 'No.' Therefore, I purchased the space and over the next six months, the newspaper placed the articles in a perfect location -- directly across from the editorial page.

Having the evidence for creation presented in a public forum again resulted in much controversy as it challenged the readers to consider the truth in areas where they have been misled. Over the next several years, over hundred letters-to-the-editor were written by 60 different authors highlighting both sides of the evolution creation controversy. Many of these were directly related to the weekly column which was published. In addition, I received dozens of requests for copies of the series. There is no doubt that presenting a public discourse on the scientific evidence supporting creation (by placing this evidence in public newspapers) helps many people to understand the foundational truths of the Bible. This is the type of effect on society that Jesus called us to have as we are commanded to be "the salt of the earth" and "a light on the hill". This effort ultimately led to this book and several others which continue to change hearts and lives.

What is Truth?

by Bruce Malone

In order to "search for the truth", the "truth" must exist. The debate over origins deals with real events in time and space. Either there was a worldwide flood... or there was not. Either God initiated the flood as judgment for man's rebellion... or He did not. Either life has existed for billions of years...or it has not. Either man came from an ape-like creature... or he did not. There are no gray areas here - only black or white. One person cannot have one truth and another have an opposing truth. One of them must be wrong. Many people have the misguided idea that evolution and creation can both be true.

There are very real consequences to accepting multiple realities. Ask your grandparents about a time not so long ago when locking doors was unnecessary and a man's word was all that was needed to believe he would carry through on a commitment. Contrast that to today when our society is permeated with lies and litigation from the schoolroom to Congress. What has happened to the moral fiber of our culture for things to change so radically?

The root of the problem is that Judeo-Christian moral absolutes have been replaced by the moral relativism of humanism. The very idea of "relative morals" is a contradiction of terms.

Once morals have been removed from an absolute source, such as the Bible, they become a matter of man's opinion instead of God's revelation. Consider sex education as an example. Most people believe they should not impose "morals" on others by telling them that it is wrong to have sex before marriage. If most adults in a community believe it is morally

I GET THESE LUSTFUL, PERVERTED, EVIL THOUGHTS. THEY STARTED WHEN...

NO... WHEN I GOT INTO PORNOGRAPHY!

...YOU WERE A BABY. YOU WERE PROBABLY FORCED TO BE RIGHT-HANDED OR MADE TO EAT ALL YOUR PEAS!

PSYCHIATRIST

THAT'S RIGHT... BLAME IT ON SOMETHING STUPID!!

Used by permission of Wayne Stayskal

acceptable to have sex with children... does that make it right? If a group of people wants to teach our children that sex with animals is just another acceptable choice... do we let them? Furthermore, why is telling children that sex outside of marriage is "wrong", any different from telling them that lying, stealing, or murdering is "wrong"? Once the tie has been severed from an absolute source of truth, everything becomes an arbitrary opinion. The Bible repeatedly claims to be THE ultimate authoritative source of truth.

The Western World is morally adrift and the blame lies squarely on the shoulders of Christians who have failed to defend the authenticity of the Bible as God's revelation to man. Creation provides the only evidence which ties the physical world to a supernatural God. By denying creation, a person is rejecting the physical evidence that the Bible is God's Word. We are already several generations down that path (with predictable consequences to Western culture).

Years ago, I laid an arrowhead on the desk of an anthropologist and explained the parallel between the creation of life and the making of an arrowhead. An arrowhead is the product of intelligent design, but it is impossible to scientifically prove. Furthermore, if someone wanted to believe that an arrowhead was the product of chance (instead of design); he would conduct experiments to try to show how that might have happened. Nothing would convince such a person that he was wrong.

The evolutionist rejected the whole analogy with a wave of his hand, stating that science can never consider the possibility of the supernatural. I pressed the point further, "But what if God has supernaturally affected the world in the past? Shouldn't there be scientific evidence of that interaction?"

His answer was very revealing, "If you want to search for 'The Truth', (tracing an imaginary 'T' in the air); you can go home and do it... but it doesn't belong in scientific endeavors." How sad that in our school system, only evolutionary explanations are taught -- even if they are total nonsense and based on faith rather than evidence.

It Does Matter HOW God Created

By Bruce Malone

"The cosmos is all that is or ever was or ever will be."[1] Thus the late Carl Sagan began his famous and influential book, **Cosmos,** with a statement which is more akin to religion than to science. *"The heavens declare the glory of God."*[2] Thus states the Bible which claims to be the inspired Word of this God.

Here, then, is the sharp contrast between the two mutually exclusive worldviews which are currently locked in combat for preeminence of thought in the Western World. The winner will determine the course of world history. But why not just say, "God used evolution to create...," and be done with the controversy?

First, Christians are always to look for the truth. Anything else would dishonor the very God in whom they profess to believe. Evolution and creation cannot both be true because they completely contradict each other. One must be wrong, if the other is right. How can we claim to be followers of the One who claimed to be *"The Truth"*;[3] if we aren't willing to search for the truth.

Second, Jesus Christ said that we could tell a tree by its fruit.[4] Have you ever heard anyone sincerely state, *"I'm glad I have learned the evidence for evolution. It has led me to the reality of God's personal love for me. Now that everything can be explained by random chance, I feel purpose and meaning in my life."* On the other hand, many people confess that hearing the evidence for creation has strengthened their faith in God's existence, in His personal involvement with His creation, and

in the Bible as God's revealed truth.

Third, the Bible is very clear that human behavior is closely tied to our beliefs. Take time to read

Romans 1:17-26. This passage states that because of the evidence of creation, no one has an excuse for disbelief in God. However, if God used evolution; then there is no evidence for God's existence from observing His Creation so this Bible passage must be wrong. The verses in Romans go on to list the results of denying God's existence: a society with widespread homosexuality, greed, envy, murder, hatred toward the God of Christianity, and many other consequences. Does this sound like America today? The primary tie of the physical world to a spiritual God is the reality of creation. This is why the Bible equates belief in God with the acknowledgment of Him as Creator. If any society accepts evolution as reality; the relevance of God decreases, and the tie to an absolute source of right and wrong is broken. The result is a drift toward humanism and the devaluation of human life.

Fourth, the Bible couldn't be

more clear concerning God's method of creation and the history of our planet. Unlike the numerous creation stories from cultures all over the world, the Biblical creation account is precise, concise, and provides testable predictions concerning the world around us. For instance, the Bible describes humanity with a tendency toward evil and every society in the history of the world has ended in tragedy and bloodshed. The Bible describes a worldwide flood and there is abundant evidence that this event happened. The Bible describes the creation of separate animal and plant "kinds" and that is exactly what the fossil record shows.

In the face of this evidence, why not consider the possibility that the Bible is exactly what it claims to be -- God's inspired revelation to humans to be read and understood in a normal, straightforward manner? Jesus was more to the point in Luke 16:31, *"If they hear not Moses [who passed down the creation account]...neither will they be persuaded, though one rose from the dead."* Jesus is largely ignored today.

A physician does not treat just the symptoms when he treats a dying patient. Our country shows many tragic symptoms of a society drifting away from God. The root cause is the denial of God's existence and the Bible's authority. This would be inconceivable had not several generations been taught that evolution is a fact.

1. Carl Sagan, **Cosmos,** Random House Publishers, 1980, p 4.
2. The Bible, *Psalms 19:1*
3. The Bible, *John 14:6*
4. The Bible, *Matthew 12:33*

No Stopping on the Slippery Slope

By Bruce Malone

Most people are concerned about the rise in crime, drug use, and suicide among our youth. Many have been led to believe that government supported anti-drug or self-esteem programs will help reduce this trend. However, studies have shown that there is no long term significant difference in the behavior of children who have been through these types of programs.[1] Religion also seems to have little effect on children's behavior.

A scientific survey showed that the behavior of churched youth is appallingly similar to that of unchurched youth. Almost all the youth in this survey professed a personal relationship with Jesus Christ, regularly read the Bible, and attended weekly youth group meetings. Yet 66% stated that they had recently lied, 36% had cheated on exams, 10% had been drunk or used drugs in the last 3 months, and 55% had engaged in sexual activity by age 18 (1994 Church Youth Survey, George Barna Research Group).

Parents who wish their children to have an unshakable moral foundation cannot rely on church attendance to provide it. So what is the solution? Allan Bloom provides the clue in his book, ***The Closing of the American Mind***. He states that, "There is one thing a professor can be absolutely certain of: almost every student entering university believes, or says he believes, that truth is relative." Western civilization has experienced a shift in thinking where the basis for morals has moved from an acknowledgment that absolute truth exists to the shifting sands of tolerance and relativism. The final Star Wars episode, seen by millions of youth in 2005, even boldly proclaimed during the climatic

JANUARY 22, 1973   ROE vs. WADE   THE U.S. SUPREME COURT DECLARES ABORTION ON DEMAND A CONSTITUTIONAL RIGHT.

THE SPLITTER SPLATTER OF LITTLE FEET!

Used by permission of Chuck Asay

scene that, *"[only evil men] believe in absolute truth."*

Absolute truth exists because God exists. An absolute truth is something which is true for all times, for all people, and under all circumstances. It is not true because it is convenient or expedient. Absolute truth is a reflection of the One who made the universe. Too many people have not realized the extent to which they have accepted our cultural dance with relativism. It is time to quit blaming society, the media, the schools, or peers for the attitudes and behavior of our children. It is time to look in the mirror and honestly assess the model we set for our children.

Jesus Christ stated that He is truth. This is not a conditional statement, and we are commanded to live by this absolute. Do we cheat on taxes, ignore speed limits, bring home items from work, not give our full effort to our employer? If so, why are we surprised when our children choose to be less than honest or honorable in other areas? Do we justify lies in order to avoid consequences? If so, why expect our children to be honest.

God is pure. Do we entertain ourselves with talk shows, dirty jokes, and the moral raw sewage emanating from TV and movies? Why should we expect our children to remain sexually pure? Do we deal with stress using alcohol, cigarettes, or legal drugs? Why shouldn't we expect our children to do the same with illegal drugs?

Absolute moral truth is a plateau surrounded by a slippery slope. Once you step off the plateau, you will slide down the slope until you put in a stake to keep you from sliding further. We often deceive ourselves into believing that our stake is the correct moral standard. Why are we surprised when our children slide further down the slippery slope before putting their stake in at a lower moral level?

Jesus stated, *"I did not come to abolish (God's moral) law, but to fulfill it."* How tragic when our actions reveal a rejection of absolute truth. If we expect our children to abstain from substance abuse and sexual sin; we must be willing to model the straight and narrow path that should characterize Christianity.

1. *Both a 1991 Kentucky Study and a 1990 Canadian government study showed no significant difference in student drug use after DARE.*

Only God can Provide a Basis for Truth

By Bruce Malone

Used by Permission of Johnny Hart

If ultimate truth exists; this truth must have a basis outside of human opinion. If we are creations; then there is a Creator. An author has the ultimate authority to interpret his own writing. Likewise, if we have a Creator; He has ultimate authority over us. Finite human opinion can never create absolute truth. An enormous number of opinions can never add up to absolute truth. Only a source of moral truth which is outside of ourselves can provide a sufficient basis for morality. Absolute truth can only exist if an ultimate being (God) exists. Therefore, as belief in a Creator declines, belief in absolute truth also declines. The two are irrevocably connected. This is one reason why Jesus emphasized that he is *"the Truth."*[1] The text does not say that He knew, told, or revealed the truth. Rather, Jesus explicitly stated that He literally **is** truth. The history of mankind is the reality of how humans have responded to God as the source of absolute truth.

The primary reason that we see such a concerted effort to remove all references to God from public life is not to protect the Constitution of the United States. God is under attack in order to remove the source of absolute truth upon which our government was founded. Whenever God's Word, the Bible, is rejected as the absolute source of truth, people's opinions become their own source of absolute truth. This is why 'tolerance' has become the most valued and treasured virtue within society. Christian tolerance values the opinions of others, but weighs those opinions against an absolute standard -- the Bible. The *new tolerance* demands that everyone's morals be considered of equal validity and that no absolute truth exists!

The *new tolerance* sounds kind and compassionate, but really it just trades one absolute belief (that God exists and has revealed the moral order of the universe through the Bible) with another absolute (that man can set his own rules of right and wrong). Furthermore, this *new tolerance* mercilessly persecutes anyone who would dare suggest that someone may be wrong or sinful. Christian absolutes are simply not tolerated.

Our government and legal system were based on the absolute moral truth defined by the One who claimed to literally be *"the truth"*. This foundation produced a nation of the greatest economic and social freedom in the history of the world. Yet, the modern definition of tolerance (that every opinion is of equal value) has replaced this viewpoint. This is a direct consequence of the belief in evolution -- which forms the foundation for relative morality (i.e. no morality.)

The whole idea that multiple truths can coexist is flawed logic. Truth, by definition, means that other possibilities are not true! Whenever Biblical truths and morals are rejected, an oppressive government ultimately begins to enforce some other set of arbitrary standards.

1. **The Bible**, *John 14:6;John 18:37; John 5:33; John 1:14*

Why Do We Have a Conscience?

By John Adam

One of many questions left unanswered by evolution is how man's conscience could have developed. How could ideas of right and wrong (which seem to be firmly ingrained into every culture) have developed by evolutionary processes? If we evolved; ideas of right and wrong must have also evolved with us. Therefore, a conscience, a knowledge of right and wrong, must have some intrinsic survival value. But does it? In a struggle for survival, will the existence of a conscience help or hinder one's survival? An evolving person without a conscience would be free to covet belongings, steal the possessions of others, and even murder without guilt. A creature with a conscience is hesitant and soul searching. Where is the survival value to the individual having the conscience? The conscience serves as a detriment to survival, not a mechanism which increases an individual's ability to survive. Unless the universe was created by a God who has established inherent values of right and wrong; it would seem that there is no survival value to the development of conscience.

If the conscience did not evolve; then it must have always existed. What could be the source of what has always existed and determines good from evil? The question in itself defines one characteristic of God.

Almost all people of every culture seem to have an innate sense of right and wrong. There

also seems to be universal guilt among humans and a desire to be free of this guilt. How could we be born with an innate sense of right and wrong? Maybe we feel guilty because we are... in reality... guilty.

People can ignore their conscience. If this happens repeatedly; their conscience will tend to atrophy the same way an unused muscle will atrophy. In Biblical language, to ignore the heart is to cause the heart to become hardened. There are many influential voices today who believe that the solution to our social problems is to deny that there is an absolute standard for right or wrong. Thus, a person with little or no conscience is as welcome in society as one with a highly developed conscience. In such a society, right and wrong is defined only by what is most expedient for those in power. Nazi Germany was such a society. Any society which denies the reality of an external source of conscience becomes a hell on earth.

Where does sacrificial love fit into such a society? Why be sacrificial in a society that teaches any life style is acceptable? The God of Christianity extols self sacrifice. This is the opposite of what evolution would produce. The Bible is full of examples of loving sacrifices but nowhere can the concept of survival of the fittest be seen as a characteristic of God.

To summarize, according to the evolutionary principle of survival of the fittest, a loving human with a conscience would have been at a great disadvantage and thus unlikely to have survived. From a humanist viewpoint, attributes of the conscience (such as self sacrifice purely for the good of others) are weaknesses. Yet it is these very attributes which make us humans and not animals.

No person has ever lived without violating his conscience in some way. Every one has fallen short of what God expects from us. So how do we make amends for the disobedience to the One who built the standard into our conscience? The Bible is very clear that we can never earn our way back into God's favor. It is also clear that God has provided a means of forgiveness through the loving sacrifice of Himself as payment for our sins. It is as if the judge at a trial took the penalty for a crime upon himself. Once we have accepted His forgiveness, we can truly start to live out sacrificial love... even toward those who hate us. What an illogical concept, if evolution is a fact of history!

John Adam is a computer programmer who lives in Granville, Ohio.

Evolution and Modern Myths

There is a preponderance of scientific evidence to support creation as the correct explanation for our existence. The misconception that evolution is science while creation is religion is propagated by a variety of "myths" surrounding the evidence for evolution. Here is the truth about a few of these icons of evolution.

Myth: *Our universe is the result of the "Big Bang" explosion of the "Cosmic Egg" billions of years ago.*
Reality: This just ignores the bigger question—who laid the "cosmic egg"? The first law of thermodynamics proves that matter and energy cannot just appear. Evolutionists must ignore the most basic law of science at the very start of their belief system. Furthermore, explosions do not result in increased organization of matter and expanding gas clouds do not form stars and planets. Has an explosion ever created ordered complexity?

Myth: *The fossil record proves evolution.*
Reality: There are no clear transitions between vastly different types of animals in either the living world or the fossil record. Lining up three objects by size or shape does not prove that one turned into the other.

Myth: *Structural and biochemical similarities prove common ancestry.*
Reality: The lack of fossil transitions strongly refute this myth. Common ancestry is only one of two possible explanations for similarities. Purposeful design can explain the same features in a more direct way. In addition, totally different organisms often display similar features. This supports the existence of a common designer.

Myth: *The rock layers of the earth form the pages of earth's history showing millions of years of evolutionary progression.*
Reality: The fossil record does not show a clear, "simple-to-complex" progression of life forms. Life is complex and well developed wherever it is found in the fossil record. Major groups of plants and animals appear suddenly in the fossil record, with nothing leading up to them. Most rock layers and the fossils they contain can be explained better by a worldwide flood and subsequent events.

Myth: *Radiometric dating methods are "absolute." They are accurate and reliable.*
Reality: Although radiometric dating methods seem to indicate great age, these methods depend upon numerous unprovable assumptions. When used to date events of known age, such as the lava flows in Hawaii or the Grand Canyon, they have been wrong by orders of magnitude. Even more revealing, recent studies indicate that there has been rapid radiometric decay in the recent past so the methods really are just a measure of the amount of decay, not the age of the rock sample. Furthermore, the vast majority of alternative dating methods indicate a very young earth.

Myth: *The human body contains many "vestigial organs" -- left overs from our evolutionary development.*
Reality: Although at one time there were dozens of features of the human body listed as vestigial, all have been shown to have important functions. Even if a few parts have lost their original function that does not prove evolution. To demonstrate evolution, you need to show the development of completely new structures, not the loss and degeneration of previous characteristics.

Myth: *The fossil record for human evolution is complete and clear.*
Reality: All too often the propagandists for evolution present their story with statements such as, *"Every knowing person believes that man descended from apes. Today there is no such thing as the theory of evolution, it is the fact of evolution."* (Ernst Mayr) The evidence for human evolution is fragmentary and reconstruction involves artistic license. Many competent scientists totally reject evolution. They acknowledge that it is not even a good scientific theory, much less a fact.

This is a condensation of an article by Dave Nutting of Alpha Omega Institute. Alpha Omega is a nonprofit creation education organization in Colorado and can be reached at www.discovercreation.org.

We Become What We Think About

By Ron Cooper

As Christians, we are commanded to *"Take every thought captive into the obedience of Christ"*[1] and to think upon the right kind of things -

*"Whatsoever things are **True**, whatsoever things are **Honest**, whatsoever things are **Just**, whatsoever things are **Pure**, whatsoever things are **Lovely**, whatsoever things are of **Good** report; if there be any **Virtue**, and if there be any **Praise**, think on these..."*[2]

The Biblical creation story is the **Truest** history on this earth. It comes from an **Honest** and **Just** God. It is a **Pure** history, straight forward and **Lovely** in its detail. It is the first report of **Goodness**. I find **Virtue** in its every detail. And I find reasons for **Praise** concerning everything it contains, in its smallest detail.

On the flip side, I can think of no thankful consequence from the belief in evolution. Evolution contradicts the most basic laws of science and is obviously **not True**. It is intellectually **disHonest** to believe the earth is billions of years old when 9 out of 10 dating methods indicate a much younger earth and God's word clearly teaches a recent creation. If evolution is true then the universe has always been ruled by **inJustice** as stronger creatures have wiped out weaker species. According to evolution, it is the **imPure** transfer of information (mutations) from one generation to the next which has resulted in upward advancement. Millions of dead ends and the happen-chance development of life can only be considered **unLovely**. God always gives a **Bad** report to those who reject Jesus and His

written word (which is exactly what evolution does). Survival of the fittest is the **opposite of Virtue**, (such as self sacrifice) which Jesus

Evolution of the Stop Sign

exhibited for us. I can think of no philosophy ever conceived by man as **unPraiseworthy** as evolution. Evolution has been (and still is) used to justify abortion, rejection of God and absolute truth, racism, slavery, euthanasia, communism, sexual immorality, genocide, and divorce.

You must choose how to direct your thoughts. Know that God is your Creator. Study the evidence that He created the entire universe in six literal days as clearly described in the Bible as six mornings and evenings of work followed by a single day of rest. The desire to remove accountability is the primary motivation behind the promotion of evolution as a fact. Evolution ultimately allows mankind to remove God from his thinking and do what is "right" in his own eyes. England went from 60%

church attending Christians during World War II, to less than 4% church attending Christians today. What happened? Could it be that, as they rejected the historical truth of the Bible, the relevance of Christianity faded? Or as Jesus said, *"If I tell you about **earthly** things and you don't believe them, how will you believe me when I tell you about **heavenly** things?"*[3]

The Bible lays the framework for understanding and correctly interpreting the evidence from biology (each creature reproduces after its own kind), geology (a worldwide flood laid down the sedimentary rock layers, filled with billions of dead organisms, all over the world), anthropology (mankind was created as man and woman and has always been highly intelligent), cosmology (in six days God created the heavens and the earth and all that is in them), and sociology (the world is the way it is because of man's rejection of God and his resulting sinful nature). Only by starting with a Biblical understanding of true history can we come to the correct interpretations of the data in all these areas of science.

We become what we think. What is the basis of your thinking?

1. 2 Corinthians 10:5
2. Philippians 4:8
3. John 3:12

Ron Cooper is president of the Ark Foundation in Dayton, A Biblical Creation Science and History Worldview group promoting the relevance and trustworthiness of the Bible. www.arky.org

The Day the Earth Stood Still

By Bruce Malone

In the classic science fiction movie, *The Day the Earth Stood Still,* the question of how mankind would respond to a choice of obedience or certain destruction is posed. A representative of life from outer space delivered an ultimatum to earth. If mankind did not stop fighting and producing nuclear warheads, all life on earth would be destroyed. The viewer was left to ponder, would humanity stop waging war and subject itself to this ultimate authority?

A brief overview of history might help resolve the question. According to the Bible, the original created set of human beings were given the same choice: obedience or death. As they chose disobedience, they died spiritually and started to die physically. *[Note: If God had not allowed for this possibility of disobedience; mankind would be no different than animals - not really possessing the freedom to love or reject their Creator]* Since that time, the history of humanity has been a history of continual conflict and bloodshed. This is not to say that mankind has not achieved magnificent artistic and intellectual accomplishments over the years, or that there are not isolated examples of sacrificial love and kindness.

However, to deny the savagery which humans are obviously capable of is to deny reality. Just in "modern times" man has been capable of these atrocities:

♦ Six hundred thousand killed during the American Civil War because of the desire for wealth based on slavery.

ONE FINE DAY AT THE MUSEUM...

Used by permission of Chuck Asay

♦ The murder of approximately 60 million people under the last 90 years of Communist oppression.

♦ The murder of 6 million Jews due to Nazi prejudice.

♦ Millions of deaths from starvation due to the Hindu religious caste system. There are enough cows to end this starvation, but they are considered more sacred than human life.

♦ The deaths of over one hundred million unborn children worldwide from abortion. The vast majority were disposed of because their births would have been an inconvenience to the parents.

Many other examples of the cruel side of humanity could be cited. The overall picture is not pretty because we continue to rebel against the absolute moral absolutes laid down by our loving Creator.

Returning to the dilemma raised in *The Day the Earth Stood Still,* history shows a consistent answer to how humanity would respond to such a challenge -- man has always crossed the line. The reality of human history is that humans are rebellious. Historically, what force has been able to restrain the evil of humanity for brief periods of time? Only three are apparent:

1. Brute government force as in the case of Communism, Fascism, Marxism, and to a lesser degree, socialism.

2. Rigid religious systems with stiff social penalties for disobedience such as is found in Buddhism, Hinduism, or Islam.

3. The freedom and liberty which comes with acknowledging the Christian absolutes as reality.

Our founding fathers clearly understood that these were the choices which any society faced. That is why John Adams said, "Our Constitution was made only for a moral and religious people. It is wholly inadequate for the government of any other." Yet our society is moving rapidly down the road which removes all influence of Christianity from public life!

One last note:

In The Day the Earth Stood Still, *a mother had no hesitation letting her ten-year-old son spend the entire day in Washington, D.C. accompanied by a total stranger. This was 1951. There was no fear letting a total stranger watch a child unsupervised. How far we have fallen in just 5 decades!*

Human Value Cannot Survive without God

By Bruce Malone

The value of anything must always be set by something outside that object. A coin is no more valuable than a pebble except by common agreement that it can be exchanged for something else. Humans are unique in their ability to assign abstract values to inherently non-functional and otherwise useless objects. A diamond ring, a thousand dollar bill, or a gold bar have no more value to an animal than a smooth pebble, a shiny rock, or a fuzzy leaf. Animals cannot even assign value to their own lives. Apart from survival instincts and some mutually beneficial biological relationships, animals either ignore each other or eat one another. Tears are never shed as one group of animals seeks to destroy another in its own quest for survival. Animals make no judgments concerning the value of biological life. Only man is capable of recognizing the value of animal life and seeking to protect it. Who is capable, though, of assigning value to human life?

If human value is set by the mutual consent of other humans; it is subject to change at any time. This has happened countless times throughout history. Many ancient cultures sacrificed living children either to appease their pagan gods or to request favors from them. Not all that long ago, the U.S. Supreme Court declared slavery legal, effectively removing human status from Negroes. Aborigines in Australia were shot and skinned less than 200 years ago because they were not considered to be human. In the last four decades, the abortion industry has profited from the destruction of 40 million

unborn children whose value and lives were eliminated by a single Supreme Court decision.

The founding fathers of our country clearly understood both human nature and the sordid history of mankind. They realized that only a source outside of mankind's existence could assign a lasting value to human life. That is why the Declaration of Independence has, as its most basic assumption, the existence of certain inalienable rights such as: "...life, liberty, and the pursuit of happiness." Inalienable rights must be granted by someone greater than the authors of the documents, otherwise those rights could be changed by the next group of people that comes into power. However, this does not imply that all forms of life are of equal value. Man has special value because he has free will and is not controlled by instincts. Most importantly, man has special value because his Creator has demonstrated His love for him through natural revelation (creation); special revelation (the Bible and the earthly visitation of Jesus Christ); and personal revelation (the personal knowledge and peace which come with accepting Him as Savior).

At present, a war of values is raging in our country. Many of us are aware of the surface skirmishes, but all too few are aware that the root cause of the war is a deep philosophical difference about reality. The basis of America's cultural war is the question of man's relationship to God. Either life's value is based on God's personal existence (meaning absolute values do exist) or man sets the standards. There are no other possibilities. The consequence of 150 years of indoctrination with evolutionary principles is the acceptance that man is part of the natural forces which shaped us. The inevitable result is the removal of any objective basis for truth. Thus, mankind either arbitrarily assigns value to things (including people) or all life becomes of equal value. In the case of the former, atrocities such as human sacrifice or passive acceptance of abortion occur. In the case of the latter, absurdities occur such as animal rights groups equating the murder and mutilation of humans with the slaughter of chickens[1]. Both are the inevitable outcome of following evolutionary humanist philosophy to its logical conclusion.

Christianity is rooted in the fact that a personal God exists. Thus, human life is inherently valuable. We have no right to do with life as we arbitrarily please. There is some thing special about all humans and no one has the right to remove their value by murder, abortion, or euthanasia.

1. Charles Nicoll & Sharon Russell, "Animal Rights Literature*", **Science** 244:903 (May 26, 1989).

Eugenics & Overpopulation

By Bruce Malone

All too frequently, there are stories which present as a fact the idea that the world is "overpopulated". This alarm has been sounded repeatedly over the last century with dire consequences if the human population is not controlled or reduced. This idea has its roots in the eugenics movement of the early 1900's. During this time, the science community, based on the evolutionary principle that natural selection would ultimately eliminate poor genetic traits, promoted the concept of reducing undesirable genetic traits from the human population by eliminating less fit people. This idea was especially popular with racists such as Margaret Sanger (founder of the infamous Planned Parenthood abortion organization) who advocated the sterilization of the poor, the sick, the blacks and other "less evolved" people. It was only after the atrocity of the Nazi party of Germany taking this philosophy to its natural conclusion that eugenics lost its luster with many people. Yet, the current public school curriculum ignores the sordid history of the population control movement and continues to push the need for population control in more subtle terms. Billions of tax dollars have been spent in attempts to coerce developing nations into stricter birth control methods, sterilization, and abortions. How should we respond to the dire predictions that the Earth is being overrun with human vermin?

To combat this subtle form of evil, we need to get the facts straight. Predictions of overpopulation have been repeatedly wrong in the same way that predictions of massive energy shortages by the end of the 1970's

THE FIRST HOMELESS

Used by permission of Chuck Asay

were totally inaccurate. Calculations of total world population are based on very tentative data which cannot predict unknown future variables. For instance, the enormous effect of AIDS on the world population was not known 10 years ago and the tendency of developed nations such as Europe, Japan, and America to voluntarily stabilize growth are seldom taken into account.

Furthermore, the entire population of the world could be placed into the state of Texas with every family given a 2000 square foot home on a 40 by 100 foot lot. This planet has more than enough resources for its growing population and almost all the problems associated with "overpopulation" are the result of greed, pride, and racial hatred rather than the total number of people present! Japan is home to 125 million people on a land mass smaller than the state of California. Most of these people live in urban areas because of the mountainous terrain. Yet the Japanese are quite satisfied with their quality of life.

In addition to these facts, some population models predict that it will take over 200 years to double the current world population. Other models actually predict a shrinking future world population.

The most important perspective to maintain is that our Creator is ultimately in control. *Newsflash* - God really does know what He is doing. The Bible clearly teaches that children are to be considered blessings, (rather than a curse to be prevented and disposed of). Nowhere in the Bible is there even a hint that it is our responsibility to reduce the number of children desired by our neighbors. Almost all methods limiting world population involve coercion at best and murder at worst. The dignity of human life is often reduced to statistics in an effort to obtain some arbitrary population growth goal. Only God knows what population this planet was built to sustain, but we are certainly nowhere near that limit. Money currently spent to control world population would be much better spent improving the quality of human life.

The next time you hear dire predictions of the effects of over population, respond with a statement of trust in God's providence rather than jumping on the "overpopulation" bandwagon. Once we start treating people with dignity and respect, someone whom the God of this universe considered worthy of dying for, we will be motivated to fund economic development instead of overseas abortions.

Same Sex Marriage Inevitable

By Bruce Malone

Legally recognized same sex marriages seem inevitable. After all, why shouldn't any two consenting adults be allowed to marry? How can Christians be such narrow-minded, bigoted, kill-joys as to interfere with the happiness of two consenting adults? Yet, if two men can be married, why not three men? Why not one man and 32 women? For that matter, why not one man and a gorilla to whom he is emotionally and sexually attracted? Given enough sympathetic television shows and publicity in favor of such "marriages", why shouldn't all of these scenarios be allowed? If the definition of marriage is based on nothing more than public opinion; there is no firm basis upon which to oppose any of these arrangements. However, if our Creator specifically designed man and woman for each other, then any other arrangement is a perversion of our design.

God created Adam and Eve, not Adam and Steve. Yet, evolution has become the "only allowed" explanation for our existence. The evidence for creation is censored from our public schools by being labeled "religion" in spite of the fact that this evidence comes from every area of science including biochemistry, geology, and physics. By suppressing the scientific knowledge we have of creation, we have also eliminated the only

factual basis upon which to set standards of morality. It logically follows that all rules of sexuality and morality become arbitrary (determined only by popular

Used by permission of Chuck Asay

opinion.) Maintaining the sanctity of marriage is a losing battle until we start with the acknowledgement of our Creator. The outcome of this issue was actually decided decades ago when the majority of Christians stopped fighting for the acknowledgement of creation in public schools. The literal creation of man and woman provides the only factual historical standard for human sexual morality. If the creation story is just a myth and we did evolve from ape-like creatures; the Bible is clearly wrong in its statements concerning our origin. If the Bible is wrong about its clear statements concerning physical matters; why should it be trusted on moral matters such as marriage? Instead of allowing the evidence to be taught that we are made in the image of God, we are allowing our children to be trained that they are

made in the image of hydrogen gas and pond slime. Instead of acknowledging that man was specifically designed for fulfillment by a woman (and vice versa), we are teaching our children that any arrangement of relationships is equally acceptable.

The real battle is for absolute truth and the reality of creation. Once creation is acknowledged as fact, homosexual marriage cannot even be a consideration. Since the public acknowledgement of our literal creation has crumbled, the passive acceptance of legally sanctioning homosexual unions is essentially unstoppable. We are debating from the shifting sands of opinion instead of standing on the rock of historical fact. Our literal creation is the foundation that determines how we deal with every other significant social issue.

It is only God's Word that provides the unchangeable foundation upon which to build our culture. God's Word, starting from the very first chapter of Genesis, is invariably confirmed by scientific research and observation of the world around us. The Bible lays the framework for correctly understanding physical evidence from biology, geology, anthropology, sociology, cosmology, and every other natural science that we had a divine Creator.

Evolution & Creation Mix like Oil & Water

By Bruce Malone

Francis Bacon and most of the founders of modern science clearly understood that science could not replace faith in Christ. They realized that without an acknowledgment of God, the present could not be adequately explained. Furthermore, these outstanding scientists had stamina to proceed with scientific inquiry only because of their confidence that an orderly universe had to have had a designer. This trust in the existence of a personal God, who fashioned an intricate, interwoven universe, provided the foundation upon which to proceed with scientific inquiry.

Today's intellectuals have lost this foundational understanding of the purpose of science. The very definition of 'science' has been altered from **"acknowledged truths and laws, especially as demonstrated by induction, experiment, or observation"** (1934 edition of Webster's New School dictionary) to **"knowledge concerning the physical world and its phenomena"** (1983 edition of Websters Collegiate dictionary). This definition removes the idea that "truth" exists and relies solely on "natural phenomena." By this modern definition, God's intervention cannot even be considered because science has been *defined* to exclude this possibility.

Truth operates regardless of the opinions of man, just as gravity operates independent of belief, understanding, or interpretation. If the universe and mankind are direct creations of a personally involved God; then man's opinions and interpretations cannot change this truth.

> **"Let not man think or maintain that a man can search too far or be too well studied in the book of God's word (the Bible) or in the book of God's works (the created universe)."**
> *- Francis Bacon , Founder of the Scientific Method*

The reason that the evidence for creation is not commonly known is because our public school system has become increasingly dominated by the philosophy of humanism. The very basis of humanism is that man, not God, is the center and measure of all things. Evolution serves as the primary justification for this belief system. Thus, evolution is presented as fact in the public school system and only evidence supporting this concept is shown to students. Yet, evolution stands in sharp opposition to a Biblical worldview in the following ways:

⇒ The Bible states ten times that life reproduces only after its own kind. This is certainly true as we observe the biological world around us. Dogs stay dogs, and people stay people. Yet evolution preaches that all life is a blurred continuum.

⇒ The God of the Bible demands unselfish sacrifice for the good of others. *"...whosoever will be chief among you, let him be your servant."* (Matthew 20:27) Would this same God use a method of dead ends, extinctions, and survival of the fittest to make us?

⇒ Belief in evolution justified the excesses of the industrial revolution, the Nazi elimination of the Jews, and the rise of Marxism and Communism. It also serves as the primary justification for disbelief in God. Although believers in evolution attempt to distance themselves from taking their theory into a social realm, these historical atrocities are the undeniable result of taking evolution to its logical conclusion.

If we are a product of biological forces; why not extend these forces into our dealing with other humans? Animal groups do not lament wiping each other out in order to survive. Why shouldn't we be the same; if we are just part of an evolutionary process which formed us? Creation is the event which ultimately gives life value because it links every human's value to our Creator who loved us enough to die for us. Evolution is the opposite.

Abundant scientific evidence exists that microbe to man evolution has never taken place. The fossil record shows no credible links between major groups of plants and animals. The chemical structure of DNA contains useful information which could not have developed by natural processes. Also, there is abundant evidence for a worldwide flood which undermines the possibility that evolution could have happened.

Evolution is a religious philosophy unsupported by the majority of scientific observations. Its power to influence society has been a detriment to true scientific advancement.

Sharing the Truth does make a Difference

By Mark & Pam Johnson

The year was 1999 and the Kansas State School board dared to modify the state science curriculum to allow the dogma of evolution to be questioned. Not to teach Biblical creation... merely to allow evolution to be critically examined. The national media went crazy, accusing Kansas of driving its children back into the dark ages. The result - every school board member was replaced in the next election and the original curriculum, allowing only the one-sided evolutionary propaganda, was returned.

Fast forward to the small, rural community of Grantsburg, Wisconson, in the fall of 2004. Population - 1364. Nothing noteworthy of special attention could happen here. Or could it? While reviewing the science curriculum, the school board decided to open the door to critical thinking with regard to origins. In doing so, the gate swung open to those that oppose such considerations for public school students. This was not a simple, run of the mill rubber-stamped review. No, this time the science curriculum was critically scrutinized in a controversial endeavor which had the potential to polarize the close-knit community. Suddenly, heads turned, petitions were put in place, and lawsuits threatened to intimidate the district. Opinions flew; tempers flared. The curriculum change was THE talk of the town with much ink in the newspaper. Even the national media turned its powerful spotlight on Grantsburg in an effort to influence the activities of this tiny town in rural America.

Creation vs. evolution was again on the hot seat. Truth hung in the balance. Could common folks have a say in what was taught in their schools? Was there any tool that enabled people to hear informative, straightforward answers concerning the creation/evolution chasm?

After hearing Bruce Malone speak passionately on Twin Cities radio station WCTS, about the need to get the evidence for creation into our schools, Jean Ekblad of Grantsburg was filled with resolve. There *was* a tool which gave clear answers. After reviewing *Search for the Truth*, Mrs. Ekblad was convinced that this was what Grantsburg needed. Soon the book was in our hands and ideas began to formulate as to how to employ the *Search* articles in our community. With well-researched, ready-to-print articles, the process was unbelievably simplified.

A small band of interested and concerned people formed -- naming our enterprise "Beacon of Truth". This grass-roots board had a mission: -- allow people, often for the first time, to read about the scientific evidence for the reality of Biblical creation. Just as Samuel Adams influenced the early colonists through his written reports, Bruce Malone's writings had the propensity to herald the truth in our community about origins -- and in communities everywhere. After establishing a connection with the *Burnett County Sentinel* editor, plans were made to begin printing weekly articles. The newspaper run would last for six months, furnishing 28 well-written articles to Burnett County subscribers. As footnotes documented each article, the information was not just opinions, but a credible presentation of scientific facts. Monies to fund the project were secured by sending letters to those who seemed to take an interest in our effort. A sample article was included with the letter to give potential supporters a taste of the writings involved. Funds flowed in and the job began. The series was launched on February 9, 2005, wrapping up with the final article in the August 17 edition.

In the midst of the newspaper run was the April school board election. The origins science curriculum was a pivotal issue and candidates were quite candid with their views. The future of origins teaching was on the line. This election came down as the closest vote in Grantsburg's history, with the scale barely tipping in the favor of those who stood for creation and absolute truth. It allowed students to view all of the evidence for their origin. Every school board member who desired to allow students the freedom to view the evidence for creation was elected. Perhaps, our humble newspaper articles caused some to stop, think, and vote for truth. Perhaps, it made others reconsider issues they deemed as scientific absolutes. We will not know this side of eternity. We do believe, though, that attempting to make a difference has made a difference.

We are a small, rural community. Our population is still growing. Good things happen when the people of a community dare to make a difference. It happened here.

Mark & Pam Johnson are concerned parents from Grantsburg, WI.

Section VI:
Creation, Christianity, and the Value of Life

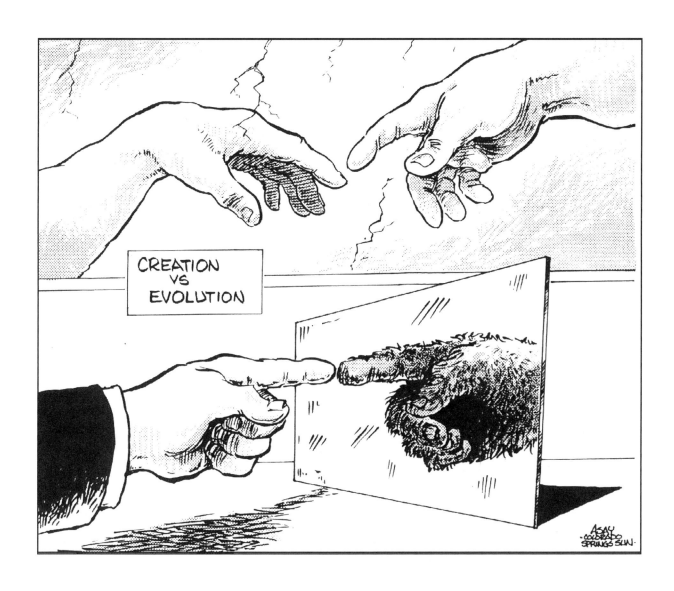

Hey Bruce,
I'm so glad you walked by my office. I can't wait to read your new book. I gave your last book, *Search for the Truth*, to my husband and it helped him come to Christ. Thank you for your ministry!

In Christ,

Sandy Mantyla

Dear Mr. Malone,
One of the pastors, visiting an inmate here left a copy of *Search for the Truth*. I stayed up all night reading the book. I was filled with the Spirit and experienced the baptism of the Spirit. A couple of articles in your book finished helping me beyond where I was able to go on my own as I also have an analytical mind and needed answers to many questions. Unfortunately, the gentleman who had your book took it with him the next day when he was bailed out. Several of us wish it was still here. Could you send more copies...

May God Bless and keep you and yours,

Brent Segars

Dear bother Bruce,

While traveling on the train in Sri Lanka the person next to me, an American, was reading *Search for the Truth*. I borrowed if from him and started reading and I thank God for raising up soldiers like you, standing for truth and boldly proclaiming the truth... Sri Lanka has 1500 abortions each day and I left my job to start a ministry reaching out to women who are thinking of killing their babies. Your book helps to show how we are designed by God. Please send more...

Yours in Christ,

Pastor Rowan Fernando

Chapter 6

How then shall they call on Him in whom they have not believed? And how shall they believe in Him whom they have not heard?...How beautiful are the feet of those who preach the gospel of peace, who bring tidings of good things!"

- Romans 10:14-15

As noted in the introduction, this book has been written for the purpose of sharing, duplicating, and distributing the good news that we have a creator and a redeemer. Unless people understand that they have rebelled against their Creator, they do not really understand that they are sinners. Therefore, the idea that they need a redeemer is foolishness to them. Not everyone is called to start a newspaper campaign to expose the faulty logic, poor science, and circular reasoning of evolutionism. However, if one person in every community would make the effort to do so, it would make an eternal difference in many people's lives. Furthermore, this is a project that anyone from a teenager to a senior citizen can undertake because the work has already been done. You may request a CD with all of the individual articles formatted in a MicroSoft Word™ document. The illustrations for each of the articles are place in a separate file so that each page can be easily formatted to fit the desired newspaper or newsletter space. In addition, the CD contains a audio file with a 45 minute talk on the relevance the Biblical creation model and a 15 minute sample of the Search for the Truth radio program. All of this comes with permission to reproduce and share with others.

It would be appreciated if you would inform us at Truth for the Search Ministries if you are planning to use any of our materials. We can be reached at ***www.searchforthetruth.net.*** Sharing the information in this book benefits everyone. The newspaper sells ad space and people in the community are exposed to a perspective they are unlikely to get anywhere else. It is a win-win situation for everybody except those who don't want the Biblical worldview to reach beyond church walls.

The most effective method of printing ***Search*** is to buy space in small community weekly newspapers. In this way ***Search*** is in every issue and the cost will be much lower than in a large circulation city newspaper. The articles tend to get lost in large city newspapers. In addition, the articles make excellent additions to any church newsletter. It is appalling how little the typical Christian knows about the scientific evidence for creation. The following tips may help as you consider whether this is something you would like to try in your community:
1. This is not an intellectual battle, but a spiritual battle.
We wrestle not against flesh and blood...but against the spiritual wickedness in high places.
(Ephesians 6:12). Pray about this. Present the concept of putting these articles into a public newspaper to some trusted friends and most importantly, take it before the Lord in prayer. If you get the confirmation to proceed; present the idea to your pastor and church. Make sure you have the full support of a core group of Christian friends before proceeding because you will likely be ridiculed and attacked. You will need their support.
2. Rotate subjects. Do not run more than 3 weeks in a row from the same subject, but try to hit all of the basics over the first 6 months. Watch the news and published stories that relate to hot topics. When the latest discovery of a new planet is announced, print an article showing the absolute impossibility of life forming by chance. On the anniversary of Roe vs. Wade; print an article on the value of life. Around Christmas or Easter print the basic Christianity series. When the latest ape-man fossil is found; print an article from the anthropology section on the bias involved in this search or the history of mistakes and deception involved in this area.
3. Sign up people to pray for the articles each week. I have found that a rotating list of seriously interested people works well. Divide up the names so there are 2 - 4 people praying each week. Send them an advance copy of the article that they are to lift up in prayer that week. This is ultimately a spiritual battle rather than an intellectual battle. Without prayer nothing will be accomplished.
4. Plan to run the articles for at least 6 months. It will take awhile to build the case for creation and shatter the blindness that has been built up over many years of evolutionary teaching.
5. Expect opposition and do not expect everyone to embrace the truth.
6. Even if you can personally pay for the project...don't. People are more intimately involved in a ministry; if they have financially contributed toward it. As hard as it is to ask for donations for a project, this helps others to buy into the vision.

7. As letters to the editor are written attacking *Search*, respond with a letter which shows how the facts of science support creation. Examples are shown in Appendix II (page 135 - 137). Every attack is an opportunity to teach the truth and letters to the editor are the most read part of a newspaper. Consider it an honor to be attacked for your Christian beliefs. It means you are having an effect. There is adequate information contained within this book to counter most objections. Feel free to reword and use any of the articles in this book, expressed in your own words, in reply to letters to the editor. Most papers will print a well worded articulate response to a personal attack. Never resort to personal attacks and name calling in your response (as many evolution believers do). This does not mean that we should not point out errors and outright lies, but we should always do it in a respectful way.

8. Add your own material or get permission to reprint materials from other authors. It will help maintain continuity if the material is related to science or creation.
   a. Keep the same format.
   b. Avoid becoming preachy. There will be time for that in personal interactions. Such a tone will cause the people you hope to reach to tune out. Do not turn the column into the sermon of the week.
   c. Have a trusted friend review and proofread your writing. We can be totally blind to our own errors and tone.
   d. Add a quote or illustration to each article to break up the text, make it more readable, and draw the reader to the article.

9. Simply do the following for each article to be published:
   a. Decide on which article to publish and provide the electronic version to the newspaper office.
   b. Proofread the final version and approve its location before publication.

Write to me if you have any comments or questions. Search for the Truth Ministries will gladly help you in any way we can. We can be reached at truth@searchforthetruth.net, or Bruce Malone, 3275 Monroe Rd., Midland, MI 48642. We would appreciate hearing about any comments and experiences you have. Hopefully, I'll be able to share them with others in the next edition!

May Jesus richly bless you as you seek to serve Him in whatever way He has prepared for you.

Suppose

By Bruce Malone

Suppose, just hypothetically, that you are an infinitely powerful god. Suppose you have the power to create the entire universe, in all of its complexity, and to see in minute detail the consequences of your actions. Because you have created the entire universe, you are not part of it and you can see everything that has happened or will ever happen within that universe from the beginning of time (time is part of the physical universe) until the end of "time".

Within this entire vast universe you decided to create one special planet made specifically for one special creature. This creature was not to be controlled by instincts but by free will. This creature was to be capable of deciding whether or not to love his maker enough to obey him. You decided upon this risky course of action because you wanted this creature to love, respond, and communicate with you from his own conscious desires. This creature occupied a very special place in your plan. In fact, everything else in the entire universe was created for the appreciation of this creature.

Suppose that this creature was mankind and this universe was our universe. Suppose that these humans you created decide to spit in your face and reject you. Since you are god, you cannot tolerate the presence of that which is now imperfect (mankind), so out of mercy you decide to curse all of creation so that imperfect man was

not surrounded by perfection (an intolerable situation). You sentence mankind to a physical death so that he will not live for eternity separated from you. However, this does not solve the problem, you still

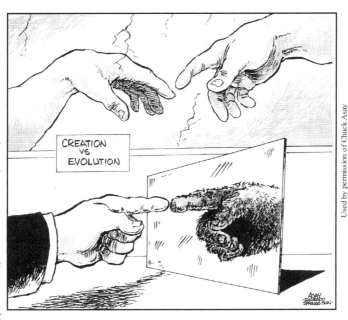

CREATION VS EVOLUTION

Used by permission of Chuck Asay

love these people and they still cannot live in your presence because they have rejected you. But you have a plan. It's the plan you had from before you ever started creating the universe.

You begin to teach mankind the eternal laws with which you built the universe. Not only physical laws, but moral laws such as, "murder is wrong", "worship only God", and "love your neighbor". And the results? Cain kills his brother Abel, men worship idols, and violence spreads across the earth. You demonstrate how much you hate sin by destroying the entire earth with a worldwide flood. The earth is filled with sediment clogged with the carcasses of the creatures you had created. Over time the sediment hardens into rock filled with fossilized bones from the

perfect world you had created. The layers of stone, sometimes miles deep, stand as a timeless silent testimony to the consequences of sin. In mercy, however, you preserved one family, because you have a plan.

Suppose that before the mud had dried, it started all over again. Instead of spreading out over the earth as you told mankind to do, they chose to stay in one place and start a monument to their own glory. Before they can complete their monument and turn to pagan worship, you confuse their languages so they are forced to spread across the globe. Now, you begin to select one special group of people for one very special purpose.

You select one man and reveal a small part of your plan to him. Your plan will span thousands of years and involve millions of people. It is a plan which could not be implemented by anyone but the creator of the universe. You promise to make a great nation of this man named Abraham and to bless the entire world through him. In spite of his repeated failures, you do not reject him but patiently continue to train him. Finally, you test his obedience by asking this father to kill his son...his only beloved son...on a lonely hillside. You start to lay a pattern for something to come.

To Be Continued...

You Have a Plan

By Bruce Malone

Suppose you are God and decide to lead a special group of people out of ancient Egypt where they had been slaves for almost 500 years. At the right time, you bring them out of Egypt with an incredible display of mighty miracles. In one final demonstration of your power, you show them that just by covering their dwelling with the blood of the most innocent of creatures -- a lamb, that they can be spared judgment. You continue to teach them a pattern. You then bring deserved judgment on an evil Egyptian nation and kill the firstborn child in every household. You separate your people from the influence of an evil world. You bring them through a sea with a wall of water on their right and a wall of water on their left to demonstrate that they are being baptized into a new life. Yet, incredibly, they immediately return to their evil ways. They build idols to other gods. They refuse to enter the land which you have provided. They are a stubborn people. But you have a plan.

Suppose you allow your chosen people to spend 40 years wandering in the wilderness in order to teach them many lessons. You teach them that they must depend wholly on you for their sustenance and that they must come back to you each day for refilling. You teach them that they will be healed only by a symbol of sin raised up on a wooden pole. You teach them that

they must put their sins upon something other than themselves because they can never pay for their own sins. You teach them that life giving water comes from a

IN JUST ONE SMALL PACKAGE GOD GAVE US HIS...
ONLY SON · FORGIVENESS · GRACE · INHERITANCE · TRUTH · ETERNAL LIFE · WISDOM · KINGDOM · SALVATION · LOVE · HUMILITY · PROVISION · RIGHTEOUSNESS · BLOOD · GUIDANCE · JUSTIFIED

Used by permission of Chuck Asay

rock. You teach them that it is only by the shedding of innocent blood that their sins can be forgiven. Each year they must bring an innocent creature - a spotless lamb - and slit its throat in a gruesome, bloody sacrifice. It makes no sense, but you are laying a pattern.

Suppose that after 40 years in the wilderness, you decide that it is finally time to bring them into a special land made just for them. You delay until the people living in that land had been given every possible opportunity to turn from their wicked ways. Then you win battle after battle for your people. You show them that you are giving this land to them. You drop walls of impregnable cities... You hurtle meteorites from space to destroy enemy armies... You stop the sun in the sky at their request... You drop giants with a single stone... You destroy entire enemy armies at the request of those who love you.

Yet, your people still refuse to obey. Time after time, you send messengers to tell your people how they are to behave. However, always they drift back into their evil ways. You tell them over and over again that you are going to send them a Savior. You tell them where He will be born. You tell them, hundreds of years before it happens, the exact day when He will enter Jerusalem and declare Himself their eternal King. You tell them that He will become their eternal sacrifice so that they can end their pitiful and hopeless pursuit of trying to work their way into your favor. You describe specific details of future events over 300 times so they will know it is you speaking with them. Their response is to kill the messengers who bring your promises and prophecies. But you love these people. Through them, you will show all people how much you love them. The time for your plan has come. The time to complete the plan which you conceived before laying the foundation of the universe -- the plan started before the first molecule was created and the first electromagnetic wave appeared... the plan laid out before the first animal was made and you breathed life, spirit, and part of yourself into these people whom you love so much... You become a man. Permanently, for all eternity, you become human.

To Be Continued...

Not What They Expected

By Bruce Malone

Suppose, at just the right time, thousands of years after history began, it was time to demonstrate to humanity what love means. You did not come to earth as an arrogant ruler... but as a humble servant to wash the feet of others. You did not arrive with fanfare and pomp, but left the glory of heaven to become a baby born in an animal stall. Your prophets had told of this... but this was not what was expected.

Suppose that you start your ministry to your people by announcing that you are the Lamb who has come to take away the sins of the world. Surely, they will understand the implication after 4000 years of teaching. You demonstrate who you are by healing sickness, casting out demons and controlling creation. Yet, they still follow you with their stomachs and not their hearts. Your prophets had told them these things would happen, but this was not what they expected.

Suppose you spend three years patiently teaching your people how to live and who you are. You repeatedly teach them that you are the rock upon which they must build their lives. You hate the arrogant lie that Your children can earn their way into Your presence. Your character is justice and justice requires payment for sin. Yet no man can pay the price. Throughout history Satan has deceived your children into believing that religion can save them. You expose the lies and hypocrisy of salvation by religious acts. You hate religion. Your harshest words are for these religious leaders. They are the ones who should know you best... but you are not whom they expected.

Suppose that the climax, which has been building since man first sinned, arrives. You pray for some other way to save mankind from his sin and to restore fellowship with you. But there is no other way.

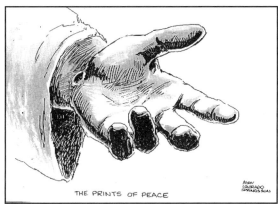

THE PRINTS OF PEACE

Used by permission of Chuck Asay

You allow yourself to be taken.

You make no defense in mock trial after mock trial because the one you represent (mankind) is guilty and deserves judgment. You allow Satan to pour his fury out upon you. You are beaten so severely that you hardly look human. You are whipped until your back resembles raw hamburger. Your beard is ripped out, thorns are thrust onto your head, you are slapped, cursed, and spit upon.

Nails are driven through your feet and wrists and you are left hanging on a pole to die. You could destroy the entire universe with a word, but you chose instead...to suffer. You become that symbol of sin lifted on a pole which will heal your people.

You become sin and take the penalty humanity deserves. You pay the price for every sin ever committed by every person in the past, present, and future. The anguish is incomprehensible. Your blood is shed for the sins of humanity. You are the innocent lamb sacrificed for others.

Suppose that three days later you rise from the dead to show them all that... at long last, they can have victory over death. Death has lost its sting. You have shown that there is nothing they can do to bridge the chasm between themselves and their Maker... you have done it all. Your forgiveness is free but they must love you more than their wickedness. You have shown them that there is no other way. There is no religious system by which they can earn their way to heaven. They have been trying to cover their sins with fig leaves from the very start. But this was not what they expected.

The plan is finally completed. The path back to you is open to all who are willing to accept it. You have done everything you could possibly do to restore fellowship between sinful man and yourself. You have satisfied the perfect justice required of your nature. You have shown absolute mercy by providing a bridge over the chasm between sinful man and a perfect God. You took the penalty which they deserved. You have made it so simple that anyone can understand it. You have done it all. But it was not what they expected.

Suppose that this is all true. It is history. It is Christianity.

It is reality.

Only One Cure for this Disease

By Bruce Malone

How can human depravity and putrid sin be explained? What would have caused the Germans in Hitler's concentration camps to torture and slaughter millions of innocent Jewish civilians? Most of those involved were not depraved maniacs, but ordinary, and often highly educated, people. Particularly puzzling is the action of the physicians involved in vile human experimentation. What would cause doctors to torture and mutilate? Robert Lifton sought an answer to this question in his book, *The Nazi Doctors*. What Lifton found was a universal denial of guilt! The doctors whom he interviewed either refused to accept responsibility, denied wrongdoing, or blamed the situation in which they were trapped. According to Lifton, "... not a single former Nazi doctor I spoke to arrived at a clear, ethical evaluation of what he had done or what he had been a part of."[1]

Such a clear window into human nature should serve as a warning beacon to each of us. We have an unquenchable desire to consider ourselves innocent. Yet, deep down, we all know that we are guilty. Abortion is ground zero in the value of life discussion. Conception is the point when a "fetus" becomes a baby. The Bible clearly speaks of unborn children as human beings[2] and makes no distinction between the value of babies before or after they are born. To discard unborn children is equivalent to playing God.

Those closest to the abortion issue - the millions of women who have had abortions, the millions of men who have coerced women into having abortions, and the tens of millions who have a friend who has had an abortion, will find it very difficult to remain objective about this subject. We all seem to have

> ## Hear
> *by Deanna Windon*
>
> **In a forest farther than remote
> A tow'ering ancient tree falls
> crashing to the earth:
> scattered limbs
> scattered bits of bark
> flying chips of wood...
> So, we philosophers sit and ponder -
> Did it make a sound
> If no one was around
> to hear?**
>
> **Hidden far away in Mama's womb
> A helpless infant child
> is shredded piece by piece
> twisted limbs
> tattered little face
> dying flesh and blood...
> So, we philosophers sit and ponder -
> Did she make a sound
> If no one was around
> to hear?**

the built in ability to guard ourselves from the pain of responsibility by denial and justification. To acknowledge guilt is to admit that some payment for the wrongful act is required. Yet, what payment could provide adequate retribution for ending the life of an innocent baby? The almost infinite ability of humanity to justify evil is part of the basic nature of sin which goes back to the very foundation of humanity. Adam's response to his sin was to hide the sin (denial); to blame Eve for the sin (rationalization), and to refuse to accept responsibility for the sin: "... *the woman YOU sent gave the fruit to me.*[3]" (Justification)

To confront abortion as an unbridled atrocity results in a shutdown of communication. However, to say nothing is not helpful to those who are already condemned by their own actions. Modern psychology has confirmed what the Bible has taught for thousands of years. Until guilt is admitted, no healing can take place. Modern man is increasingly trying to deal with guilt by denying that sin, or even guilt, exists. Other people are guilty... but never us. All religions, except Christianity, attempt to "pay off" guilt by some retributive behavior. Neither of these strategies for dealing with the reality of guilt will work. Humans feel guilty because they live in the reality of a holy God's existence. We are guilty. The very nature of a just God requires repentance before forgiveness can take place. Until we admit our sins, repent, and accept His sacrifice as payment, we can never be truly free.

As painful as it may be to admit wrongdoing, the benefit of knowing you are forgiven by the Creator of the universe is worth the pain of acknowledgment. After admission of guilt there must be more than regret. Admission of guilt is just the first step and regret is not the same as repentance. Repentance is a 180 degree change in thinking and actions. It is only by turning away from the darkness you can see the light.

1. Lifton, Robert, *The Nazi Doctors*, New York: Basic Books, 1986.
2. Psalm 139:13-16, Isaiah 49:1, Jeremiah 1:5, Judges 13:3, 6-7, Job 3:3, Job 10:18-19, Ecclesiates 11:5.
3. Genesis 3: 10-13

Verbicide: The Murder of a Word

By Bruce Malone

Over 80% of born again Christian youth no longer accept that unchangeable truth exists.[1,2] One of the consequences of this rejection of absolute truth is passively accepting the manipulation of words to advance a cause. For instance, although the word "gay" was traditionally defined as a state of happiness, it has been appropriated to describe a group of people who clinically exhibit a much lower level of happiness than the general population. "Choice" has been used as a banner to remove the most basic freedom (the freedom to live) from the most innocent of life (an unborn child). "Family" has had the long standing definition of a mother or father with children. It is currently being redefined to mean any group of people who reside together for any length of time. Rather than adding dignity to non-family groups, it undermines traditional families, the basic building block of society. Of particular concern in our society is the negative use of the word "fundamentalist".

Fundamentalist is frequently used as a label for any individual or group of people who are accused of having closed minds and of being hate filled and bigoted. It is typically used as the ultimate insult for those who dare oppose the politically correct values of the liberal media. However, accepting the fundamental beliefs of Christianity does not make you a dangerous fanatic. On the contrary, those who truly accept the classic fundamentals of the Christian faith undergo a remarkable change to become more productive citizens. What are these fundamentals? That the Bible is inspired by the Holy Spirit and therefore without error (interpretation can be erroneous but not original content); Jesus Christ is God; He died to pay the penalty for our sins and only by believing this and receiving Christ as Savior can you "get right" with God (John 1:12); He rose from the dead; He will return again. **Either these things are true or they are not.** Believing them makes you a Christian and a fundamentalist regardless of your particular denomination. Likewise, not believing them means you are not a Christian in the Biblical understanding of the term.

The Christian faith has never been a blind faith. Christianity describes the world around us, explains our history, and has a positive effect upon the lives of those who embrace it. This is not to say that Christians are perfect people or that the Church has never erred. Christians are wrong whenever they exhibit a hateful attitude. A true follower of Jesus will freely admit this. Although, the absolute truths of Christianity teach love, care, hope, and justice for all people, they do not hesitate to point out behavior which is harmful or sinful (the two are actually synonymous). To neglect to speak out on these issues is not love, but apathy.

Chuck Colson is a living example of how acknowledging Jesus Christ as Lord and Savior, and the Bible as truth, can change a person's life and attitudes. He was Richard Nixon's right hand man during the heyday of President Nixon's power. By his and others' admission, he would have steam rolled over his own grandmother to maintain his position. Twenty-five years after his conversion to the fundamental truths of Christianity, he still runs a worldwide nonprofit ministry to prison inmates. He daily confronts inmates with the reality of their sinfulness, but always with love toward the person. Chuck will often hug inmates who are dying of AIDS as a demonstration of his love for human beings made in the image of God.

The next time you hear about a fundamentalist don't picture someone who has a closed mind or is hateful and bigoted. Rather picture someone who would lay down his life in defense of the Christian principles upon which America was founded.

> **Verbicide:**
> "The murder of a word...Men often commit verbicide because they want to snatch a word as a party banner to appropriate its selling quality."
>
> *- C.S. Lewis, late Oxford English professor, from an essay entitled "Studies in Words"*

1. Josh McDowell, ***The Last Christian Generation***, Green Key Books, 2006.

2. George Barna, ***Revolution***, Tyndale House Publishers, 2005.

That's One Body that will Never be Found

By Bruce Malone

Christianity centers on the resurrection of Jesus Christ almost 2000 years ago. Did it happen or not? If this event actually happened; it is not only the focal point of Christianity, it is the most important event of all human history. If Jesus Christ rose from the dead after three days in the grave just as He predicted on four occasions prior to His death; then why would we doubt other statements He made while here on earth? How do we know that the account of the resurrection of Christ was not a complete hoax? How do we know that Jesus Christ even existed?

Historians judge the accuracy of ancient documents by several criteria. The most important of these criteria are the total number of ancient manuscripts, the time-span between the actual event described and the oldest manuscript, and how well the events described by the manuscript are confirmed by other historical events or manuscripts. No other ancient document even approaches the Bible for accuracy, total copies available, or effect upon Western culture and thought. For instance, we have only 10 ancient documents describing the Gallia wars of Julius Caesar and the oldest available document is 1000 years removed from the events described. We have only 5 ancient documents describing the life and work of Aristotle and the oldest copy is

1400 years removed from the events described. In contrast, there are over 2,000 ancient manuscripts of the New Testament Bible which are essentially identical to our modern translation.[1] The oldest

manuscript has been dated to within a single generation of the events described. If Caesar or Aristotle were real people and if we have an accurate account of their lives and statements; there is far greater evidence for the existence of Jesus Christ, the accuracy of His statements, and the reality of the events surrounding His life. This is the account of Jesus death:

Prior to His death, Jesus claimed to be God and stated that He had not come to earth to bring peace among men but to make the ultimate sacrifice in payment for mankind's rebellion against God. Because He claimed to be God, the religious authorities had him crucified. This form of death was so excruciatingly painful that no Roman citizen was allowed to be put to death in this way. Before Jesus was nailed to the cross, He was beaten beyond recognition. His final words were, "It is finished." The exact same words were written on paid bills to mean, "Paid in full."

The body of Jesus was pierced with a spear to assure that He was dead, tightly wrapped in strips of cloth coated with spices, and placed into a sealed tomb. After His execution, his closest friends fled and even denied

that they knew Him. In spite of this demonstration of cowardice by His followers, the religious leaders feared that they might try to steal the body. Therefore, they had the tomb sealed by the Roman government and guarded the tomb around the clock. Several days later, the tomb was found empty, except for the burial cloths which made it appear as if the body had just disappeared out of them (they had not been unraveled). The massive stone sealing the tomb had been moved away from the entrance. Jesus appeared on numerous times to many groups of people. On one occasion He was recognized by 500 people. The body was never found...

EITHER THESE EVENTS HAPPENED…...OR THEY DIDN'T.

The documents describing these events were widely distributed during the lifetime of those who had witnessed them and could have been refuted were they not factual. Not only were the accounts not refuted, Christianity transformed the entire Roman world in spite of incredible persecution. The amazing effect that Christianity has had on Western civilization is undeniable. In the face of these facts, what excuse do we have for denying the claims of Jesus Christ?

1. McDowell, Josh and Hostetler, Bob, ***Don't Check your Brains at the Door***, pp.52, Word Publishing, 1992.

History Validates the Resurrection

By Bruce Malone

Christianity is a faith based on real events which really happened in time and space. It is not a mystical faith based on good feelings. The miracles of Jesus were His calling card; i.e., the validation of His claim to be God. The resurrection was His proof of identification. Even more importantly, the death and resurrection of Jesus were God's method for sinful mankind to stand forgiven before Him. God's nature demands payment for wrongdoing, yet He is merciful beyond comprehension. How can these two contrasting sides of God be reconciled?

Without acknowledgment of the factual nature of the resurrection, Christianity is nothing but smoke and mirrors; just another spiritual attempt to explain reality based on man's opinion. The two most prevalent attempts to explain away Christ's resurrection will be examined in this article. In spite of the obvious historical accuracy of the Bible, there have been many alternative explanations for the missing body of Christ. Liberal theologians have even speculated that Christ's body ended up in a ditch. Yet, Jewish laws would never have allowed this.

The most popular excuse for rejecting Christianity is the idea that Christ did not really die on the cross. Although this has been suggested in recent years, rational

I EXPECT THAT'LL BE ABOUT THE LAST WE'LL HEAR FROM MR. CHRIST!

FAMOUS LAST WORDS

Used by permission of Chuck Asay

thinking will discard this idea as pure nonsense. The very idea of a man reviving after he has been brutally beaten, nailed to a cross, pierced with a spear, and tightly wrapped with suffocating cloth is ridiculous. For such a person to push aside a huge stone and sneak past trained guards is ludicrous. Even more remarkable was the effect the appearance of Jesus had on His disciples. They were transformed from a group of sniveling cowards into men who traveled the world, preaching that Jesus was God and had risen from the dead. Because of their message, all but John died horrible deaths of torture. Merely changing their story would have spared them this persecution. They had absolutely nothing to gain and everything to lose if their story wasn't true. Would a half-dead Jesus, who had dragged Himself from the tomb to their doorstep, have inspired this response?

The second attack on reality has been around since before the moment of resurrection -- the idea that the disciples stole the body. The religious leaders who had Jesus murdered, feared this possibility and took the logical precautions to prevent this from happening. The sealed tomb was guarded day and night. How could a group of "rag tag" Jewish fishermen have overpowered a group of highly trained and motivated guards? How could they have moved a huge stone and sneaked away with the body unseen and unheard? The very fact that guards were posted adds credibility to the fact of the resurrection. If any of the details reported in the Bible were false; they would have been successfully refuted by the Jewish leaders. Although they tried, they were unsuccessful in their attempt to discredit the facts of the resurrection. Evidence for the truth of the resurrection was apparent to the thousands who converted to Christianity soon after the event. The rapid spread of this persecuted faith is perhaps the greatest evidence of its reality. The facts of the resurrection were checked by converts of that day and led to changed lives. They still do today.

Christianity has nothing to fear from those honestly searching for the truth. It is based on logical evidence surrounding real events in time and space.

Pro-Abortion Arguments are Deceptive

By Bruce Malone

Justification is not a neutral term. It implies that something has been done that needs to be excused. Wherever there is justification, there is sin. A myriad of common excuses are used for the purpose of justifying abortion. Perhaps the sheer number of excuses is an indication of just how difficult it is to justify.

IT'S A FETUS - NOT A BABY

Calling a baby a fetus is mere semantics. Labeling an unborn child by the scientific name is purely an effort to depersonalize the baby in order to make the process of disposing of the baby less emotionally painful. Any woman who plans to keep her child immediately refers to the child as a baby. No one asks, "What are you going to call your fetus?" As soon as sperm and egg combine, a new human is the result. Biologically and physically, the baby is a completely separate entity from the mother. The baby is only dependent on the mother for time and nutrition to survive. Women do not give birth to guppies, cabbages, or blobs of tissue. The only reason for calling a baby anything other than a baby is to depersonalize it in order to justify its disposal.

IT'S MY BODY, I'LL DECIDE WHAT TO DO WITH IT

As soon as a woman becomes pregnant, her body becomes two bodies. At first a young baby may not resemble a human, but it is one, and not long after conception, it is easy to recognize as human. The developing baby is a different entity from the mother and, half the time, is of a different sex. An unborn child carries innumerable characteristics that distinguish it from its mother.

The most basic purpose of any society is to provide justice and assure order. Almost every law places some kind of control over how we use our bodies. We are not free to strike other people except in self defense, drive a car in a reckless manner, or steal the property of others. For the good of

society as a whole, we are not even allowed to use certain addictive drugs or commit suicide. Justifying the disposal of an unborn baby by claiming it is part of the woman's body is biologically illogical and culturally inconsistent with other laws which protect innocent life.

EVERY CHILD SHOULD BE A WANTED CHILD

Everyone is "unwanted" by someone at sometime, but this is never considered adequate justification for murder. Why should it be considered valid justification for the disposal of an unwanted child? There is no shortage of dedicated couples who would gladly adopt and raise a child rather than see it aborted. Mother Theresa pleaded with mothers to send their children to her rather

than killing them before birth. This was no idle gesture. Dedicated Christians are willing to raise these children regardless of race or other circumstances surrounding the child's conception. If the money our government has put into encouraging abortions was used to streamline and encourage adoption; there wouldn't be any unwanted babies.

SOME BABIES ARE BETTER OFF NOT BEING BORN

Does the prospect of poverty or physical handicap justify disposing of a child before it is born? If so, why not use the same rational to dispose of a child after it is born? Countless accounts of marvelous accomplishments by physically handicapped people attest to the remarkable value of every human life. Helen Keller (deaf and blind) and Steven Hawkins (a brilliant physicist who can currently control nothing, but eye movement) are just two examples that show a person's worth is not dependent upon a perfect body. Even more numerous are people who have risen to the height of human accomplishment from the depths of human poverty.

If there is any established fact of human existence, it is that material wealth does not assure happiness and fulfillment. Disposing of babies based on affordability is the ultimate in selfishness. It is also the clearest possible representation of a lack of trust in the providence of God! Women in poverty are a social concern, but allowing them to destroy their unborn children has obviously not removed their poverty. Furthermore, our society has certainly not improved in the 40 years since it has become "legal" for mothers to kill their unborn children.

The Intolorance of TRUE Tolorance

By Bruce Malone

The most highly valued virtues in our culture were once honesty, bravery, hard work, and compassion. Today, the most highly valued virtue is tolerance. If you doubt this, ask your child what they believe is the most important teaching of Jesus. I was shocked a few years ago when the response of my son was, "Do not judge others".

Only God can accurately judge a person's heart and we are commanded to forgive others but... we are also told to hold each other accountable. How can we hold each other accountable without judging actions against some absolute standard? Even when Jesus forgave the woman caught in adultery his parting words were, *"Go and sin no more."*

A prime example of the removal of any absolute standard for moral judgement is the acceptance of homosexuality. The Bible clearly teaches that men and women were created separately for the purpose of forming a permanent union in order to complete each other. The Bible also clearly and repeatedly states that homosexuality is a sinful perversion of God's creation. However, in recent years, both the authority of the Bible and the acknowledgment of creation has been rejected by our society. Therefore, upon what basis can anyone argue that there is anything wrong with homosexuality? Once a source of absolute truth outside of ourselves (such as the Bible) is rejected, there is no logical basis upon which to condemn any activity

as immoral. In other words, unless you are willing to defend the Bible as absolute truth (and there is plenty of good objective evidence upon which to do so), you have already lost the battle. You are

"HEY, NO PRAYING HERE ... THIS IS A PUBLIC BEACH!"

merely stating your opinion as to what is morally acceptable. Why should your opinion be more valid than someone else's opinion?

As soon as we stop reasoning from a foundation which acknowledges an absolute source of right and wrong (and our entire legal system was founded on this principle), it is only a matter of time before we are forced to accept whatever norm society decides is acceptable. As we are no longer basing right and wrong on the absolute truth of the Bible, it will not be long before every organization from the Boy Scouts to churches is forced to accept homosexuals as leaders. After all, how dare such organizations be allowed to be intolerant.

Part of the problem is that the working definition of tolerance has been distorted. Today, the world insists that all opinions are to be respected as equally valid.

Unfortunately, this rule holds true only insofar as the world's beliefs are concerned. Take for instance, the stance on evolution. Evolutionists insist that their view of our origin is the ONLY correct answer, but do not consider themselves "intolerant." However, any Christians who insist that Biblical creation is reality ARE labeled as intolerant.

Biblical tolerance is acknowledging the dignity of all people because they have been created in the image of God. Biblical tolerance is loving homosexuals even as you cry over their spiritual blindness. Biblical tolerance is not persecuting another person just because they are wrong in beliefs or actions. However, this does not mean that there will not be consequences to their actions. True love, compassion, and tolerance confronts someone who is destroying their lives with sin.

If you doubt that the definition of tolerance has shifted; try telling your co-workers that homosexuality is a sin or that abortion is the execution of an innocent human being. You will be labeled intolerant so fast it will make your head spin. It doesn't matter that this is clearly what the Word of God states. It doesn't matter that the scientific evidence supports that homosexuality is an unhealthy life-style and that abortion is the killing of another human being. Since opinions must all be given equal validity in the name of tolerance, stating that someone else's opinion is wrong makes you intolerant.

Why Should the Innocent Pay?

By Bruce Malone

This article examines More of the numerous excuses used to justify abortion.

SEX EDUCATION WILL END THE NEED FOR ABORTIONS

This line of reasoning assumes that teaching children how to have sex, without having children, will prevent abortions. However, like many abortion justifications, this flies in the face of reality. Experience has shown that morally neutral or valueless sex education increases experimentation, pregnancy, and sexually transmitted diseases. Since 1970, when our government started major contraceptive programs, teenage pregnancy has increased 87% and teenage abortions are up 67%.[1] "Safe sex" is a farce... Scientific studies have shown that even under properly controlled situations condoms fail to prevent pregnancy as much as 15% of the time.[2] Giving them to teenagers and implying they allow for "safe sex" is ridiculously irresponsible. Human beings, including teenagers, are not animals controlled purely by hormones. Pregnancies can be prevented much more successfully by teaching young people the important and logical reasons why it is preferable to wait until marriage to have sex.

RAPE OR INCEST VICTIMS SHOULD GET ABORTIONS

Life isn't fair. We have not lived in a paradise since Adam and Eve chose rebellion over obedience. We do not even have the right to expect perfection or fairness. Throughout life, many people have had to bear different burdens. Fortunately, God promises comfort and help in bearing these burdens if we will only turn toward Him instead of away from Him. Why should the baby resulting from rape pay the death penalty while the man responsible for the violent act gets off with a lesser penalty? What did

SOUND FAMILIAR?

the baby do wrong? Should a child conceived in an act of violence have to pay the price for that sin? If so, why? For those who insist on absolute fairness, what is fair about ending the life of the unborn child because of what a sinful man has done to an innocent women? Furthermore, it will do nothing to remove the agony which the woman has already endured and often just piles guilt on top of the pain. Two wrongs never... ever, make a right. Encouraging adoption is the more compassionate response for victimized women.

THE ABORTION PILL WILL END NEED FOR ABORTIONS

Similar promises were made when "THE PILL" was developed in the 50's with the promise of sex without consequences. Abortions really became popular after that promise failed.[1] "Have sex, take a pill, be happy" seems to be the theme surrounding the "morning after" abortion pill. These chemicals are designed to cause a woman's body to kill and spew out the baby which is growing inside her or to prevent the baby from attaching to the mother's womb. In widespread use, they are likely to cause the deaths of many women from uncontrolled vaginal bleeding.[2] In addition, they are only 80% to 95% effective so many women end up with later term surgical abortions to finish the job the abortion pill botched. Taking an abortion pill does nothing to quell the guilt which often accompanies the killing of an unborn child. Perhaps it should be marketed in a twin pack along with a conscience killing pill.

One final fact: The abortion pill will not protect women from the more than 20 incurable and potentially deadly venereal diseases which run rampant among the general population. Once marketed, it will be relied upon to the detriment of the users. The abortion pill is yet another subtle evil which will bring harm to the women whom it is supposed to help.

1. Elise F. Jones, *"Contraceptive Failure in the United States,"* **Family Planning Perspectives**, 21:103 (May/June 1989).
2. Lamsey, Lauie, *"Abortion Made Easy: The RU486 Peril,"* **Citizen Magazine**, Vol. 3, No. 8, Aug. 1989.

Death with Dignity

By Bruce Malone

Evil often masquerades as good. There is no more fitting example than the righteous facade of the "right to die" movement. The organizers of this movement sound so caring and compassionate that many people find themselves unwittingly supporting the concept without comprehending its consequences. They do not realize, or perhaps refuse to acknowledge, the effect of legitimized suicide on society.

The crux of the *"right to die"* discussion is not whether any person has the right to end his/her life. The real argument is about whether our government should sanction the killing of one person by another. The right to die crowd never speaks of the issue in these terms because it is so much easier to sell the idea of *"death with dignity"* or not *"forcing"* a person to live in pain. In this day of rights for everything, the right to be killed by the physician of your choice seems to be the latest in an ever growing list.

The fact remains that people can kill themselves any time they want to. No government on earth can prevent its citizens from killing themselves. From drug overdoses to carbon monoxide poisoning, there are dozens of ways people end their lives. What the right to die advocates are really after is the legitimization of suicide. By making an activity legal, it quickly becomes legitimate in the eyes of many. Euthanasia advocates ultimately wish to use the government to sanction and promote assisted suicide. Modern examples of the speed with which legitimization takes place can be found in both the abortion *"rights"* and homosexual

Used by permission of Wayne Stayskal

"rights" movements. Who would have believed that only a few decades after legalizing abortion, over 40 MILLION babies would be disposed of before birth?

The inevitable result of a society which accepts assisted suicide as a social norm will be the subtle (and later not so subtle) pressure on older Americans to allow themselves to be killed. Assisted suicide laws start with many limitations, but history has shown the limitations are soon ignored. As the massive group of baby boomers head toward retirement, the pressure on older Americans to commit suicide will mushroom. By pushing to legalize murder and make the act of suicide easier, we are creating our own hell on earth.

Rather than speculating on the cultural effect of legalizing doctor-assisted suicide, a look at the Dutch system which has allowed the practice for decades should be enough to chill the effort in other countries. The disposal of people is so common in Holland that many elderly are afraid to drink their orange juice in hospital for fear they may be *"helped along"* in their deaths. As many as 25% of all deaths in that country are now assisted.[1]

Few deaths are without pain or discomfort. As our bodies wear out, discomfort is inevitable. One person's unbearable pain is another person's testimony to character. I have witnessed the painful and slow death of loved ones. Had those individuals been pressured to opt for the easy way out, hundreds of others would have missed living testimonies of courage and faith. Death with dignity is trusting your Creator rather than pretending that you don't have one.

We live in an age where there are more drugs for pain suppression than at any other time in history, yet we are on the verge of legalizing murder as the compassionate solution to stopping pain! Death is a door through which each of us must pass. Let us leave the handle of that door in the hand of Jesus, who knows what we have left to accomplish for Him on this side of the door.

1. Rita Marker, The International Anti-euthanasia Task Force, from an interview with James Dobson broadcast on the Focus on the Family radio program, Oct. 1991.

From Goo to You by Way of the Zoo

By Bruce Malone

On June 10, 1993, President Clinton signed a document allowing for taxpayer money to fund research using aborted baby parts. With the stroke of a pen, abortion was given an appearance of legitimacy. In anticipation of this event, Newsweek magazine devoted its February 22 , 1993 cover story to *"Cures from the Womb."* Dr. Gary Hodgen, a researcher at Eastern Virginia Medical College, stated that President Clinton's January 23 announcement supporting fetal tissue investigations was "the greatest day for science since the Scopes' Monkey Trial."

Why would these two seemingly unrelated events be singled out as the most significant advances in science in the last century? Why bypass all of the incredible scientific advances of the twentieth century and link the Scopes' monkey trial to the legitimization of research on aborted babies?

To answer this, the reader must understand both the reality of fetal research and the significance of the Scopes' monkey trial. Some fetal research is most effectively carried out on fetal parts which are as fresh as possible. Brain cells and organs of a baby deteriorate rapidly once deprived of oxygen so they are more valuable for research if they are extracted while the baby is still alive. However, this is a complication for the abortionist because legally every effort must be made to keep a breathing baby alive once it has been removed from the mother's birth canal. Therefore, one abortion technique is to use forceps to pull everything except the baby's head out of the mother's body. The skull is then

PARTIAL-BIRTH ABORTION (FULL VIEW)

STEP 5 BRAIN REMOVAL

STEP 5 CONSCIENCE REMOVAL

Used by permission of Chuck Asay

crushed and the brain is sucked out. After the brain has been removed, the baby's body is sliced open and other desired parts are extracted.

Even at 3 months, the baby looks like a miniature human being. It has brain waves, a functioning heart, and miniature human organs (which is why the researcher is interested in extracting them). What events have led our society down this immoral, barbaric, low road?

In 1925, the ACLU set in motion the events leading to one of the most famous trials in history - the Scopes' monkey trial. There has been both inaccurate and biased reporting of the events surrounding this trial, but the result is undeniable. The Scopes' trial was a turning point in American education. The accuracy of the Bible was openly ridiculed and evolution replaced creation as the most widely accepted explanation for our origin. Thus, almost a century after this historic trial, we have reached the point in America where our children are being taught that evolution is a fact and that we all came from simple life forms by natural processes. Is it any wonder classes on self esteem are now necessary?

As one writer aptly described the situation, we are teaching our children that, "You came from goo by way of the zoo." The atrocity and injustice of using the most helpless of human lives for research could be tolerated only after our society was conditioned to accept that there is nothing particularly sacred about human life. If we are just highly evolved animals; then why not do everything possible to understand our biological situation and improve it -- even if this entails sacrificing a few million babies in the process?

As the great Christian philosopher, Francis Schaeffer, predicted, once a source of absolute truth is denied, we will increasingly ignore injustice and tragedy in order to maintain personal peace and affluence.[1] Complacency has replaced the striving for truth and freedom upon which this country was founded. The right for an unborn child to live has already been removed. We should carefully ponder whose rights and lives will be curtailed next.

1. Francis Schaeffer, **How Should We Then Live?**, Crossway Books, 1976.

Trust is Faith Acted out in Obedience

By Bruce Malone

Two words summarize most of the teaching of the Bible, and if followed, lead to an incredibly fulfilling life. Yet, few people succeed in implementing this simple Biblical principle. Obeying these two words will save you from countless hours of mental and physical anguish and sleepless nights. These words are simply, *"Trust Me"*.

God values two things above all else in our lives – faith and obedience. These two things together are what define "Trust". Without faith, we can never please God and obedience is the action which demonstrates that our faith is real. Trust is simply faith acted out in obedience.

Mankind's natural tendency is to trust the world and ourselves rather than God. That is why we are told to, *"Die [to yourself] daily."* (I Corinthians 15:31) Furthermore, we are locked in an invisible spiritual battle of which most people are not even aware. We have an enemy who longs to destroy us and his primary weapon is to deceive us into putting our trust into something other than our Maker. Throughout our lives, we will be tempted to transfer our trust away from God and into material wealth, friends, our own accomplishments, or religion. Yet each will prove itself unsatisfying and we will look for some other source of meaning, purpose, and peace. Only a real relationship with the One who created each of us can fully satisfy our deep desire for meaning in life. So how do we hold onto this trust in God? One way is to maintain an unshakable understanding of who God is as our Creator.

Used by permission of Chuck Asay

1. God is not part of the created universe any more than a painter is a part of his painting. God made the universe, He actively holds it together, and He entered into it as Jesus Christ… but He is not trapped inside what He created.

2. Time is a part of the physical universe. Time is not constant but varies with mass and acceleration. God is not trapped inside time anymore than a chef is trapped inside his souffle. As one prophet stated, *"God inhabits eternity."* (Isaiah 57:15).

3. Since God is outside time, He instantly sees the past, the present, and the future. Even before the first molecule was created and time began, God knew every person, action, tear, and tragedy that would ever happen. Nothing surprises God.

When the reality of these three truths really sinks in, you become free to completely trust God. You understand that He is in absolute control. Even though He chooses not to violate our free will, His ultimate plan cannot be thwarted and He has promised that He will not allow anything in our lives without giving us the ability to endure it. (I Cor. 10:13)

Furthermore, we are promised that all trials and tribulations will ultimately be for our own good and for His glory. (Romans 8:28). Finally, God has the ability to take care of our financial, physical, emotional, and spiritual needs (Matt. 10:28 - 31). If He chooses not to give us what we think we need, this too is for our own good (Jn 16:33).

If you only trust Jesus with your heart; you will live on an emotional roller coaster waiting for the next spiritual high. If you only trust Jesus with your mind; your faith will be dry and powerless. If you only trust Jesus with your strength; you won't be able to tap into His strength so you will ultimately burn out.

Trust Jesus with all of your heart, all of your mind, and all of your strength.

131

Appendix I:
Original Creation Class Notice

Only one view of human origins is currently taught in our public schools and colleges. As a result, many people are not aware of how well the scientific evidence supports a different view.

"Human Origins: Scientific Evidence for Creation" will be the topic of a ten-week seminar held on Sunday mornings at the First Presbyterian Church, 65 N. Third St., Newark. All sessions are free, open to the public and start at 9:15 a.m. Child care will be available. We invite you to attend any or all of

SEPTEMBER 9 - OVERVIEW OF THE COURSE
Why are there widely varying interpretations of the same physical evidence? How can science speak to this issue? Why is this subject directly relevant to your life and thinking? This class will include clear definitions of the evolution and creation models of life's origin.

SEPTEMBER 16 - THE FOSSIL RECORD
Fossils are superficially used as the best evidence for evolution: But do they support or refute evolution? A close examination of what fossils tell us about the history of the world. Which model of origins do they best fit? Why are there still no fossils linking major animal groups after 100 years of extensive searching?

SEPTEMBER 23 - WORLDWIDE GEOLOGY
Does the geology of the Earth show slow gradual change over eons of time or rapid catastrophic change? We will examine evidence that the geology of our present world is the result of massive catastrophic forces of the past. We will discuss the implications of viewing most geology as the result of a worldwide flood event.

SEPTEMBER 30 - THE ICE AGE, THE ARK, AND DINOSAURS
Where did the water for a worldwide flood come from and go to? Is the story of Noah believable, How does the ice age fit in? Where do dinosaurs fit into the creation view of earth history?

OCTOBER 7 - THE ORIGIN OF MAN
Your children are taught that it is a fact that man evolved from ape-like creatures. An examination of where the search for ape-man stands.

OCTOBER 14 - CHEMICAL ORIGIN OF LIFE
A look at the chemistry of life. The probability that this chemistry could have happened by chance. What are the required conditions and chemistry at each stage of the proposed evolutionary scenario?

OCTOBER 21 - THE AGE OF THE EARTH & DATING METHODS
The mathematical assumptions involved in all dating methods. How valid are these assumptions? A look at many methods which indicate a "young" earth. Why the most widely accepted dating method (carbon 14 dating) gives excessively old dates.

OCTOBER 28 - THERMODYNAMICS AND NATURE
Why the most basic law of science rules out the development of life from non-life. The world around us testifies to design, purpose, and interdependence. A look at how living organisms don't fit the evolutionary model for their development.

NOVEMBER 4 - MOUNT ST. HELENS EXPLOSION
Undeniable evidence for how massive geologic changes can take place rapidly. A documented slide presentation on the rapid deposition of hundreds of feet of layered rock strata, the rapid development of massive river beds, and a mechanism for rapid coal formation.

NOVEMBER 11 - SO WHAT?
This will be a summary session re-examining the evidence from all of the areas of science. Is there enough evidence to determine the true origin of life? What are the implications of your belief system about origins? Come, let us reason together.

These fellow workers, friends, and scientists believe the data fits the creation model for origins:

Name	Credential	Name	Credential	Name	Credential
Jerry Adkins		John & Lavina Grubaugh		Wayne & Carol Nichols	BS Elec. Eng.
Gus Andrews		Susan Gualtieri		Mitch & Shelley Nicholson	
David Aschenbeck	Ph.D. Chem. Eng.	David & Donna Haas		Joseph & Carol Ogg	
		Peg & Charles Hardy Jr.		Claudie & Allene Owens	
Pearl Bell		Molly Harris		Ray Palm	
Bill Bertram		David Hartman	BA Chem. & MS Plas.Eng.	Fred & Bernadine Paul	
Paul & Linda Busta		Jeff & Lynn Hartman		Betty Place	
Roger Bilen	BS Mech. Eng.	John & Marilyn Hauck	M Ed. Adjunct Prof.	Mary Priest	
Earl Bishop		Lew & Joy Hildreth		Linda Rector	
Robert Blamer		Doug Hofmann	MS Geology & Minerology	Paul & Mary Rector	
Ken Bow	BS Elec. Eng.	Brian Hopkins		Jack & Jeanette Redman	
Fred Bretz		Robbe Hotchkiss		John Reeb	
Don Bugg	BS Chem. Eng.	Tom Huff	Ph.D. Chemistry	Mr. & Mrs. Carl Rinehart	
Kathy Bullock	BS Biology & Chem.	Ron Iden		Mr. & Mrs. Larry Ritchey	
Karen Burkey		Denzil & Mae Jones		Dave Roodvoets	BS Pkg. Eng.
Walte & JoCarey Carlisle		Joe Jones	MS Eng. Physics	Kevin Rose	Science Lab Tech.
David Chaas		Jean Jones		Steve & Virginia Rosenow	
Ronald & Emmy Clark		Rob & Beth Kelch	MS Chem. Eng./BA Sci. Ed.	John & Betsy Salladay	BS Chem. Eng.
David & Jeanette Coakley		Mark & Monica Kocik		Steve & Sharyl Sands	
Ron & Eve Deibel	BS Chemistry	Mark Kovac	Science Lab Tech.	Jerry Severson	MS Chem. Eng - PE
Mr. & Mrs. Henry Derexson		Dr. Keith Kulow	BS Biology & Med. Doctor	Dave Shelly	
Sheila Dailey		Al & Linda Leech	BA Science Ed.	Creston Shmidt	BA Botany
David & Melissa Dahlberg	BA Science Ed	Mike & Mary Levingston		Don & Sharon Shmidt	BS Chem. Eng./ RN
Kim Dershem		Mr. & Mrs. W. Lockhart		Carl Strauss	Ph.D. Polymer Sc.
J. Michael Demko		Mark Long		William Streicher	MS Ceramic Eng.
Jeff & Carol Dudley	BS Ch. Eng./BS Ch Eng.	Paul Lumbatis		William & Nancy Sweeney	
Russ Elright		Joe & Pat Mahon	RN	Kellie Tanner	
Virginia Elliott		Becky Mahon	BS Chemistry	Tom & Marilyn Thompson	MS Mech. Eng.
Sheryl Ewing		John & Linda Mattis		Quey Tsay	Ph.D. Chem. Eng.
Faith Felomiee		Bruce & Robin Malone	BS Ch. Eng./BS Ch. Eng.	Don & MaryAlice Turner	
Bob Furbee		Mary Mantonya		John Uible	
Shante Gambrel		Larry & Mary Mansfield		Charles & Gladyse Vanoy	
Gaye & Laura Gibson	RN	Angie & Ruth Miller		Dorothy Velts	
Wayne and Laura Gibson	Ph.D. Chem. Eng.	Carl and Sharon Miller		Steve & Shelia Vogelmeier	Elec. Eng./RN
David & Laurel Gilem		Susan Moeller	BS Chem. Eng.	Dee Weekly	
Paul & Margaret Gleckler		Eula Montgomery		Mark & Lee Weick	BS Chem. Eng./BA educ.
Clair & Sue Graham		Mr & Mrs. P. Morehouse Jr.		Jim Wells	BS Mech. Eng.
Florence Gregg		C. Arthur Morrow		Jim & Deanna Windon	BS Ceramic Eng.
Jim & Taree Grimes	Science Lab tech.	Theresa Muston		Andra & Richard Wright	
JoAnn Gross		Kevin & Edie Nethers		Mary & Brian Wright	

If you cannot attend, ask them about the facts behind this model of origins.

Appendix II:
Typical Letters to the Editor

Creationism has no place in science education (Midland Daily News 12/29/99)

To the Editor,

...It is my opinion that the study of a science education program should remain pure, relying on scientific theories, facts, and methods. It should remain free from all creation myths, religious doctrines, and political authority decisions. [Malone and others] would like to accomplish in Midland what creationists have been advocating in America for years - the inclusion of the Biblical story of Genesis in the teaching of evolution science. If incorporated into the Midland public schools' science program; this would deprive Midland students from getting a sound science education. Students should be given the opportunity and support to develop free minds and learn unadulterated science, free from religious doctrines, supernaturalism, and political authority decisions.

[As explained in certain popular evolution books] it would truly be a wonderful experience for students to learn the scientific theories of nuclear, chemical, biological, and anthropological evolution. However, with the interjection of creationism into the science education program, the excitement of learning these theories would be diminished. Alternatively, for those students who are interested in creation mythologies, they should be given the opportunity to study mythical creation stories in comparative religion or mythology couses.

As a free thinker, I would be incensed, deeply troubled and feel denied of my human rights to a science education; if a political authority decided that I would not be tested on my knowledge of the theory of evolution and I would be denied the opportunity to learn the Big Bang theory. Further, the interjection of the story of creation as told in Genesis into the study of evolution science would deprive me of developing a free and open mind. The Kansas Board of Education and Creationism smack of authoritarianism...

- Richard Maltby, Midland, MI

Some facts a reader wants taught
(Midland Daily News 12/29/99)

To the Editor,

There have been several items in the MDN lately discussing the origin of the universe and the human species. Unfortunately, much of the discussion has focused on the religious aspects of the arguments, while the facts have been ignored.

As a father, I hope our schools can get beyond the blind dogma and teach our kids the facts and how to think about them critically. I would like to see my children taught in the Midland Public Schools:

No scientist has experimentally created life out of lifeless chemicals, nor has anyone demonstrated the mutation of one kind of creature into another. No one has detected life anywhere but on Earth.

...In 1842, coal miners in Germany found an obviously human skull in the middle of a coal seam. In 1958 coal miners in Italy found a human jawbone in what was thought to be "20-million-year-old rock". In 1975, a rock collector in Utah found the lower halves of two human skeletons in "100-million-year old rock".

...The moon perfectly blocks out the sun during a solar eclipse. If its diameter were just 140 miles smaller, we would never see the sun's beautiful corona. The moon is 400 times closer to us than the sun and its diameter is exactly 400 times smaller. The chance of even this one design feature happening by accident is remotely small.

...The present world population on Earth would have developed from a single family in *just 4,000 years* if the growth rate were 0.5%, or an average of only 2.5 children per couple. That is 1/4 of the current world population growth rate and easily accounts for long periods of no growth due to wars and famine.

It is unfortunate that the U.S. Supreme Court ruled in 1987 that states cannot provide a presentation of a creation alternative to the theory of evolution in the public schools... For many years, I subscribed to the mandated view. I religiously watched PBS programs and read *Discover* and *Scientific American*, all of which chanted the evolution mantra. But they never really answered the questions with hard facts -- they just told stories.

I finally asked God to help me understand the truth. He did. I found lesser known books highlighting the kind of facts stated above. I went and looked for myself -- the American Southwest is full of evidence of a massive flood and rapid mountain building -- not millions of years old as commonly preached. Anyone who goes there with open eyes will see it too. Your readers should ask God to open their eyes. He will happily oblige.

- Richard Worden, Midland, MI

Intelligent Design not Really About Science (Midland Daily News 5/25/01)

To the Editor,

The claim that "intelligent design," as an alternative to evolution, is just another scientific theory, raises a question: If only a tiny minority of practicing scientists subscribes to this viewpoint; why does it deserve equal time in the classroom?

Scientific progress inevitably involves conflicts between rival interpretations of observations. Disagreements can be acrimonious, and sometimes endure for generations. Nevertheless, I can't recall another field in which a dissenting camp of scientists sought to promote its viewpoint by sponsoring laws to force its presentation in pubic schools. Scientists don't operate this way. The battle between competing hypotheses is carried out in professional meetings and journals, not in state legislatures. Scientists proposing new ideas focus on selling them to their peers, and assume that textbooks will be revised appropriately, if they succeed.

The fact that "creation science" advocates (who are mainly non-scientists) have sought to short-circuit the normal peer review process is a dead giveaway that their real agenda has little to do with science. Rather, they are continuing a more than 30-year-old campaign to modify the presentation of biology in the public schools to remove conflicts with the tenets of fundamentalist protestant Christianity. This movement has been forced to alter its tactics several times when previous approaches were invalidated by the courts. The current strategy, which involves down playing the religious motivation behind the legislation and invoking intellectual freedom, is disingenuous.

The harm in reducing the emphasis given to evolution in education is that without this unifying framework, the facts of biology lose much of their relevance, as well as much of their fascination. The intricate tapestry of life's history is reduced to a jumble of unrelated threads. This would be a disservice not only to students with the potential for careers in bioscience and medicine, but also to society at large. In the coming century, issues related to advances in biology are likely to assume a prominence in public policy... A society whose members are better educated in matters biological will be better equipped to face these challenges.

- Alan Wolfe, San Francisco, CA

Evidence Suppressed (Midland Daily News 6/14/01)

To the Editor,

It never ceases to amaze me the extent to which people will suppress evidence that contradicts their beliefs. On May 18, a letter was published which stated that the scientific evidence for creation should not be shown to students because creation was religion - yet no attempt was made to refute the factual nature of the evidence. A second letter stated that creation evidence should be suppressed because it does not fit the current narrow definition of science – yet "science" has been arbitrarily redefined in the twentieth century to specifically exclude the conclusion that an intelligent designer was involved. A third letter on May 25 stated that students should not be allowed to see the scientific evidence for creation because the majority of scientists don't support it. The same poor logic was used to suppress the truth of Galileo's observations that the earth revolved around the sun in 1633. The battle against Galileo was not started by Catholic officials, but by Galileo's colleagues and scientists, who were afraid of losing position and influence. They used the power of the church to do their dirty work. Today the majority scientific opinion (using a definition of science which excludes the consideration of evidence pointing to an intelligent designer) uses our public education system (instead of the church) to accomplish the same suppression of truth. How little human nature has changed in 400 years.

Dr. Michael Behe, professor of biochemistry at Lehiegh University, makes the following concluding statement after filling his 250 page book, *Darwin's Black Box*, with scientific evidence for intelligent design, *"The results of the cumulative efforts to investigate life at the molecular level is a loud, clear, piercing cry of 'design!'...this triumph of science should evoke cries of 'Eureka' from ten thousand throats...Instead, a curious, embarrassed silence surrounds the stark complexity of the cell."* The reason for this embarrassed silence when confronted with the intelligent design of the cell is three–fold. 1) Allegiance to the relatively recent redefinition of science which eliminates the consideration of intelligent design. 2) Fear that if God is ever acknowledged, "intervention by god" will be used to explain everything. 3) Unwillingness to ever acknowledge that an intelligent creator exists because this implies accountability.

Not one of the recent letters, defending the current one-sided teaching of only evolutionary evidence, had the goal of encouraging students to seek the truth. Let's make searching for the truth the real goal of science education by allowing students to see all of the evidence for both creation and evolution.

- Bruce Malone, Midland, MI

What Science Is and Isn't
(Midland Daily News 11/30/05)

To the Editor,

Science is the understanding of how the natural world operates through verifiable experiment, and the use of that knowledge to predict future actions. This understanding is gained through observation, hypothesis, and experiment...

The reliance of science on natural laws not changing is not based on one's "worldview." The concept of gravity is not true because Sir Isaac Newton put his "faith and trust in science," but because it has been proven valid and has led to the explanation of many natural phenomena (the tides of the ocean, the rotation of the planets around the sun).

The Kansas State Board of Education recently voted to remove the statement that science is the study of "natural explanations for the world around us," which means that, in the State of Kansas, science can also include the study of the supernatural. There are two objections to this action. First, what is scientifically valid is not determined by the vote of a political body. Secondly, the definition of the supernatural is that which cannot be defined by natural laws , i.e., science.

Scientists and engineers...do not rely on the supernatural to prevent chemical reaction from running out of control in their everyday operations; they rely on tried and true scientific concepts that do not change at the whim of the supernatural.

There also seems to be a misconception among religious fundamentalists that if one accepts science, then one must disavow God. This is absolutely not true. Science is used to explore and understand how the world works; it does not explain how it began, why we are here, or why only humans have a moral conscience - a soul. However, such discussions are outside the realm of science, as the arguments to these questions cannot be tested by experiment. They are best left to the fields of theology and philosophy, not the science classroom.

As to the debate over evolution, it has been tested over time and is the basis of large fields of biology and modern medicine (genetics, molecular biology, virus research on aids, and influenza). Intelligent design (creationism) is based on beliefs that cannot be tested by experiment. What experiment can prove, or disprove, that all things were designed by some unknown entity? There isn't one. Intelligent design is theology masquerading as science.

- Scott G. Gaynor, Midland, MI

No Proof
(Midland Daily News 12/21/05)

Scott Gaynor's letter of 11/30/05 is typical of the litany of logistical errors promoted by those who wish to keep the evidence for creation out of our schools. The following strategy is repeatedly used by those who advocate "evolution only" education: 1) Define science to exclude the possibility of a creator. 2) Claim that all the evidence for our designer is "not science" and therefore cannot be shown. 3) Repeat, like a mantra, statements such as "evolution is the basis of [science]" that imply that microbes to man evolution is a proven fact. Then give examples of minor changes within organisms as "proof" that one organism can change into a completely different type, while using the same word, 'evolution', for both the small and the enormous changes.

The actual scientific evidence for major evolutionary transformation is non-existent. No experiment ever preformed has come remotely close to showing how life could form from chemicals. Major problems with origin of life experiments are systematically hidden from students – after all, we can't have students considering the only other alternative (creation), can we? No experiment has shown how useful functioning information can be added to the DNA molecule by random changes. Yet it can be experimentally demonstrated that every known mutation results in a net loss of original functioning information. Why aren't we training students to ask the big question - where did all of this original functional information come from? Acknowledgment of a designer gives a mechanism that agrees with known scientific observations; evolution relies on faith that denies experimental reality.

Evolution believers say creation is not science because it is not testable or repeatable. In actuality, the creation model is far more testable than the concept that microbes have turned into man by random mutational changes. Any sequence pattern even remotely similar in form or function to the DNA code, beamed to earth from outer space, would immediately be acknowledged as evidence of an intelligent originator. Yet the same evidence for a designer, found in every DNA molecule, cannot be acknowledged as such in classrooms! Mutation rates have been accelerated by a million-fold with fruit flies, yet no new creature or even any new functioning feature has ever developed. Fossils are an undeniable record of the sudden appearance of distinctly different animal forms with huge gaps between distinctly different kinds of creatures. Creation theory explains the fossil record as a consequence of a real worldwide flood and the reality of this ancient global flood has been repeatedly confirmed by careful scientific observations. Yet, these evidences are systematically suppressed because of a dogmatic faith in evolution.

Those setting the standards for our public school science curriculum have merely replaced the acknowledgment of our Creator's existence with a definition of "science" that excludes the possibility of God's existence. Their belief system cannot survive if all of the evidence is allowed to be viewed. Therefore, evolution continues to be promoted by suppressing the evidence for creation and redefining "science". Our culture has sadly replaced what science should be – a tool for searching for the truth. God, who desires for us to have a personal relationship with Him, must be crying over our stupidity.

- Bruce Malone, Midland, MI

Appendix III: Resources for Further Study

INTRODUCTORY BOOKS WITH EVIDENCE FOR CREATION:

A Closer Look at the Evidence, Richard and Tina Kleiss, Search for the Truth Publications, 2005.
Bones of Contention: Creation Assessment of Human Fossils, Marvin Lubenow, Baker Books, 1992.
The Darwin Conspiracy, James Scott Bell, Broadman & Holman, 2002.
Defeating Darwinism by Opening Minds and Reason in the Balance, Phillip Johnson, Intervarsity, 1995 & 1998.
Footprints in the Ash, John Morris and Steven A. Austin, Master Books, 2003.
The Fossil Book, Gary and Mary Parker, Master Books, 2006.
In the Minds of Men: Darwin and the New World Order, Ian Taylor, TFE Publishing Co., 1987.
One Blood: The Biblical Answer to Racism, Ken Ham, Master Books, 1999.
Refuting Evolution & Refuting Evolution 2, Jonathan Sarfati, Master Books, 1999, 2002.
Taking Back Astronomy, Jason Lisle, Master Books, 2006.
The Revised and Updated Answers Book, Don Batten (ed.), Master Books, 2002.
Thousands...Not Billions, Don DeYoung, Master Books, 2005.

TECHNICAL BOOKS WITH EVIDENCE FOR CREATION:

Frozen in Time: The Woolly Mammoth, The Ice Age, and the Bible, Michael Oard, Master Books, 2004.
Grand Canyon - Monument to Catastrophe, Steven Austin, Editor, Master Books, 1995.
Genetic Entropy & the Mystery of the Genome, John Sanford, Ivan Press, 2005.
In the Beginning: Compelling Evidence for Creation and the Flood, Walter Brown, CSC, 2001.
Proceedings of $1^{st}, 2^{nd}, 3^{rd}, 4^{th}, 5^{th}$ Conf. on Creationism, Creation Science Fellowship, 1986, 1990, 1994, 1998, 2003.
Radioisotopes and the Age of the Earth, Vardiman, Snelling, & Chaffin, Master Books, 2000.
Starlight and Time, Russell Humphreys, Master Books, 1994.

BOOKS ACKNOWLEDGING MAJOR PROBLEMS WITH EVOLUTION (WRITTEN FROM A SECULAR PERSPECTIVE):

Darwin's Black Box: The biochemical challenge to evolution, Michael Behe, Free Press, 1998.
Darwin on Trial, Phillip Johnson; Regnery Gateway, 1991.
Evolution: A Theory in Crisis, Michael Denton, Adler & Adler, 1986.
Icons of Evolution: Why Much of What We Teach About Evolution is Wrong, Jonathan Wells, Regnery Pub., 2000.
In Six Days: Why Fifty Scientists Choose to Believe in Creation, edited by John Ashton, Master Books, 2001
Of Pandas and People, Percival Davis & Dean Kenyon, Haughton Publishing Company, 1993.
The Mystery of Life's Origin, C. Thaxton, W. Bradley, R. Olsen; Philosophical Library, 1988.
Tornado in a Junkyard, James Perloff, Refuge Books, 2000.

CHIDREN'S BOOKS ON DINOSAURS FROM A BIBLICAL PERSPECTIVE:

Dinosaurs by Design, Duane Gish, Creation-Life Publishers, 1990.
The Great Dinosaur Mystery, Paul S. Taylor, Chariot Publishers, 1987.
Life in the Great Ice Age, Michael Oard, Master Books, 1995.
Noah's Ark and the Lost World, John Morris, Master Books, 1991.

PERIODICALS WITH EVIDENCE FOR CREATION:

Acts and Facts - Free monthly newsletter with both general and technical information
Answers Magazine - A bi-monthly non-technical magazine of creation articles
Bible-Science News - Monthly newsletter of current creation information, non-technical
Creation Research Society Journal - Quarterly technical journal of latest creation research
TJ - A tri-yearly peer reviewed technical journal of creation research

CREATION ORGANIZATIONS:

Institute for Creation Research, P.O. 2667, El Cajon, CA. 92021 (619) 448-0900 www.icr.org
Answers in Genesis, 7080 Industrial Rd., Florence, KY, 41042 (859)727-2222 www.answersingenesis.org
Alpha Omega Institute, P.O. Box 4343, Grand Junction, CO 81502 (970) 523-9943 www.discovercreation.org
Creation Research Society, P.O. Box 8263, St. Joseph, MO 64508 (816) 279-2312 www.creationresearch.org
Creation Science Fellowship, P.O. Box 99303, Pittsburgh, PA. 15233 (412) 341-4908 www.cfspittsburgh.org
Creation Moments, P.O. Box 260, Zimmerman, MN 55498 (763) 856-2552 www.creationmoments.tc
The Ark Foundation, PO Box 33071, Dayton, OH 45433-0071, (937) 256-ARKY, www.arky.org
Twin Cities Creation Science Association, www.tccsa.tc - Contains a great list of over 75 other creation organizations
Northwest Creation Network, www.nwcreation.net - A good source for powerpoint creation talks and other info.

Index of Illistrations

Subject Index

OTHER CREATION BOOKS

OUR BEST SELLER

A CLOSER LOOK AT THE EVIDENCE

A one of a kind devotional organized in 26 different scientific areas with each page tying God's Word to God's World. Softcover, 414 pgs.

CENSORED SCIENCE: THE SUPPRESSED EVIDENCE

There has never been a creation book like this! Every page is a visual masterpiece. Written in an understandable, fascinating, and storytelling style. Learn what is being left out of textbooks and museums. This book is the key to unlocking the mental hold secular science has on truth. Available in softcover or as a "coffee-table-quality" hardcover, 112 pg. **Significant savings on multiple copies!**

SEARCH FOR THE TRUTH

Extensively illustrated one-page summaries of creation evidence interwoven with the store of what happens when the evidence for creation is placed in public newspapers. Softcover, 144 pgs.

BY HIS WORD

Written for Christians who simply don't understand why creation matters to Christianity. Softcover, 128 pgs.

READY TO GIVE AN ANSWER

A handbook of Christian evidences which confront the major objections to Christian truth. Softcover, 176 pgs.

Books Priced To Share With Others

CHRISTIAN RESOURCES

PROTECTING HIS WORKMANSHIP

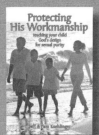

Help for the parent/child "sex-talk"! This biblical workbook will equip your child to stay pure in today's sex-saturated society. Softcover, 112 pgs.

MT. ST. HELENS PANORAMA

A gorgeous print of a significant creation geology event. This panorama is a wonderful teaching tool and conversation starter. Available as a three-foot print, a five-foot print, or framed in solid cherry or oak.

BORROWING GOD'S GLASSES

Answers to teenage girls' questions! This down-to-earth book helps young ladies discover who they are, who God is, and who they are created to be. Perfect for small group study! Softcover, 208 pgs.

DVD RESOURCES

CREATION "101"

Two Foundational lectures on the Evidence for Creation.

EXPLOSIVE EVIDENCE

A very visual overview of the geological evidence for creation

A MATTER OF TIME

How dating methods work and the evidence for a recent creation

MONKEY BUSINESS

The deception and misinterpretations surrounding the ape-to-man links.

Search for the Truth Mail-in Order Form

Send completed order form with check or money order to:
Search for the Truth Ministries
3275 E. Monroe Rd.
Midland, MI 48642
989.837.5546
truth@searchforthetruth.net

Normal delivery time is 1 – 2 weeks; for express delivery, increase shipping to 20%

Price List
Call or e-mail for case pricing

	Single Copy	2-9 copies	10+ copies
Censored Science (Hardback)	$19.95	$14.95/ea.	$10.00/ea.
Censored Science (Softback)	$14.95	$11.95/ea.	$7.50/ea.
Search for the Truth (Book)	$11.95	$8.95/ea.	$6.00/ea.
Borrowing God's Glasses (book)	$11.95	$8.95/ea.	$6.00/ea.
A Closer Look at the Evidence (Book)	$11.95	$8.95/ea.	$6.00/ea.
By His Word (Book)	$9.95	$5.95/ea.	$4.00/ea.
Protecting His Workmanship (Book)	$11.95	$8.95/ea.	$6.00/ea.
All DVDs	$11.95	$8.95/ea.	$6.00/ea.
(4) audio CD radio show series – sixteen 15-minutes talks	$11.95	$8.95/ea.	$6.00/ea.
Mt. St. Helens panorama - 36" by 12"	$10.00	$5.95/ea.	$4.00/ea.
Mt. St. Helens panorama – 60" by 20"	$15.00	$9.95/ea.	$6.00/ea.
Oak Framed Mt. St. Helens panorama - 36" by 12"	$75.00		

Resource	Quantity	Cost Each	Total
Censored Science (Hardback)			
Censored Science (Softback)			
Search for the Truth (Book)			
A Closer Look at the Evidence (Book)			
Borrowing God's Glasses (Book)			
By His Word (Book)			
Protecting His Workmanship (Book)			
Why America is Losing its Heritage (DVD)			
A Matter of Time (DVD)			
Explosive Geological Evidence for Creation (DVD)			
Monkey Business (DVD)			
Mt. St Helen Print (specify 36" or 60")			
36" framed Mt. St Helen Print (specify oak or cherry)			
Quarterly newsletter (including one-hour creation talks CD)		Free	Free
SHIP TO:		**SUBTOTAL**	
Name:		MI Residents add 6% Sales tax	
Address:		Shipping add 15% of subtotal Poster/Framed Prints (Call)	
City/St./Zip:		Total Enclosed	